Comparative Peace Pro

Comparative Peace Processes

JONATHAN TONGE

polity

First published in 2014 by Polity Press

Polity Press
65 Bridge Street
Cambridge CB2 1UR, UK

Polity Press
350 Main Street
Malden, MA 02148, USA

ISBN-13: 978-0-7456-4289-5
ISBN-13: 978-0-7456-4290-1(pb)

A catalogue record for this book is available from the British Library.

Typeset in 9.5 on 13 pt Swift Light by
Servis Filmsetting Ltd, Stockport, Cheshire
Printed and bound in Great Britain by Clays Ltd, St Ives plc

The publisher has used its best endeavours to ensure that the URLs for external websites referred to in this book are correct and active at the time of going to press. However, the publisher has no responsibility for the websites and can make no guarantee that a site will remain live or that the content is or will remain appropriate.

Every effort has been made to trace all copyright holders, but if any have been inadvertently overlooked the publisher will be pleased to include any necessary credits in any subsequent reprint or edition.

For further information on Polity, visit our website: www.politybooks.com

Contents

Acknowledgements

A large number of debts have been incurred in the publication of this book, but I particularly wish to thank colleagues in the Department of Politics, the School of Histories, Cultures and Languages and the Sydney Jones Library at the University of Liverpool, for offering an environment conducive to research. Polity has been a very patient publisher and I thank them for their generosity. Researching and writing the book has taken a considerable period at the expense of quality time with Maria, Joseph, Frances and Connell. I am very grateful to my family for their considerable forbearance, and this book is dedicated to them.

Abbreviations

AIPAC	American Israeli Public Affairs Committee
AMODEG	Mozambican Association of the War Demobilized
ANC	African National Congress
CIRA	Continuity Irish Republican Army
DDR	Demilitarization, demobilization and reintegration
DUP	Democratic Unionist Party
EA	Basque Solidarity
EAE-ANV	Basque Nationalist Action
EHAK	Communist Party of the Basque Homelands
ELA	Basque Workers Solidarity
ELN	National Liberation Army (Colombia)
ETA	Basque Homeland and Freedom
FALANTIL	Armed Forces for the National Liberation of East Timor
FARC	Revolutionary Armed Forces (Colombia)
FMLN	Farabundo Marti National Liberation Front (El Salvador)
GAL	Anti-Terrorist Liberation Group
GDP	Gross domestic product
GFA	Good Friday Agreement
GNP	Gross National Product
HDZ	Croatian Democratic Union
HET	Historical Enquiries Team
ICC	International Criminal Court
ICTY	International Criminal Tribunal for the former Yugoslavia
IFOR	Implementation Force
IPKF	Indian Peacekeeping Force
IRA	Irish Republican Army
JVP	People's Liberation Front (Sri Lanka)
KAS	Patriotic Socialist Coordination (Basque Country)
KLA	Kosovo Liberation Army
KPNLF	Khmer People's National Liberation Front
LAB	Nationalist Workers Committee
LTTE	Liberation Tigers of Tamil Eelam
MPLA	People's Movement for the Liberation of Angola
NATO	North Atlantic Treaty Organization
PDK	Party of Democratic Kampuchea

PIC	Peace Implementation Council
PIRA	Provisional Irish Republican Army
PLO	Palestine Liberation Organization
PKK	Kurdistan Workers Party
PNU	Party of National Unity
PNV	Basque Nationalist Party
PP	People's Party
PRK	People's Republic of Kampuchea
PSOE	Spanish Socialist Workers Party
RENAMO	Mozambican National Resistance
RIRA	Real Irish Republican Army
RUC	Royal Ulster Constabulary
SDA	Party of Democratic Action
SDLP	Social Democratic and Labour Party
SDS	Serbian Democratic Party
SFOR	Stabilization Force
SWAPO	South West Africa People's Organization
TELO	Tamil Eelam Liberation Organization
TNA	Tamil National Alliance
TULF	Tamil United Liberation Front
UFF	Ulster Freedom Fighters
UN	United Nations
UNF	United National Front
UNIFIL	United Nations Interim Force
UNITA	National Union for the Independence of Angola
UNSCR	United Nations Security Council Resolution
UUP	Ulster Unionist Party
UVF	Ulster Volunteer Force

About the Author

Jonathan Tonge is Professor of Politics at the University of Liverpool and a former Chair and President of the Political Studies Association of the UK. He has published 14 books and more than 50 journal articles and chapters, mainly on political aspects of peace processes and conflict, including pieces in *Political Psychology, Party Politics, West European Politics, Political Studies, Terrorism and Political Violence, Irish Political Studies, Representation, Parliamentary Affairs, Nations and Nationalism* and the *British Journal of Politics and International Relations*. His 2010 book on *Former Prisoners and Conflict Transformation in Northern Ireland*, co-authored with Peter Shirlow, Jim McAuley and Catherine McGlynn, won the Political Studies Association of Ireland prize for the Politics book of the year. Professor Tonge has completed six Economic and Social Research Council and two Leverhulme Trust funded projects over the last decade.

Introduction

Recent decades have seen the growth of the term 'peace process' to describe the often protracted period of ceasefires, negotiations, settlement and implementation of deals designed to achieve peace. The proliferation of peace processes does not herald a more peaceful geopolitical environment. Many peace processes end in failure, some catastrophically, but their expansion does highlight the capacity and desire for peace-building. The persistence of wars has been accompanied by burgeoning attempts to ameliorate conflict via processes embracing mitigation, conciliation and reconciliation, increasingly via third-party intervention. Realist perspectives will continue to point to the anarchic nature of the world system, shaped by nations having permanent interests rather than enduring allies, maintaining the inevitability of war. They point to the mediocre record of peace processes as hopes against history or actuality. Longitudinal examination of conflicts demonstrates that peace processes offer only a modest record in solving conflict. Nonetheless, there is tentative evidence that this record is improving and that peacemaking and peacekeeping capacities are becoming more adept. Successful peace processes have now been developed in every region of the world (Wallensteen 2011). It is necessary to explain how and why this progression is evident.

This book undertakes a number of tasks, adopting a distinctive analytical approach. It marries analysis of the growth of peace processes, assessment of the tools of conflict management and analysis of the increasing importance of post-conflict restorative justice with a series of case studies. Whilst comprehensive coverage of all peace processes is obviously impossible, this book chooses a particular selection of the most successful processes in terms of reductions in violence, such as those in Bosnia and Northern Ireland and the most unsuccessful, such as in Sri Lanka, which had a catastrophic end, and that in Palestine, bereft of any obvious chance of political success. The book thus avoids the possible trap of choosing winners and readily acknowledges the limitations of even the most successful processes. Thus alongside the major political progress in the Bosnian and Northern Irish cases there has been only modest societal reintegration. A key feature of the book is its detailed exploration of consociational power-sharing as a means of conflict management. Given the shift in conflict away from inter-state to intra-state forms and the predominance of inter-ethnic rivalries, power-sharing between antagonists has become a key tool of diverting conflict into politics. The focus on consociation does not make great claims for its success and acknowledges its limitations, but stresses its importance as a model now regularly deployed, one which can be re-defined according to circumstance to at least have some utility.

In undertaking this combination of universal and local conflict analysis, this book assesses the growth of peace processes and considers their sequencing, analysing what might be considered the essential and probable components of successful processes. The book explores which types of process succeed and why, discussing key variables such as the nature of conflict – inter- or intra-state; the length of war and the ability to utilize external brokers. The volume also examines the rise of a wide range of measures designed to offer a fair political settlement to antagonists. It considers vexed problems of imple-menting peace and achieving restorative and retributive justice for different groups, ranging from families of victims to war criminals. The focus of the work is upon the political tools available to broker, implement and maintain peace. The book is deliberately aimed at the politics of peace processes, not upon the military aspects of conflict which pre-date (and often accompany) peace processes.

In attempting these tasks, the book is divided into two sections. The first outlines the development of peace processes. Chapter 1 begins with an assess-ment of the growth of the term 'peace process' and explores its usefulness weighed against realist assumptions of the ubiquity of violence, empirical evidence of the persistence of conflict and the failure of a majority of peace processes. The chapter highlights the rise of peace processes amid the partial displacement of inter-state wars by intra-state conflict and discusses which type of conflict may be easier to settle. The chapter examines the common sequencing of peace processes, from secret talks to ceasefires, implementation and future prevention. The essential and useful features of peace processes are identified and the relative importance of endogenous and exogenous factors considered.

Chapter 2 begins with a critical assessment of ideas of ripeness for peace, contending that asymmetry may be as liable to yield peace as a supposedly mutual hurting stalemate. The chapter then examines the utility of various political prescriptions applied to conflict arenas, including consociation, partition, secession and devolution. Amid a growth in ethno-national conflicts around issues of identity, the chapter assesses the extent to which power-sharing deals based upon proportionality for ethnic pillars can endure, amid sectarian retrenchment and polarization.

Chapter 3 looks at the difficulties of implementing peace processes. The chapter examines the capabilities of United Nations peacekeeping forces in physically preventing re-ignition of conflict and assesses how reconstruction can take place after war. It then turns to an exploration of the psychological healing attempted as the denouement of peace processes, via such mecha-nisms as truth and reconciliation commissions. It contrasts the 'soft' approach of truth commissions with the 'hard' retributive ending of war crimes trials.

The second section of the book offers empirical scrutiny of a selection of peace processes of recent decades. There is little point in merely selecting the most recent or the most dated such processes, but much greater value in analysing how the modus operandi of peace processes have varied across different types of conflict and across time. Moreover, to select peace processes which appear to have worked would offer scant value. As such, the case studies include some deemed broadly successful; others far less able to resolve underlying problems and an example of one which collapsed amid slaughter precipitated by the successful pursuit of victory by one side.

Chapter 4 analyses the peace process in Palestine. It assesses the scope for dilution of the territorial claims (infused to different degrees by religious perspectives) of Eretz Israel or a full Palestinian state based on pre-1948 borders. The chapter focuses upon fundamentalist Israeli and Palestinian (Hamas) political-religious narratives. It examines the failure of previous attempts at conflict management, assessing whether blame was attributable primarily to the structure of the deals or the flaws of the agents. The chapter concentrates particularly upon the false hope of the Oslo Agreement of the 1990s and explores whether territorial boundaries can ever be agreed for the much-vaunted two-state solution.

Chapter 5 assesses the Lebanese peace process which produced the 1989 Ta'if Agreement and discusses the extent to which loyalty to the state of Lebanon has been secured in subsequent decades. The attempts at establishing internal fidelity to 'project Lebanon' and to engage in state-building are discussed in the context of persistent external interference within the Lebanese polity and the development of Hezbollah as a governing force across much of the south of the country.

Chapter 6 examines the Northern Ireland peace process. It explores the extent to which the 1998 Good Friday Agreement secured a definitive peace in establishing consociational power-sharing political structures. The chapter measures the extent to which it has been possible to diminish sectarianism amid institutional recognition of ostensibly competitive Protestant-British-Unionist and Catholic-Irish-Nationalist identities. The persistence of low-level violence via spoiler groups, in the form of 'dissident' IRAs, is also assessed.

Chapter 7 dissects the peace process in Bosnia-Herzegovina. It explores the consociational and confederal aspects of the 1995 Dayton Agreement and assesses the contribution of each to freezing ethno-national hostilities between Croats, Serbs and Bosnians. The chapter examines the degree to which reintegration has been evident since the end of hostilities. It discusses the importance of external intervention in forcing and implementing peace, and evaluates how the avoidance of blame inherent in the Dayton deal gradually shifted towards the determined pursuit of war criminals.

The final two chapters examine what happens when peace processes collapse entirely, amid very different levels of violence, but with the state determined in both cases to ensure the absolute defeat of insurgents without offering any tangible rewards for their rebellion. Chapter 8's exploration of the Basque peace process stretches the label of 'peace process', as what has mainly occurred is a gradual petering out of ETA's violent campaign to achieve an independent Basque homeland. The chapter discusses the Spanish government's pressure upon ETA and also discusses how the govern- ment has responded politically to demands for greater Basque autonomy or independence. The various ETA ceasefires are explored in the context of the organization's difficulty in sustaining a credible armed campaign.

Chapter 9, in its dissection of Sri Lanka, shows how a peace process can col- lapse via a determined onslaught from a state. Here, the promise of peace deals dissipated amid the rout of the Tamil Tigers by the Sinhalese government. The chapter traces the reluctance of both sides to clinch a permanent agreement and assesses whether the Tamils' demand for an independent homeland was ever viable. The denouement of this 'peace process', the destruction of the Tamils, was accompanied by numerous allegations of war crimes against the Sri Lankan forces.

Through its initial comparative approach and the deployment of these case studies, the book attempts to establish the central and peripheral aspects of peace processes. It explores whether the political tools associated with the management of conflict have become more nuanced and successful in, as a minimum requirement, harnessing conflict in new political institutions or constitutional structures. Alternatively, are attempts at managing conflicts through the prism of ethnic identity politics ultimately doomed to failure, as issues of sovereignty and territory continue to preoccupy antagonists?

CHAPTER ONE

The Concept of a Peace Process

Peace studies have grown in scope and depth since the Second World War. Peace research has historical roots in the field of international relations and retains the multi-disciplinary focus of that discipline, but has developed a wider remit than inter-state relationships and conflict. Peace research offers a holistic approach to the prevention of conflict and maintenance of peace. Cross-national attempts at formulating international peace are not new; the Hague Peace Conference was held at the end of the nineteenth century, but peace research was piecemeal and uncoordinated during the first half of the twentieth century.

The late 1950 and 1960s saw a collectivization of peace research, via the formation of organizations such as the Peace Research Institute Oslo, the Conference on Peace Research in History and the International Peace Research Association (see Van den Dungen and Wittner 2003). By the 1970s, peace studies had expanded vastly in scope and size, reflected in the growth of research institutes, the launch of academic journals such as the *Journal of Peace Research*, the creation of university departments and appointments of peace scholars. Allied to the importance of the research conducted, these developments facilitated a growth in confidence within the field, to the point where peace research was claimed as a discipline in its own right (Boulding 1978a). Central to the development of peace research has been the belief that scholarly research can have practical application, contributing to the management or resolution of conflict. Within the field of peace studies, deployment of the term 'peace process' is fairly recent, but has become extensive. The label has become an often unsatisfactory catch-all badge for episodic or sustained attempts at resolving conflicts.

As the world order shifted from a West versus East paradigm before the close of the twentieth century, local wars and intra-state civil conflicts assumed greater prominence. Such conflicts had always existed, but they became the subjects of greater focus and intensified peacemaking efforts, amid the demise of the rigidities of the old bipolar geopolitical perspective which had dominated much post-1945 thinking. Although the focus on regional conflict was soon accompanied by a global 'war on terror', the concept of peace processes continued to embed. The unfreezing of the old United States versus Soviet Union, West versus East, inter-bloc hostility facilitated a focus on other inter- and intra-state and inter-communal conflicts. The thawing of Cold War hostilities encouraged fresh thinking about war and terrorism, allowing the 'superpowers' greater influence in brokering peace beyond their boundaries, rather than using countries as proxies for the pursuit of inter-bloc enmities. It is within that context that the term 'peace process' became regularly deployed to cover attempts at ending violence. The term was already developing amid the collapse of white settler regimes in African countries (Angola, Mozambique, Namibia, Rhodesia and South Africa). An apparent resurgence in ethnic pluralism, previously suppressed within Soviet-influenced countries or dormant elsewhere in much of the northern hemisphere following the Second World War, created new conflicts and from these arose numerous peace processes.

Wars are more commonly inter- rather than intra-state clashes, and the majority of peace processes relate to internal conflicts. Indeed nearly four-fifths of conflicts are now labelled as predominantly internal (International Institute for Democracy and Electoral Assistance 2006: 26). However, the boundaries of states are often contested, leading to dispute over what constitutes inter- or intra-state violence. Between 1990 and 2002, civil wars accounted for 90 per cent of conflict-related deaths, overwhelmingly occurring in non-democracies (Lacina 2006: 276). Even when inter-state conflict is evident, it may not necessarily be termed 'war'. Britain's retaking of the Falkland Islands in 1982 from Argentina, whose forces briefly captured the territory earlier that year, was not preceded by a declaration of war by either of the two antagonists, yet a war it was. The conflicts in the Balkans during the 1990s erupted not through formal declarations of war, but through the determination of constituent parts of Yugoslavia to secede from that state, as each pressed claims for self-determination.

Defining and Studying Peace Processes

In analysing the concept, development and outworking of peace processes, there is a need for precise terminology over what constitutes war and peace. Superficially, this may appear straightforward, in that 'war' is associated with considerable conflict, whilst 'peace' is seen as a common label for non-war, a catch-all term covering an absence of violence. Yet war and peace may be much more difficult to identify. States may be reluctant to label internal conflicts as war, preferring to identify political violence as 'terrorism', the problems in the Basque region, South Africa, Northern Ireland and Sri Lanka all offering examples in recent decades. In these cases, the state has been reluctant to confer status upon an organization contesting its legitimacy, with the result that ETA, the ANC, the IRA and the Tamil Tigers have never formally been acknowledged as armies, their 'status' confined to that of terrorist guerrilla group.

Acceptance of the term 'peace process' requires understanding that transitions towards non-violence and the permanent eradication of conflict are non-linear, subject to regression and rarely short. Peace processes rarely have definable start and end dates and may be marred by fractured ceasefires. How is a 'peace process' best defined? Given the different methods of brokering peace, regularity of breakdowns and sometimes indeterminate length of bartering, there is an inevitable imprecision in establishing what constitutes a peace process. The peace process generic label covers a multitude of aspects of the possible ending of conflict. It is applicable where a conflict is subject to attempts at mediation, transformation or resolution. Few conflicts are immune from such efforts and the outright failure, or longevity, of such processes ensures that the concept of a 'peace process' is imprecise. Given its elasticity, the ready deployment of the term is vulnerable to criticism of over-use. The label of 'peace process' assumes that there is at least some momentum to efforts to resolve a conflict. It is regularly deployed in the Middle East amid, at times, an absence of either peace or a discernible process. However, it is possible to attempt a workable definition regardless. A peace process is defined as the active attempt at the prevention and management of conflict between and within states, a remit covering the treatment of inter-state, inter-communal and intra-communal violence. The term peace process requires the following: the involvement of most combatants; the cessation of conflict (peace); the formulation and implementation of political arrangements, whether interim or comprehensive accords; the prevention of the re-ignition of conflict (process) and the attempted political management of differences.

Peace is not a singular event, but a conglomeration of incidents, ideas, tactics and developments. An all-embracing peace process fuses the military, political, humanitarian, psychological and restorative aspects of movement away from conflict. The use of the term 'process' acknowledges that war does not end suddenly, but is contained, managed and (possibly) resolved over a lengthy period of time. Concepts of peace can also extend towards the need for harmony in societal and inter-personal relationships, or even the psychological need to be at ease with oneself (Rinehart 1995). Whilst cognizant of Galtung's (1969) contention that issues of social justice arising from peace processes may affect issues of inter-personal harmony and aware of the need to avoid reductionist definitions of peace (see Johnson 1976), the focus of this book is upon the political development and management of non-personal conflict.

Peace is not merely the temporary absence of war and process is not merely an avowed willingness of combatants to negotiate. Bloody conflicts have followed both these circumstances and the term 'peace process' should only be utilized when sufficient ingredients are in place to indicate movement from hitherto fixed military and political positions. Peace as merely the non-presence of war is a largely static concept, bereft of dynamism, one which does not tackle the basis of conflict. Defining peace in such a negative fashion does not tell us what peace could or should comprise and indicates only what to avoid, not what action to take (Cox 1986). Temporary ceasefires need a political process to remove the conditions underpinning the conflict, or end the political paralysis arising from antagonistic relationships.

It is possible for decades of peace to have been evident without a permanent resolution of a problem, in which case the term 'political process' may appear more useable than that of 'peace process'. To take one example: Cyprus has enjoyed peace and has become a popular tourist destination in recent times. Yet the island was partitioned (although the partition was not recognized by the United Nations (UN)) following the Turkish invasion of the north of the island in 1974, a move which followed years of inter-communal violence between Greek and Turkish Cypriots. Decades of cold peace have resulted, with 30,000 Turkish troops deployed to 'protect' the Turkish sector and a UN buffer zone separating the two sides. Attempts to unfreeze the divide and re-unite the island have not been successful. Most notably, the 2002 Annan Plan was rejected by Greek Cypriots in a referendum (see Diez and Tocci 2009). The question begged is whether the negotiations leading to the Annan Plan consti-tuted a peace process, given the lack of immediate prior violence. Those argu-ing that peace processes need to challenge division and not merely address the absence of war would argue yes. Guelke (2003) notes how peace processes may come to be seen almost as substitutes for a settlement and that continual search for a solution almost becomes a surrogate for enduring peace. Cyprus, paralysed by a lack of movement and yet perennially supposedly on the verge of a 'breakthrough', offers one prolonged case.

Alongside the growth of peace processes, there has been considerable debate over the scholarly and practical value of their study. Much of this discussion has attempted to gauge the value of purely academic peace research, relative to the need for the practical application of peace studies. Anatol Rapoport (1970) claimed long ago that radical research raising fundamental ques-tions was discouraged by governments, which withheld funding for projects challenging existing modes of thought. As a consequence, too much peace research consisted of technical matters of a narrow empirical character, with little wider value in improving knowledge of why wars start or how peace begins. Whilst acknowledging the validity of the criticism of the blinkered, narrow approach of some peace research, Kent's (1971: 47) rejoinder suggested that no radical 'would want or would expect government support for his anti-government campaigns. He [sic] can and should look elsewhere'. For Kent, the problem was that too few scholars 'know how to relate normative and empiri-cal studies' (Kent 1971: 50), a difficulty which has not entirely dissipated. The argument of Galtung (1975), amongst others, was that peace research needed to deploy objective scientific study, beyond the control of any particular government or organization and that such research needed to be of practical and emancipatory value. For Galtung, the major challenge confronting peace researchers is to encourage the state's exercise of power in a non-violent direction, using a multifaceted approach embracing research, education and action, and concerning itself with human development as well as violence. Peace studies embrace a broader range of concerns than 'security studies'. More recently, Patomaki (2001: 726) expressed similar sentiments to those of Galtung, urging a realist ontology which, nonetheless, asks fundamental questions of existing concepts, is critical of asymmetric power relationships and is intentionally transformative:

> Peace research is an applied science charged with the task not only of presenting how things actually are, but also of telling how they should be. Just as the normative objective of medicine is health, the objective of peace research is peace. Therefore, not only are peace researchers expected to produce original high-quality studies, they must also be relevant.

Scholars of peace processes have divided into two very broad methodological schools; positivist empiricists and a critical peace research school (Dedring 1987). They have engaged in a somewhat artificial and sterile debate. The empiricist school argues that quantitative and behavioural approaches are the most appropriate means of studying processes. This approach stresses the need to test falsifiable or verifiable hypotheses, measure essential variables and produce an objective, scientifically-rigorous approach to peace processes, often based upon mathematical modelling (Singer 1971, 1972). Using rational choice modelling and factoring in local variables, this approach may allow forecasting and analysis of how peace can be attained. The criticism offered by the quantitative school of non-quantitative, qualitative work is that such studies risk being normative, judgemental, value-laden, descriptive and unscientific.

In response, the critical peace research school argues that much of the quantitative research on peace processes is neither objective nor value-free. Moreover, it adds little to our understanding of how to avoid future conflict, which ought to be the primary purpose of the research. These critics argue that game-theory and modelling are eschewed by policy-makers dealing with the real world (a point rebutted by those who argue that modelling is increasingly used by peacemakers) and as such may have only minor value. Qualitative research may involve detailed work and discussion with combatants, ascertaining ground-level perceptions of the righteousness of their cause and determination to persist, arguably a more value-learning process than research constructed around a series of elaborate but abstract hypotheses. Critics of approaches grounded exclusively in quantitative studies also argue that they risk being reductionist in their definitions of war and peace. For researchers in the critical peace school, genuine peace is more than the mere absence of war, bringing into question the value of the conflict data utilized by the empiricist school. Data is thus value-laden, designed and filtered according to the values of the researchers. Quantitative research is based upon pre-ordained conceptual ideas and as such offers little value-added. Despite the mathematical modelling, it has rarely offered any reliable predictive capacity.

The objectivity of peace research has been a source of contention, more particularly when developed via qualitative studies. In particular, the search for relevance has sometimes led to a blurring of the relationship between peace research and peace activism. Van den Dungen and Wittner (2003: 367) argue that peace researchers ought to (and do) 'occupy a middle ground [between government and activists] which allows them to tackle questions in a more objective manner', yet they also claim that most peace researchers 'evince an affinity with activism' and could legitimately be termed 'activist scholars'. This type of scholar believes that activism provides value-added to the research, although the extent to which peace activism contributes to change remains difficult to assess. For example, Cortright's (1993) thesis that citizen activism was a primary factor in the demise of the Cold War is appealing given the extent of the 'People's Uprising', but has strong counter-arguments based on the ruinous economic cost to the Soviet Union of the arms race. A further illustration of the limitations of peace activism was provided by the 'Peace People' in Northern Ireland. Their visible demonstrations for peace enjoyed huge popularity during the 1970s, their leaders receiving the Nobel Peace Prize in 1976, but a further two decades of conflict followed.

Articulation of the differences between what might be called the quantitative and critical schools (the distinction is far from absolute) has to some extent been a redundant dialogue of the deaf. Clearly there is a need for empirical testing of what may constitute salient variables in contributing to the development of peace processes. Moreover, peace and war are palpably identifiable in many instances. There is, however, scope for nuanced qualitative interpretation of, for example, grassroots perceptions of how wars start and end. The debate over methodology is difficult to resolve fully, as it highlights a gap between differing conceptualizations of peace and demonstrates a gulf in the desired objectives, scope and outcomes of academic study, in addition to the dispute over the value of applying mathematical modelling to conflict scenarios.

Early research into the peace studies field found the profession equally divided between those who defined the concept of peace as the control or elimination of war and those who preferred the broader, more positive, definition of both the prevention of war and the advancement of human rights and justice (Parker 1978). Negative definitions, revolving around the mere absence of war, reflected the pessimism evident among peace scholars of prospects for permanent global peace (Everts 1973; Kemp 1985). For the 'Galtungian' school, conceptualizing peace as merely the absence of war discredits peace research, ignoring structural violence. Galtung's (1985) human rights-based conceptualization of peace was a product of his location in Rhodesia, where the second-class citizenship and oppression of blacks was not accompanied by substantial inter-racial violence. On a strict 'war' and 'peace' definitional criteria, this was the latter, highlighting the inadequacy of the minimalist definition of peace. Research on peace processes has also focused increasingly upon the 'aftermath' of conflict in terms of state-building and social healing, as much as the negotiations which prevent violence. The reconstructive has thus begun to assume greater parity of status with the preventative.

The term 'peace process' is now common currency, covering the apparatus of establishing, implementing and maintaining peace, defined on the
minimalist Uppsala model as the absence of violence for more than one
year (Wallensteen and Sollenberg 2001). In the final decade of the twentieth
century alone, there were 23 peace agreements reached. Two of those deals
broke down entirely and at least sporadic violence followed all the remainder,
with an unhealthy overall recidivism rate. The overall success rate for peace
processes in the six decades following the Second World War, measured in
terms of a non-return of violence two years after a deal, was only 41 per cent
(Doyle and Sambanis 2000; Ramsbotham et al. 2005: 222–4). Wolff (2006:
131) highlights the cynicism surrounding peace deals in citing an observer
of seemingly perennial conflict in the Democratic Republic of Congo: 'The
peace agreement was signed on Tuesday. Just in time for the massacre on
Thursday'.

The grim statistics are not necessarily surprising, given that peace processes
involve new thinking, rapprochement, painful compromises and often further hurt for families of victims of the conflict, as perpetrators may re-enter
society, sometimes even assuming senior political positions. Although a self-
evident aside which has acquired cliché status, it is worth remembering the
observation of the former Israeli leader, Yitzhak Rabin (if also attributed to
Moshe Dyan and Olaf Palme) that one does not make peace with one's friends,
but rather with one's enemy (Rabin 1996). Propensity towards compromise
creates danger for leaders willing to deal with the enemy; Rabin was assassinated by a Jewish ultra shortly after making his observation.

Peace processes are never a quick fix and should not be conceptualized
in terms of a single 'big bang'. Although common stages are identifiable,
some may have to be revisited and issues returned to via new agreements.
Breakdowns or reversals of peace processes are common. To cite one of hundreds of examples, Bosnia-Herzegovina had a potentially viable 'Vance–Owen'
peace plan in 1993, based upon ethnic cantonization, which soon collapsed,
but within three years an enduring deal had been reached, emphasizing that
peace processes are not dead due to the collapse of a single plan. Despite this,
there remains a tendency to focus on the 'big deal', rather than the confidence-
building pre-deal agenda, or the problems of post-agreement implementation.

There is no comprehensive checklist of essential features of peace processes,
but there are a number of ingredients sufficiently common to indicate they
are key elements. In isolation, these features are necessary but insufficient
ingredients; the sum of the parts, however, may yield a durable process. Darby
and Mac Ginty (2003: 2) offer five such components: negotiations conducted in
good faith; inclusion of the main combatants; a willingness to address the key
points of dispute; the disavowal of force; and prolonged commitment.

A peace process without the above essential components is not worthy of
the name. A lack of commitment or unwillingness to include the main groups
fighting, regardless of past heinous actions, means that a peace process is

doomed to fail. Peace processes require acceptance by all significant partici-pants of the impossibility of total victory, although symmetry of position on entering negotiations is unlikely. Nearly half of all conflicts do result in a total victory for a particular side, with the defeated army crushed, often amid serious human rights abuses or even genocide, as seen in the Sinhalese mas-sacre of the Tamil Tigers in 2009 (see chapter 9). Where there is such disparity in prospects, a peace process is superfluous; few states or armies negotiate seriously around what might readily be taken on the battlefield. It is when the costs of victory are too great, in terms of human and financial resources, or when the prospects of success are low, that actors enter a peace process. The process may allow undefeated, but non-victorious armies, some share of the peace process spoils, but the original demands of one set of antagonists may need to be heavily diluted, amid uneven compromise. This scenario is common in the asymmetrical conflicts involving terrorist campaigns, where the terror group cannot be entirely vanquished, but the inability to achieve its fundamental goals leads towards inevitable compromise.

Concepts of peace have developed beyond negative avoidance of war towards increasingly positive ambitions of permanent peace through change in a region. Emancipatory definitions of peace have been accompanied by pro-grammes for the rectification of social inequality and injustice. The search for transformative peace was ushered in amid realization that many of the wars of national liberation or anti-colonialism stemmed from ill-treatment of a native population by a colonial power. There is a danger of over-emphasizing a neat chronology of change in assuming that decisive movement from inter-state to intra-state, internal struggles against colonialism occurred following the termination of the Cold War. Civil wars have been more numerous than inter-state wars for at least two centuries, although the gap has widened further in recent decades (Mack 2005). Moreover, the labelling of conflicts as civil wars can be contentious. For example, Lacina (2006) claims Northern Ireland as the only post-Second World War European civil war that lasted more than four years, but the organization committing the majority of killings in that con-flict, the IRA, saw it not as a civil war, but as an anti-colonial uprising against 'foreign' British rule (see chapter 6).

The concentration upon avoiding nuclear war between superpowers was at the expense of a focus upon how 'positive' peace might be attained in the numerous anti-colonial struggles or social conflicts. It was the framework of analysis that changed towards regions and nations more than the nature of conflict, given that regional and intra-state conflict was already prevalent. The demise of bipolarity and rise of unipolarity encouraged the proliferation of new thinking on how to create peace and improved the context for peace processes. The end of bipolarity also removed the 'proxy' argument against creating peace. Right-wing forces, most obviously the apartheid regime in South Africa, could no longer claim to be a bulwark against expansionist com-munism; left-wing forces no longer received backing from the Soviet Union.

As concepts of peace were refined, there was a concomitant development of peace processes, bolstered by policy learning and knowledge transfer in how to anticipate, broker and maintain peace. Predictive capacity, in terms of the ability to forecast future arenas of conflict, remains low, meaning that peace initiatives have often been fire-fighting, reactive entities. Yet this makes the greater political sophistry acquired through decades of peace processes even more valuable. Two case studies in this book add to scepticism over predictive capabilities of peace scholars. It was impossible to find any academic predicting the war with a huge death toll in the Balkans that erupted in the 1990s, or warning in the 1960s of the onset of decades of violence in Northern Ireland. 'Peace learning' has been more successful in terms of prevention of conflict recurrence and the amelioration, eradication or management of existing conflict than in anticipating where and when the next outbreak of violence will occur. The capacity for peacekeeping and peacemaking has exceeded that for conflict forecasting. Nonetheless, broad holistic models of scenarios under which conflict is likely to occur have been developed, utilizing variables including the opportunity for ethnic rebellion; immigration and refugee numbers; the level and type of repression; environmental upheaval; size and performance of the economy and distribution of wealth (Gurr 1970; Baechler and Spillman 1996; Collier and Hoeffler 1998; Ramsbotham et al. 2005). That such a multiplicity of conflict causes exists highlights the difficulty of predicting where violence might erupt, but relative deprivation and 'second-class citizenry' – the ill-treatment of particular ethnic groups fuelling grievance – are the most persistent factors in explaining conflict causation.

External Inputs and Knowledge Transfer

A comparative approach to the management of conflict was a logical development arising from studies of international relations examining why and where violence erupts. As Galtung (1985: 153) comments, 'one cannot build a general theory of peace for the world on relations between Nordic countries alone, or a theory of disarmament on the basis of Costa Rica'. Equally limited is theoretical work which has no practical value or collapses at the first hint of empirical testing. The comparative approach allows peace scholars to determine what matters most in the construction of peace, using key cross-national tests of consistency of applicability and viability. It is through this approach that factors common to most peace processes, such as verifiable, monitored ceasefires, demobilization, prisoner releases, external aid and healing mechanisms, such as truth or victims commissions, have become familiar features. The knowledge accumulated from a succession of peacemaking initiatives may allow the success rate of peace processes and agreements to improve. As the range of tools available to peace-brokers increases, along with cognizance of when best deployed, a concomitant rise in the number of successful peace processes is possible.

Cross-national policy learning and transfer has been aided by the growth of academic studies of peace and by the numerous examples of the 'export' of experienced peace-brokers across various conflicts to offer brokerage or mediation roles. The United States diplomat Richard Holbrooke was involved in efforts to create peace in Vietnam, Morocco, East Timor (one of the most enduring conflicts, which had persisted since 1975), Bosnia (where he did much to broker the 1995 Dayton Agreement) and Afghanistan. Senator George Mitchell successfully brokered the talks leading to the Good Friday Agreement in Northern Ireland in 1998 and subsequently acted as United States peace envoy to the Middle East. Finland's Marti Ahtisaari has been involved in peace processes in South Africa, Northern Ireland, Indonesia and Kosovo. External actors extend well beyond the diplomatic corps, with, for example, the Roman Catholic and Protestant churches playing brokerage and mediation roles in Argentina, in a dispute with Chile and amid civil war in Mali (Mitchell 2003). External brokers play a wide variety of roles, ranging from those of flatterers (warring parties may, perversely, enjoy the international attention warranted by their actions) to enforcers, with a range of intermediate remits in teasing out positions, facilitating compromises, guaranteeing deals and overseeing the implementation of agreements.

Encouraged by the promotion of international norms of peace by the UN, external brokerage of negotiations has become an important component of many peace processes, given that local groups are often unable to settle differences amid the unilateral pursuit of blinkered interests. Honest brokers require a host of skills to function effectively: historical knowledge, confidence-building, an ability to mediate and facilitate deals, confidentiality and the ability to present the offerings of the other side as concessions and compromises. They may also need to be deadline-setters and enforcers. The honest broker acts as a conduit for rival forces, given that they may not engage directly with each other.

This honest broker requirement is nonetheless problematic, as brokers are often not regarded as neutral, one factor in the failure of the United States to referee Middle East peace. Supposed honest brokerage has often been usurped by physical intervention, in which a particular regime type has been imposed. Interventionism has also been justified on the basis of forcing people to be free. Neo-conservatives and neo-liberals have tended to share the same assumptions concerning the value of intervention, regarding it as undertaken for the good of the local population. This belief has elevated interventionism to a regular feature of Western foreign policy, even if its results in pursuit of the belief that states can be transformed into capitalist democracies have been, to be charitable, only mixed. Moreover, external agents cannot remove the antagonisms which fuel many conflicts (see Lederach 1997). As one example, a variety of non-governmental organizations in Europe and South America staged dialogues on political and economic change with Colombia's Revolutionary Armed Forces (FARC) and the National Liberation Army (ELN) during the early

2000s, sponsored by the German, Swedish, Mexican and Cuban governments, but as talks proceeded the conflict merely intensified (Chernick 2003; Jeong 2010). Other factors, such as the level of state repression and the breadth of FARC organization (with over 60 FARC fronts in existence) were more salient factors than the quality of external brokers (Holmes et al. 2007).

At best, external agents can achieve transformation and management by moving conflict into a potentially more peaceful setting, but such agents do not resolve, only referee, the problems which caused the conflict. There is also an ongoing debate over the extent to which external brokers or mediators may bring their own cultural understandings or misunderstandings to the broker-age process. This is potentially dangerous and can collapse the process where violence is culturally-based (Galtung 1990). In contrast, those who see conflict as rooted more in the need for human security and who believe that there are holistic approaches to diplomacy are more sceptical over the importance of cultural understandings to long-term conflict resolution (e.g., Zartman 1995). This is not to suggest that those diplomats, peacemakers and policy advisors are merely the peace process version of the doctor on call, prescribing reme-dial treatment to make the patient better. Nonetheless, in the way that patient treatments have grown in range and sophistication, the same is true in terms of the political sophistry which can be applied to manage conflicts. Moreover, as a doctor also relies upon patient willpower and commitment to improved health, so peacemakers are reliant upon sincere commitment to peace and progress amongst combatants. The export of peace process knowledge and policy transfer by practitioners – part of what is sometimes referred to, not always flatteringly, as the 'peace industry' – has been accompanied by rapid growth in multi-disciplinary peace-oriented academic studies.

External input to peace extends beyond diplomacy. The use of force to 'create' peace has also been a prelude to peace processes. The invasion of Iraq by the United States and United Kingdom ended Saddam Hussein's oppression of his own people, but precipitated civil war, with the allies remaining until a new constitution was agreed and a relative, often fractured, peace imple-mented. The deployment of the same countries' armed forces in Afghanistan as part of the 'war on terror' proved unsuccessful in ousting the Taleban when accompanied by a supposed peace deal (the Bonn Agreement), which attempted to ignore their presence. Creating peace through militarism may be possible; sustaining that peace and building a post-conflict society is more problematic, as the transition from coercion to peace-building may take years. The issue of legitimacy is particularly difficult, given that a government imposed following external intervention may be seen as a puppet regime of foreign powers, even if democratic elections take place. Security issues may require a long-term, non-local, military presence, exacerbating the percep-tion of external governance. The longevity of military intervention for peace inhibits the establishment of purely local judicial systems, whilst foreign financial aid is invariably needed. Institution-building and state-building are most difficult when accompanied by a continuing post-conflict military presence.

Agreements and Crises: the Limits of Peace Processes

Peace processes rarely succeed quickly. They tend to originate in cost–benefit analyses of peace versus war by combatants, influenced by policy priorities and with compromises offered on the basis of viable exchange (Schwarzer 1998). Concessions to violent protagonists are far from guaranteed to succeed and a total breakdown of the political arrangements which led to the suspension of hostilities is not uncommon (Call 2008). If war really is, to paraphrase Clausewitz (1873), politics by other means, then adequate political arrangements are self-evidently most likely to bring about peace. That war and politics are seen as interchangeable highlights the difficulty of moving from conflict management to conflict resolution, as only the latter eliminates the risk of a resumption of violence.

As Mac Ginty (2006) argues, too often the focus is upon bringing about peace via an agreement, rather than considering whether an agreement is likely to hold. It did not, as one example, take great prescience to foresee that the 1990 unification deal between North and South Yemen might collapse due to a lack of commitment from the respective leaderships. Mac Ginty suggests a need to re-orientate the emphasis of peace processes upon sustainability rather than the big event of a deal. Whilst the focus on the attainment of peace is understandable, too little thought is given to the possible after-effects of deals, which may contribute to longer-term destabilization. There is considerable empirical evidence to support the concerns over flawed agreements. Much more rarely, the focus upon the 'big agreement' risks overlooking those conflict cessations where no deal has been struck, but where the conflict has simply petered out.

Whilst there tends to be a transparent climax, in the form of an agreement between warring parties, some violence may follow and implementation of a deal may be followed by collapse and a worsening of the situation. The collapse of the 1993 Arshua Accords in Rwanda, followed by two million deaths, provides one stark example. The agreement between rebel Tutsis of the Rwandan Patriotic Front (RPF) and government Hutus was designed to settle an ethnic-economic conflict (the economic element was principally over competition for arable land) but was followed by a rapid descent into genocide, with a staggering one million deaths within three months. The fragility of the deal was emphasized by the assassination of President Habyarimana, an act which plunged both sides back into civil war.

Failure may be frequent. As one example, a succession of peace initiatives, accompanied in the mid-1990s by a major UN peacekeeping intervention, failed to bring peace to Somalia, where conflict has ranged from endemic to episodic. A 1988–92 ceasefire agreed by the combatants was followed by invasion by United States forces, appearing to end the conflict between rebel movements and the Presidential government of Siad Barre. However, the country disintegrated post-ceasefire amid further violence. Autonomy was awarded to Somaliland in the North West and Puntland, where power-sharing between the Presidential forces of Abdullahi Yusuf Ahmed and rebel militias was partially successful. A struggle ensued for control for the capital, Mogadishu, and much of the South. The US-backed Ethiopian invasion in 2007, designed largely to prevent the growth of Islamic movements, exacerbated the problem. By 2011, many of the country's inhabitants were facing starvation. The Islamist group, Al-Shabaab (The Youth), an armed militia opposed to Western influence, emerged from the Islamic Courts Union and gradually extended control, particularly in southern Somalia, in the absence of an authoritative central government. The failure to observe peace agreements and foreign incursions (Kenya invaded the south of Somalia in 2011) led to further violence.

Conflict is even more likely to re-ignite where there has been a failure to clinch a political agreement to consolidate the peace offered by ceasefires. Violence in Bodoland in north-eastern India, where the National Democratic Front demands a separate sovereign state, provides one example. A ceasefire agreement in 2005 was not accompanied by a fully agreed political arrangement and the cessation of violence duly collapsed. In Myanmar (Burma), the Karen National Union's armed wing, the Karen National Liberation Army, demanding a federal Karen state in Eastern Myanmar, renewed hostilities with the military government in 2005, after barely one year's cessation of violence, reviving a conflict which has persisted in varying degrees of intensity since 1949. Concurrently, fighting resumed between the Shan State Army, demanding an independent Shan State, and the same government.

The Sequencing of Peace Processes

Although definitive starting points are rarely observable, peace processes usually contain identifiable stages. Dialogue is often secret and informal initially, constructed on the basis of deniability, between representatives of the combatants and trusted third parties. These exploratory and indirect 'feeler' discussions help establish the terms for a cessation of violence. This pre-negotiation stage then tends to be followed by a ceasefire, the durability of which may form a crucial test of the bona fides of combatants in seeking peace. In some cases, the ceasefire may be preceded by a broad declaration by one or more interested parties, often the states involved in brokerage, of the outline contours of what a future political agreement might contain. An example here is the 1993 Downing Street Declaration in the Northern Ireland conflict, which held out the prospect of an 'agreed Ireland' without providing much detail on the contents of a formal deal, its finer points being negotiated several years down the track. Another, far less auspicious, example from the same year was the Oslo Agreement, which lacked precision on how a settlement would take shape in the Middle East, but made various pronouncements concerning peace and security and offered recognition of the Palestine Liberation Organization (PLO) by Israel. Movement towards recognition of the political aims of combatants is crucial. In South Africa, the African National Congress (ANC) moved rapidly from pariah status to becoming an official negotiating body; as did Sinn Féin in Northern Ireland and the People's Liberation Movement in Sudan.

It is usually only after ceasefires and other confidence-building measures that serious discussions take place to achieve an agreement. Even then, direct negotiations between former combatants may be rare or non-existent. Proxy talks are common and there may be the need at this stage to agree an honest broker to handle negotiations and engage in rule-making. Dialogue normally opens with articulation of statements of position, followed by exploratory examination of the possible scope for compromise, moving beyond the repetition of selective historical narratives by combatants. A further important stage may include reverse role-playing, where members of one side are asked to consider and articulate the case of the other. This can have a profound effect, forcing antagonists to consider conflict from the position of the 'enemy'. In the Northern Ireland conflict, this process had already occurred and impacted upon Irish republican thinking prior to negotiations. English (2004) records how Irish republican prisoners were forced to adopt loyalist-British perspectives during internal debates, a development which rendered those republicans uncomfortable over the certainties of their position.

Self-analysis at an early stage of the negotiation process can cut through the self-delusion, deception or myopia of a particular position and require combatants to see how fixed beliefs can antagonize the other side. It does not require outright *repudiation* of beliefs, or rejection of the righteousness of the cause, as that would be far too ambitious, especially at this early stage. Introspection may nonetheless assist awareness of the claims and rights of opponents and encourage meaningful dialogue at the expense of monologue. It may be the first occasion on which the hurt imposed upon others, rather than that suffered by one's own side, is seriously considered. From this self-assessment may follow a desire to address opponents as equals and accept that hurt has been inflicted upon rivals. Introspection helps foster the cognitive awareness necessary if the causes of conflict are to be addressed. If introspection is undertaken in a cursory fashion, it is difficult to conceive how movement from fixed positions can be attained.

The next point in the process is for deadlines for negotiations to be agreed. The key criteria are 'reasonableness' and 'seriousness', along with a willingness by participants to agree deadlines that may be produced by external brokers (du Toit 2003: 66). For fulfilment of the reasonableness requirement, there needs to be sufficient time for details to be finalized, as ambiguities and omissions will invariably complicate any agreement later. The seriousness criteria means that deadlines need to stick, or the process loses credibility. Seriousness can be a high hurdle, particularly if participants are lukewarm and the deadlines are imposed by external mediators. The sanctions that can be imposed by outsiders are very limited. They do not want to collapse the process by being over-insistent and participants are aware of this, thus the incentives to meet deadlines may be modest. Accepting his role as Middle East peace envoy under the Obama US Presidency, Senator George Mitchell emphasized how peace processes can be extraordinarily prolonged, a feature scarcely surprising given the longevity of the conflicts which precede them. Referring to his previous role as chair of peace negotiations in Northern Ireland, Mitchell (2000) noted how all ethnic rivals agreed to share power only after he insisted that talks were truncated, given that political representatives would have talked forever had they been allowed. Moreover, a peace deal in the region was concluded:

> [A]lmost 800 years after Britain began its domination of Ireland, 86 years after the partition of Ireland, 38 years after the British army began its most recent mission in Ireland, 11 years after the peace talks began and nine years after a peace agreement was signed. In the negotiations we had 700 days of failure and one day of success. For most of the time progress was non-existent or very slow. (Mitchell 2009)

Mitchell used the Northern Ireland example to emphasize that 'there is no such thing as a conflict without resolution', no matter how protracted. This belief sustained the fragile peace process in the Middle East, where Mitchell claimed a bystander had remarked, in reference to the conflict in Ireland lasting 800 years, 'Ah, 800 years; so recent a conflict' (Mitchell 2009).

Mitchell earned a reputation as an honest, neutral broker, yet there have been convincing, if counter-intuitive, assertions that biased mediation can be more successful as a means of brokering agreements of greater quality and sustainability. Cetinyan (2002), Walter (2002) and Svensson (2007, 2009) all contend that biased mediators have more credibility with antagonists and can thus sell a difficult deal more readily, hold greater detailed knowledge and can use a special relationship with a particular side and make offers to, or withhold resources from, that side. In particular, demobilization, confidence-building guarantees and amnesties are more likely to feature if the mediator is drawn from the ranks of either the government or anti-state allies. There are credible examples of partisan mediation being successful, such as Kenya's brokerage role in the peace process in Mozambique, but the role of the United States in the Middle East offers an obvious empirical rebuttal of the argument.

In terms of movement towards a deal, clearly 'facts on the ground' are crucial. Conflict containment may create sufficient space to facilitate agreement. Perhaps surprisingly, only 60 per cent of peace process agreements include ceasefires as a formal provision (Harbom et al. 2006: 624), although de facto or actual ceasefires may already be in place prior to the deal, with permanent cessation assumed rather than stated. A series of confidence-building measures, embracing one or more of demobilization, verifiable disarmament and decommissioning, may then be required. The problem of spoilers, or ultras, determined to ignore an agreement and fight on, is attendant to virtually every peace process (Stedman 1997). Using a rational choice model, successful peace-building requires broadly symmetrical perceptions to be held by combatants, in terms of mutual recognition of the limited utility of continuing violence. Yet such perceptions are rarely universally held amongst all combatants, placing considerable pressure on the leaders of warring groups to deliver the inevitable compromises of peace amid the threat of fragmentation of their side. Amid pressure from below for continued violence, military and political leaders have to offer a vista of gains through peace which may be difficult to contemplate given what has occurred to date. Presentation of how a switch from war to peace will bring better results requires considerable skill. Violence may have brought rewards prior to negotiation, as might belligerence and aggrandisement afterwards. Ethnic entrepeneurship, communal advancement and continuing threatening actions towards opponents during negotiations are common features. Peace processes may offer conflict management rather than conflict resolution in such cases; the volcano may be rendered dormant, but not extinct.

Should an agreement be concluded, it is necessary to recognize its limitations. Peace processes are not necessarily designed to resolve conflict, but may merely manage a problem with an aspiration (but no more) towards its long-term dissipation. As Boulding (1978b) argued, stable peace does not necessitate the resolution of conflict, but does require recognition by former combatants of the lack of utility and purpose of a resumption of violence. Antagonists need to declare for peace and eschew war as costly and ineffective, whilst political action, economic exchange and greater integration need to be promoted as appropriate replacements. Successful peace processes achieve conflict transformation, changing the conditions of enmity from those where violence is seen as essential and may be endemic, towards a position where non-violent methodologies are considered as viable alternatives. If conflict transformation embeds, there is the prospect of successful conflict management and even full resolution.

Conflict resolution represents the potential endgame for peace processes, but is not a requirement, as mere management may suffice for success to be claimed. Conflict resolution requires movement beyond agreement and management, which may merely freeze the antagonisms or grievances that contributed to the onset of violence. Conflict resolution within peace processes is the process of addressing the structural and ideological causes of conflict and moves beyond agreement towards settlement. This stage of the process may be accompanied by removal of personnel from the theatre of conflict if they are seen as warmongers, to allow political progress and movement from fixed ideological and political positions. Conflict resolution is about more than peace-building or peace-solidifying. It attempts to embed peace through problem-solving and is the most ambitious aspect of a peace process. The political element of a peace process may not extend to conflict resolution, if management is seen as the limit of what is attainable. The division between management and resolution is nonetheless rarely absolute. Although much of the Northern Ireland peace process was concerned with merely managing division and transporting it to an institutional setting, the 'equality agenda' of the process might be seen as a form of conflict resolution, removing any lingering traces of the political and structural inequalities which fuelled the hostility of some Irish Catholic Nationalists to the state.

The success of conflict resolution measures can be gauged empirically along an axis which moves from the end of war towards full political participation of former combatants, the elimination of economic and political ascendancy of particular groups and the reintegration of society within an institutionally reconstructed polity. Full conflict resolution may include the establishment of democratic elections as a permanent political feature; the removal of militarism or paramilitarism as an adjunct to political activity; the reintegration of former combatants into civic society; equality legislation; the establishment of a consensual legal and judicial system and economic reconstruction. A best-case scenario is that societal reconciliation accompanies conflict resolution. This may take different forms, including the de-ethnicization of society; support for cross-community initiatives; truth and victim commissions and reparations. Aside from the difficulty of achieving these features of resolution and reconciliation, there is an ongoing debate as to how far some aspects of reintegration, particularly in the educational, cultural and territorial spheres, should be pursued. Reintegration which tramples on cultural pluralism, religious rights or communal safety and belonging may aggravate tensions. Reconciliation amid amnesties for antagonists and amnesia over crimes may be difficult to achieve.

There are several variables which influence the likelihood of whether a peace process can be successful. The scale of conflict matters, as low intensity wars are easier (or less difficult) to resolve, as does the number of armed groups; the lower the number the more likely a solution to the conflict. Geographical confinement of the problem is also helpful, diminishing the risk of a spillover of war. The difficulty of creating a durable peace process in Africa's worst-ever conflict, in the Democratic Republic of Congo, is highlighted when considering these variables. Six other states, Angola, Namibia, Rwanda, Uganda, Zambia and Zimbabwe have been involved in the conflict, albeit to very differing degrees, and 25 armed groups have featured. Over 5 million people have died, many not directly through armed combat, but as a consequence of famine and disease arising from the mass displacements of populations and money diverted towards arms procurement. The Democratic Republic of Congo has housed various armed groups keen to bring down neighbouring regimes, with Rwanda and Uganda having been targets, and as such these states, already subject to years of internal wars, have become embroiled in further conflict. Although a peace deal was reached at Lusaka in 1999 and a UN peacekeeping force deployed, the lack of a serious accompanying political process and delays in full implementation meant that violence remained.

Models of Peace Processes

Realist models of conflict accept the likelihood or inevitability of violence as a mechanism for solving global problems. Conflict is regarded as an endemic feature of human activity, fuelled by the pursuit of national or ethnic self-interest above universal considerations. Realists differ over whether the root causes of the pervasiveness of conflict are predominantly psychological-genetic, suggesting a human disposition to violence which, although intuitively possibly appealing, is difficult to substantiate; contextual-physical, based upon a drive for security; or economic, fuelled by the need to secure scarce resources. In respect of the lattermost, it is worth noting that most inter-state conflicts are confined to countries with low standards of living and poor health and educational records. The orthodoxy is that violence is the most appropriate measure to gain or hold territory, or to rectify grievance. This assertion has been questioned by modern interpretations which view the greed of individuals for power and control as more important than the addressing of grievance or defence of territory (Shearer 1997; Ramsbotham et al. 2005). Faith in the utility of peace processes relies upon rational choice assumptions that remedial action and fair brokerage, rather than the appeasement of greed, are the cornerstones of peace-building. The logical conclusion of the 'greed' theory is that coercive responses, such as arrest, imprisonment or invasion, rather than gentle brokerage, are the only viable responses to create 'peace'.

Pessimism over the capacity of peace processes to end violence is exacerbated when the location of violence is considered. During the twentieth century, killings by state forces of their own citizens amounted to 170 million people, four times the number of deaths in inter- and intra-state wars (Rummel 1995; Patomaki 2001). Thus even successful peace processes in their current remit, dealing with identifiable conflict but not usually internal tyranny, will not eliminate genocide. Internal secrecy, sovereignty and suppression all contribute to the inability of the international community to extend the same processes of dialogue, management and resolution to slaughter within a state as might be applied in cases of civil war or inter-state conflict.

Empirically, the persistence of conflict offers much succour to Realist approaches. The nineteenth and twentieth centuries witnessed over 450 wars (Mack 2005). There were 244 armed conflicts between 1945 and 2009, across 151 locations, with over half of these conflicts being in existence since the end of the Cold War (Harbom and Wallensteen 2010: 501). Yet the number of inter-state wars has fallen dramatically, with no such conflicts recorded in 2009, although there were several cases where combatants in one country received support from another (Harbom and Wallensteen 2010). The diminution of inter-state conflict has, however, been 'compensated' by the continued proliferation of other conflicts, predominantly intra-state in nature, with 36 armed conflicts in existence in 2009, across 27 locations (Harbom and Wallensteen 2010: 501). There were nine conflicts in which the death toll exceeded 1,000 (the somewhat arbitrary requirement for classification as war) in 2010, and the Libyan and Sudan civil wars and internal conflict in Syria increased the number of high intensity wars in 2011 and 2012.

The rise of internal wars is associated with struggles to assert ethnic or religious identity, often within newly formed political entities, with peace reliant upon inventive capacity for multi-ethnic statebuilding. In South Sudan, for example, a bloody conflict between the Murle and Lou Nuer tribes saw hundreds killed in 2011, months after the declaration of the independence of the region. The government of the newly-independent state was beset by tribal rivalries and unable to utilize an effective police force or army to quell the problem. There is little to suggest that this growth in ethnic confrontations will be checked in the near future, although the political tools available to peacemakers dealing with ethnic conflict are being continually refined.

The Realist approach begs the question of whether peace processes amount to mere interludes in conflict. The pervasiveness and durability of wars offer succour to this view. However, against this are several arguments against any 'inevitability' thesis. There is an uneven geographical distribution of conflict, with 60 per cent of conflicts taking place in Africa and Asia and Realist perspectives do not fully explain why the violent pursuit of power is so geographically skewed. The nature of war has changed and few would have predicted the near-demise of inter-state wars. Moreover, the success of some peace processes provides grounds for empirical contestation that war is an inevitable facet of human organization. One-third of the post-Cold War conflicts have ended in peace agreements (Harbom et al. 2006: 617) and the overall trend, albeit uneven, is towards a reduction in the number of conflicts.

Whilst the Realist model holds the advantage of empirical backing in terms of the regularity of conflict, it may underestimate the capacity for policy learning apparent in peace processes, by which models of peace may be exported and refined at the local level. The capacity for conflict-building may be replicated, or even replaced by, the ability to build peace. To assume otherwise is to assume that a propensity to fight wars is an in-built human condition, a pessimistic, if understandable, interpretation given that there has never been full 'world peace', but also a hypothesis that cannot be proven. Realists tend to stress that peace is most probable where the (physical) balance of power between competing forces is appropriate and place less emphasis upon carefully designed political balancing acts inherent in liberal models of peace processes. Given its scepticism over permanent commitments to non-violence and enduring prospects for non-violence, a Realist interpretation of peace processes stresses the value of pressure being brought to bear upon insurgents through security measures and preventative actions. Under this interpretation, policies within peace processes may need to be coercive, in terms of retribution, arrests or imprisonments, reducing the capacity for armed activity and denying propaganda opportunities for combatants. Pressure for peace will develop as a functional consequence of this squeeze, rather than through a noble conversion to the values of non-violence. Whilst this approach is useful where terrorist groups are fairly weak or geographically isolated, as in, for example, the case of ETA in the Basque region, coercive approaches have less utility amid large-scale conflict where rival groups may each be heavily armed and disinclined to de-escalate conflict.

The logical conclusion of the liberal model of peace processes is that eventually they will ameliorate most global conflict, an unpersuasive argument even to those critical of Realist pessimism. The liberal model tends to assume that peace *per se* is a good thing, a laudable goal to be pursued in its own right and that this can then be followed by appropriate long-term political solutions. After all, who can possibly be against peace? Liberal models of peace processes contain the advantage of belief in a substantial human dimension, capable of rectifying problems. As Cochrane (2008: 1–2) argues, 'we do not have to accept war as integral to the human condition. Large-scale wars and smaller low-intensity conflicts are driven by political, economic and cultural imperatives. These forms of violence emerge as a means to an end and are not normally an end in themselves, even if the causal factors are difficult to determine'.

The difficulty with the liberal model is that its pursuit of peace as the ultimate intrinsic good ignores the capacity of peace processes to implement unfair and unjust agreements. Such a criticism is common in neo-Marxist critiques of peace processes, which tend to share similar short-term assumptions of the inevitability of violence as Realist models, but with more radical remedies. Dominant powers have the ability to dictate the terms of peace. National claims for self-determination and the creation of ethnic states may be approved within a very short time in some cases and rejected permanently in others, according to whether the dominant nation in the region is capable of subjugating the claims of ethnic groups, or is obliged to capitulate under pressure. Whilst it would be comforting to assume that rights of nationhood are conveyed on a logical, coherent basis during conflicts, this is not the case. Thus the rapidity with which the West recognized the claims to self-determination of countries in the Balkans conflict of the 1990s, perhaps justified on the grounds of undoubted Serbian aggression, contrasted with the persistent rejection of (highly contentious) claims to Basque self-determination within Spain. Given its internal problem with the Basques, it is unsurprising that the Spanish government is regularly one of the most reluctant countries to concede the claims to nationhood of others. The liberal assumptions of 'peace good, conflict bad' may also overlook the injustice bequeathed upon populations by the shaping of the contours of agreements. Thus the 'options' for Palestinians in their peace process comprise *how much* of their territory they are willing to permanently concede in a two-state solution – that they must permanently lose ground is unquestioned. Peace processes are about what is possible within a largely pre-ordained context and it is not necessarily the local population which sets the parameters for what can be agreed.

Peace Processes and the 'War on Terror'

The utility of common assumptions regarding peace processes has been questioned by Realists and liberals since the post-9/11 'war on terror'. The very term 'war on terror' assumed that negotiations and the normal rules of peace processes were not applicable; terror could only henceforth be defeated by war. As General Mike Jackson of the British Army pointed out, terrorism was not Al-Qaeda's end goal, so a war on the terror in isolation was inadequate; the defeat of Islamic fundamentalism was what was required (cited in English 2009: 130). Peace processes had hitherto been seen as sufficiently adaptable to deal with different types of conflict: inter- and intra-state, ethno-national and ethno-religious. There tended to be an assumption that, with the growth of secularism, conflicts would be predominantly ethno-national, another perspective substantially revised in recent years. Most of those ethno-national conflicts involved a small number of states. Moreover, peace processes often enveloped conflicts between armed non-state terrorist groups and state forces operating in a single country. Jihadist movements have shifted their focus from South Asia, where they have been pressurized by external and local forces, towards African countries. These include Algeria (where they have been similarly pressured), Mali, Nigeria (via Boko Haram), and Somalia, Al-Qaeda in the Islamic Maghreb offering a broad-ranging and sometimes internally divided challenge to national state forces and Western economic interests.

That Jihadist-related terrorism might possibly be seen as amenable to negotiated peace is unsurprising: as has been noted, terrorism is 'fundamentally and inherently political' (Whittaker 2003: 5). It has been defined as 'a form of political behaviour resulting from the deliberate choice of a basically rational actor, the terrorist organization' (Crenshaw 1981: 380). As a rational (in its own way), politically-inspired activity, terrorism was seen as amenable to political processes, which could respond to the political instrumentality underpinning terrorist groups (Taylor and Horgan 2006). 'New' terrorism has led to the questioning of this assumption. 'Old' terrorism, as a holistic concept or label, was inevitably loaded and contested. As English (2009: 143) contends, deployment of the label invariably created 'fruitless arguments between sides merely accusing each other of being the real terrorists'. In terms of solutions to terrorism 'old' and 'new', English offers a series of prescriptions, falling short of full peace or political processes, but potentially facilitating both, designed to ameliorate the impact of terrorism and limit its growth. These include stoical public and governmental responses, expressly designed to avoid over-reaction; adherence to existing legal and judicial frameworks;

avoidance of overbearing quasi-military responses; strong and coherent political counter-argument, and effective, often discreet, counter-intelligence (English 2009). Several of these propositions are echoed by Mueller (2005) in stressing that the direct effects of terrorism are limited and should therefore not be outweighed by indirect effects. The tendency of terrorist groups towards factionalism and splits may also diminish their strength. This 'little to fear except fear itself' advocacy may be sage, but often difficult to achieve amid the clamour for rapid response, the sense of threat, particularly given the disinterest in sparing civilians in the 'new' terrorism and demands for revenge or shows of strength that may emanate in frenzied climates from a range of sources, ranging from the media to victims' groups.

Schmid (1993: 12) argues that terrorists who 'adhere to the rules of war' and attempt to spare civilians should be given special treatment, whereas those who target civilians are guilty of war crimes and should be treated as war criminals. Indeed there is now a tendency to see 'old' terrorism more favourably, compared to newer, less discriminating forms. Pre-9/11, terrorism tended to be based upon a set of local demands, such as Basque independence or a united independent Ireland. Although terrorists could be drawn from a particular ethno-religious community and their demands could include the emancipation of an oppressed religious group, more commonly their demands were territorial. Although some terrorist groups claimed the mantle of revolution, the most enduring were those with specific anti-colonial demands which could be settled or negotiated. Post-9/11, it was difficult to contemplate how a peace process could even begin to be relevant in terms of diluting the demand for global jihad from Al-Qaeda, a network formed in the late 1980s and financed and operated largely independently of states. Al-Qaeda possessed an 'executive' (the Shura) drawn from individual countries and associated itself with Islamic struggles in individual countries or regions, but its ambitions extended well beyond these immediate theatres. Addressing the distinctive of national problems and local grievances, the normal aspects of peace processes, was therefore unlikely to be particularly fruitful. The motivation for violence rests upon a fundamental interpretation of the Koran and desire for a particular form of Islamification seemingly impervious to the efforts of negotiators to reconstruct or diminish it in terms of its outworking. The normal democratic apparatus – which offer post-conflict societal reconstruction; elections, referenda; parties, government – carry little credence. As Rapoport (2012: 54) argues, this wave of terrorism 'appears explicitly antidemocratic because the democratic idea is inconceivable without a significant measure of secularism'. This rejection of 'Western' intervention extends to the UN and its promotion of international values, given that the US is seen as the most important player within that organization.

There is nonetheless disagreement over the extent to which Al-Qaeda and what may loosely be labelled Islamic terrorism really constitutes a 'new' terrorism, immune from the treatments afforded to previous forms and carried out by diffuse, non-hierarchical organizations with which it is impossible to coordinate negotiations. In addition to the traditional considerations of the efficacy of terrorist techniques, this debate has covered several areas: whether the tactics of terror are new; whether the 'new' terror groups can be clearly identified and whether they can be incorporated into peace processes. The use of suicide bombings, whilst most dramatic on 9/11 and commonly associated with religiously fundamentalist groups, has (albeit more sparingly) also been used by secular groups such as the Kurdistan Workers Party (the PKK) and the Tamil Tigers (the LTTE). Thus the suicide terrorism of Al-Qaeda is not novel, having been used as a strategic logic in four other countries containing no significant Islamist militancy during the 1980s and 1990s (Pape 2003). Whilst it has been claimed that terrorists use suicide terrorism because it works, empirically this is difficult to sustain, given the eventual defeat of the Tamil Tigers and the limited successes achieved by Hamas. As a method of striking fear and establishing the 'credentials' of a terror group, however, suicide terrorism appears far more effective.

Duyvesteyn (2012) argues that Al-Qaeda-sponsored terrorism is essentially political, not nihilistic. In respect of the tactics deployed, although civilians are more at risk, targets remain mainly symbolic and terrorism is territorially organized, in common with previous forms. Islamic terror groups have reached political agreements on territorial issues. The Moro Islamic Liberation Front concluded a deal with the government of the Philippines in 2012 to establish Muslim-dominated Bangsamoro as an autonomous political entity. Terrorism exercised by single-religion groups is hardly novel, although to compare the importance of religion within, say the IRA, to that of Al-Qaeda, appears fatuous. The lack of a cohesive political outlet is not a new feature of terrorism. Weinberg (1991) found that only just over one-third of terrorist groups were linked to political parties.

The actions of Al-Qaeda and its affiliates have nonetheless revised approaches towards peace processes. Whilst successful processes involving the defeat of terrorism have previously tended to involve a subtle and coordinated interplay of political carrots and military sticks, these lessons were overlooked in some responses to post-9/11 Islamic jihad, mistakes not fully exonerated by the difficulty and novelty of dealing with global fundamentalism (English 2009). Whether peace processes can be conducted locally via national wings of the loose affiliation that Al-Qaeda embodies remains to be seen. Terrorist groups purporting to support the principles of Islamic Jihad, often only very loosely affiliated, if at all, to Al-Qaeda, exist in more than 20 countries, although their strength varies considerably, from being a major factor in, for example, Nigeria and Somalia, to a minor player in Lebanon and southern provinces of Thailand. Moreover, Islamic terrorist groups are not always operating under the Al-Qaeda umbrella: in Algeria alone, 60 extremist groups, many an assortment of religious zealots or political Islamists (Whittaker, 2003: 156–7) have been identified. Ollapally's (2008) analysis of ostensibly 'religious' terrorism

has considerable roots in geopolitical identity and responses to external interference. Dingley's (2010) analysis also disputes the novelty of 'new' terrorism,
in highlighting the ordinariness of its advocates and in arguing that terrorist
violence is a response to the disturbance of stability amid social dislocation.
Both make the point that, given that the development of terrorism is a
response to political or structural factors, it can be 'treated' via political processes. Indeed, Ashour (2009) has highlighted how previously Jihadist groups
have moderated their outlook.

Given that Al-Qaeda offers a very limited vertical chain for national Islamic
groups and that horizontal connections, at least in terms of common ideological goals, appear greater, what is the best approach of any peace process, even
assuming (a very large assumption given the fundamentalism of each group's
demands) they may be amenable to potential incorporation within peace
dialogues? For a peace process to be realizable, national territorial aspirations
for these groups, which can be the subject of discussion or negotiation, would
need to outweigh global religious ambitions for a peace process to be viable.
Yet even where Islamic militant groups have become largely nationalistic in
outlook, the Taleban in Afghanistan providing perhaps the most prominent
example, their fundamentalism may outweigh any possibility of participation in a peace process. Whilst the isolation of such groups might force them
towards a process, regional sympathy (from sections of Pakistan's Army in the
Taleban's case) is a sufficient counterweight. Arguably the most difficult challenge for peace processes over the next few decades will be how to formulate
political solutions to conflicts in which nationalist Islamists, holding socially
conservative values very different from much of the West, are enticed into
post-conflict governing structures. This process will be acutely difficult if terrorist groups acquire weapons of mass destruction.

Conclusion

Realist perceptions of the ubiquity of war are understandable given the apparently endemic nature of conflict. However, the position is not static in terms
of the nature and intensity of those wars. Moreover, the capacity of human
agency to confront what appears to be an endemic condition should not be
underestimated. In tackling modern forms of conflict, peace processes rely
upon decades of accumulated empirical evidence to assist scholars in gauging
how the management of peace processes can be improved. As the nature of
war has altered, so has the dexterity of the political formulas seeking its eradication. Inter-state conflict has diminished and it is possible that intra-state
violence may take a similar course. For such a development, the policy learning evident in peace processes has to have greater import in regions seemingly
impervious to the processes of compromise and prioritization of avoidance of
loss of life which have begun to embed elsewhere. The persistence of belief in
conflict as an inevitable form of human activity does not adequately explain

the geographic variability of violence, nor does it explain why 'new' forms of terror have emerged, in terms of the religious, or ethno-religious conflict which has been evident in recent times.

Collective studies of peace processes indicate a reasonably clear sequencing, beginning with secret exploratory dialogue, followed by the public emergence of discussions and negotiations, brokered increasingly by external mediators. Amid much grandstanding over formal peace deals, there has been a welcome shift towards dealing with vexed problems of implementing and sustaining peace, maintaining political institutions and managing post-conflict issues such as moving combatants into civil society. The achievement of a peace deal is merely one step towards managing a conflict. Resolution of the conditions or divisions which yielded violence requires a much longer term effort. Peace processes are thus sustained, non-linear constructions, beset by regular reversals, given that, at their most comprehensive, they cover decades of shifts from violence to constitutional politics; the management of division and, ultimately, the resolution of the underlying problems which precipitated violence.

CHAPTER TWO

Prescriptions for Conflict Management or Resolution

A range of political remedies have been adopted as the outworking of a peace process. Inter-state wars have fewer political options than those of internal conflicts, but may involve a redrawing of borders to reshape local political geography and may also rely heavily upon external brokerage and peacekeeping. Clashes between different communities, or rebellion against the state, yield different solutions. Gurr's (1993, 1995) typology of ethno-national communities suggests various forms of resolution: increased autonomy, which may involve devolution or federal restructuring as described below; greater access to state resources, which may consist primarily of an equality agenda designed to eradicate discrimination; power-sharing and control within the state; or secession, the exit option used when the demands of antagonists are irreconcilable within existing state structures. The growth of peace processes has seen the development of a plethora of political provisions, including the formation of new governments; the co-option of antagonists into that government; the establishment of new political parties (often led by former combatants); the creation of new structures of local or regional autonomy; referenda; power-sharing (at national or local level); and federalism (Harbom et al. 2006). New structural arrangements require political legitimacy, but devices such as the staging of elections risk precipitating a renewal of hostilities if held prematurely, or if they produce clear losers (Snyder 2000; Brancati and Snyder 2011; Dunning 2011). This chapter explores the plethora of possible political and territorial solutions to conflict, but begins by examining how conflicts may arrive at the point where political dexterity becomes possible.

Mutually Hurting Stalemate and Ripeness for Peace

The predictive capacity of scholars of conflict and peace has often been questioned. Few predicted the demise of the Soviet Empire and the events of 9/11 and Jihadist 'struggles' were not widely anticipated. The primary role of a peace process is to end conflict, but should students of war and peace also be better able to anticipate when conflict might cease? Much of the predictive and analytical work on assessing prospects for peace has relied upon game theory in identifying how conflict might be turned into non-violence. Game theory itself utilized various adaptations of the prisoner's dilemma which indicated the lack of logic behind non-cooperation (Rapoport and Chammah

1965). Two prisoners are faced with a choice between 'defecting', i.e. confessing to the police, or cooperating with each other (remaining silent) with each prisoner uncertain over the intentions of the other. The prisoner's dilemma works on a classical rational choice model that the most likely course of action would be that seen as maximizing individual benefit. This is perceived by each prisoner as achieved by confessing (shorter sentence or earlier release from jail) even though had each prisoner remained silent they may have received only a minimal sentence or none at all if the police lacked evidence.

Applied to conflict and peace, the rational choice model grounds the chances of peace as most likely when it is in the perceived self-interest of each set of rival combatants to move towards cessation. Thus peace is not a derivative of an amalgam of rival interests, but is built from a mutuality of separately constructed perceptions. Peace does not arrive from altruism, benign goodwill, cognizance of rival arguments or self-doubt (although there may be elements of this within the thinking of combatants), but is instead arrived at via calculation. What benefits will peace bring to our side and will these benefits outweigh continued warfare? Mutual benefit may indeed accrue from ceasefires embracing all combatants, but shared interest is not the initial consideration in bringing about peace. In movement towards peace, a series of 'prisoner's dilemma' equivalents may be evident, as combatants tiptoe towards ceasefires often unaware of the intention of their enemy (Axelrod 1984). The most appropriate strategy for each individual set of combatants may be initial cooperation with enemies, followed by persistent copying of the strategy of opponents, to prevent outflanking. To always cooperate with the enemy is to risk humiliation; to persistently defect, i.e. betray the enemy and eschew cooperation may be self-defeating.

It is within the context of the desirability of attaching a predictive capacity to studies of peace processes that the concepts of mutually hurting stalemate and 'ripeness' for peace developed. Mutually hurting stalemate may be an objective reality, but for it to be converted into a basis for peace negotiations, it requires transformation into a subjective awareness held by the participants in conflict that outright victory is unattainable and the costs of its pursuit unacceptable. Combatants, or at least their leaders, come to realize that they have reached a 'costly dead-end' (Zartman 1989: 268). This may be due to a plateau having been reached in terms of the level of conflict, in which decisive further casualties cannot be inflicted, or a precipice, in which the escalation of conflict may be too catastrophic to contemplate. Ripeness for peace is thus a perception (Zartman 1989, 2003); in the absence of perfect knowledge of the enemy's capabilities and intentions, it cannot be anything else. Ripeness may be created by one or more of a large loss of life and escalation of the conflict; the impossibility of unilateral actions solving the war; or the risk of loss of support for combatants if they continue with violence.

Using a rational choice model, the assumption is that combatants utilize violence to further their goals. Desired behaviour is brought about by the threat of loss, or inability to make further gain. This assumption may be rooted in a zero-sum game model of conflict in which gains for one side ensure losses for the rival; thus violence exercised by one set of combatants may weaken the enemy. When these sides each develop cognitive awareness, either through self-realization or through the work of a mediator, that non-violence might be more productive for their own cause, or even more promisingly, if unlikely, that there might be mutual benefit in ceasing violence, a conflict may be ripe for peace. Incompatible objectives are supplanted by a desire to end conflict for pragmatic reasons. The obvious question begged is how this awareness is reached amid the blinkered visions evident in war. Mutually hurting stalemate requires a number of features to be labelled as such: broadly equal desire for compromise; the ability of leaderships to deliver and sell the deal; and acceptance of an agreed set of procedures by which an agreement can be formulated (Haass 1988; Kleiboer 1994). Stedman (1991) refined the concepts of mutually hurting stalemate and ripeness, downgrading the importance of the existence of a deadlock as a prerequisite for peace and acknowledging the existence of factionalism amongst groups, which may lead to differing subjective perceptions over the utility of compromise. A perception amongst some combatants that the conflict will worsen, along with skilful mediation, are instead the key contributors to ripeness.

It has been claimed that mutually hurting stalemate and ripeness have become the orthodox mode of assessing the amenability of conflicts to management or resolution (Ramsbotham et al. 2005). Ripeness for peace arising from stalemate has been claimed as a key agent of peace in, as examples, Angola, El Salvador, Morocco (the Western Sahara conflict with the Polisario Front), Namibia, South Africa and Northern Ireland. Yet sometimes the supposed ripeness turned sour with appalling consequences. Angola was arguably ripe for peace by the 1980s, amid a stalemate between the National Union for the Independence of Angola (UNITA) and the People's Movement for the Liberation of Angola (MPLA). The 1991 Bicesse Agreement was reached after the two sides had apparently fought each other to a standstill, yet UNITA returned to war for a time in 2002, its leader Jonas Savimbi unable to accept the objective reality of a mutually hurting stalemate. It took his death, rather than the broader conflict scenario, to reinstate ceasefires.

The attraction of stalemate and ripeness as explanatory aspects of peace processes is obvious, in that they provide a rational explanation as to how conflicts move from deadlock. They demonstrate why and when negotiations begin and form a basis for action. Thus in El Salvador, as one example, there was a recognition by the government and the military that the Farabundo Marti National Liberation Front (FMLN) could not be entirely defeated, given that the rebels controlled one-third of the country and that the government could not afford further sustained military offensives. Equally, the FMLN, although strong, was incapable of taking command of the remainder of El Salvador. The mutual recognition of the illogicality and lack of utility of continued violence led to a series of peace accords during the early 1990s. A similar stalemate was evident in Namibia between the South West Africa People's Organization (SWAPO) and South African state forces, as SWAPO's fight for independence created an upsurge of violence during the late 1980s (Bertram 1995). Perceptions of a mutually hurting stalemate were also influential in the onset of peace in the Cambodian conflict of the 1980s and early 1990s. The People's Republic of Kampuchea (PRK) forces, backed by the Vietnamese, had been pitted against those of the former government, the Party of Democratic Kampuchea (PDK) and the Khmer People's National Liberation Front (KPNLF) which, along with other small groups, formed the Coalition Government of Democratic Kampuchea, backed by China. Neither side could oust the other and, amid the decline of support for the Cambodian forces from their external agents (Vietnam and China), ripeness for peace developed, mediated by third parties and enforced by the United Nations in 1990–1 (Amer 2007).

In East Timor, a mutually hurting stalemate was evident between the Indonesian forces controlling the area and East Timorese guerrillas, the Armed Forces for the National Liberation of East Timor (FALANTIL), demanding independence for the region. Those guerrillas had conducted an armed campaign for over two decades, leading to nearly 20,000 deaths and could not be entirely eliminated, whilst the demand for independence extended well beyond the armed group. Equally, the FALANTIL were incapable of achieving their aims through force. It was correctly argued that the required ingredients were the 'presence of valid spokespersons for the principal protagonists, and widespread perceptions of a mutually hurting stalemate', to develop the 'necessary formula for the way out' (Salla 1997: 463). These spokespersons arrived via diplomatic representatives from Indonesia and Portugal, with the formula being that of a referendum, overseen by the UN, which facilitated self-determination for the East Timorese. The vote in favour of secession for East Timor led initially to violence from those opposed, but independence was finally awarded in 2002. The existence of a mutually hurting stalemate has also been credited with producing ripeness for peace between Azerbaijan and Armenia for control over Nagorno-Karabakh in the early 1990s, amid a conflict which produced 25,000 deaths and nearly one million refugees. The costs were high to both sides and the outcome, in which Nagorno-Karabakh remains nominally overseen by Azerbaijan, but with no real power exercised by that country, was unsatisfactory for both sides. Accordingly, Mooradian and Druckman (1999: 726) conclude that ripeness for peace may be created by negative conditioning, as 'settlement depends more on the "push" of a hurting stalemate than on the "pull" of an anticipated outcome'.

Yet mutually hurting stalemate and ripeness have been heavily criticized as approaches to identifying the onset of a peace process. Firstly, ripeness for dialogue and the construction of possible formulas of peace by combatants may not be tantamount to ripeness for a peaceful solution, yet the two processes tend to be conflated. When dialogue breaks down, the assumption is that the situation was unripe. Secondly, it is not apparent whether the conditions for ripeness appear, or whether they have to be deliberately created, or are contrived by mediators. Zartman (1989: 273) claimed that 'conceptually, the moment [of ripeness] stands out, but in reality is buried in the rubble of events'. It is unclear how this claim can be verified. If reality is buried, then it does not become a subjective perception, which leaves it only as an objective reality – which is not how ripeness is constructed by its adherents. A core, universal set of indicators of either the existence of a mutually hurting stalemate or a ripe moment for peace remains elusive. Thirdly, very few conflicts reach a point where there is, objectively or subjectively, a symmetrical mutual hurt, or a realization by two or more sets of combatants that this position has been reached. Adherents of complexity theory argue that no decisions can ever be made 'with full knowledge of the complex interaction of a multiplicity of variables' (Little 2009: 254; see also Geyer and Rihani 2010). Such full knowledge is rarely evident amid conflict.

Many peace deals have been concluded amid little optimism that a hurting stalemate had been recognized and that the conflict was ripe. The 1977 bilateral accord between Israel and Egypt, for example, confounded those who assumed that, in common with Israel's relations with other neighbours, the problems in the region were insurmountable. Static positions in conflicts are rare. A more common position is that of shifting alliances and levels of backing for antagonists. As one example, rival Kurdish forces were frequently subject to the changing loyalties of their leaderships during the Iran–Iraq war of the 1980s and were used as proxies by both sides in what appeared to be a stalemate, until finally siding against the Iraqis in 1986, following Saddam Hussein's deployment of poison gas (Jeong 2010). Stalemate theses may underestimate the capacity of groups to alter the balance of forces or develop alternative transformative strategies, including a shifting of goals.

Mutually hurting stalemate also assumes that the capacity to inflict hurt upon an opponent is static, when a more realistic position is that this can be adjusted or improved. The most serious criticism is that the concept of ripeness is tautological. Although Zartman (1986) insists that ripeness should not be judged retrospectively, i.e. by the outcome of the peace process, there is a tendency amongst ripeness adherents to do precisely this. Zartman (2003: 20) asserts that 'not all ripe moments are so seized and turned into negotiations', but if this is indeed the case, how do we know they were ripe? When peace processes break down, the conflict is then judged as having been unripe for peace, a position discouraging confidence in predictive capability. Having observed the collapse of several embryonic peace dialogues, Lederach (2003: 31) argues that ripeness theory offers mainly a 'rear view mirror'; a retrospective take on why peace did or did not take hold. In many cases, stalemates and apparent ripeness do not mature into fully developed peace processes. To then dismiss the situation as having been unripe is palpably unsatisfactory. Possible ripeness for exploratory dialogue, which may exist, needs to be disaggregated from ripeness for conflict management or resolution, requiring a far greater level of commitment than cognizance of stalemate or mere acknowledgement of the possible benefits of peace.

Managing Modern Ethno-National Conflict

Nationhood and issues of self-determination for ethno-national groups have been major elements in producing conflict. The worst conflict in Europe since the Second World War, in the former Yugoslavia, was produced by the desire of ethnic groups to achieve full statehood, nationalist fervour and the demand for self-determination far outweighing commitment to the Communist federal construction. Acts of violence to achieve self-determination may be construed by dominant state actors as terrorism rather than war, requiring a different approach to that needed for 'traditional' inter-state or even intra-state conflict. 'Terrorism' may be defined by states as criminality, to be crushed amid the assertion of asymmetrical relationships, rather than seen as an arena for negotiation. Thus following the Chinese invasion and occupation of Tibet in 1950, resistance by the Tibetans and their promotion of rights of self-determination have been persistently faced down by a combination of killings, martial law and religious and cultural repression (Jeong 2010) rather than processes of dialogue and reconciliation.

Conflicts between different ethno-national and ethno-religious groups within the same state are amongst the most common types of hostility, yet they take many different forms and have prompted an extremely varied range of solutions, embracing partition, consociation, integration, devolution, federalism and independence, each of these accommodations taking on particular forms according to local conditions. The need to take account of local factors is crucial, as is the requirement to avoid imposing western values. Lieven (2012: 12) may overstate his case in asserting that 'much of western political science is hopelessly wedded to general theories based on schematic versions of western societies and institutions and is remarkably impervious to even the strongest evidence of local experience', but the insistence of western leaders and political scientists upon imposing *their* view of how a state should be designed may be fatal for a project. Lieven highlights how the absence of a bottom-up, localized strategy in Afghanistan beyond original 'Blairite nostrums about "people everywhere wanting freedom"' results in withdrawal amid 'embittered clichés about "tribalism" and "fanaticism"' (Lieven 2012).

Most intra-state conflicts have an ethnic background (see Guelke 2010) and ethnicity is a powerful agent of mobilization. It is worth stating, lest we run away with the idea that expressions of ethnic identity are retarded or dangerous, that in a majority of multi-ethnic states there is peaceful, harmonious co-existence and an absence of conflict. However, where there have been problems, there is considerable divergence over the most appropriate means of 'treating' ethnicity, linked to the ongoing debate over the essentialism of identity. Some regimes have attempted to smother separate identities, as in the old Soviet Union and this has been the approach in Russia and China. Russia's difficulties with Chechen militants remain ongoing. An alternative approach is to foster rival ethnic identities, relieving pressure on an authoritarian regime by dividing opposition, as occurred via programmes of separate development in South Africa (Esman 2004). This may extend a strategy of hegemonic control by an ethnic minority in a multi-ethnic state, but 'divide and rule' is impermanent as a means of retention of control (Lustick 1979). The South African model was unsuccessful in preserving the apartheid white regime and the Russian and Chinese governments have been only partially successful in quashing expressions of ethnic identity.

Western governments have used force against those attempting to crush ethnic expression, NATO's bombing of Serbia to deter aggression against Kosovo being one example. Genocide to crush ethnic rivals was evident in Saddam Hussein's actions against Kurds in Iraq, a practice also adopted by the Iranian regime, and the crushing of ethnic groups has also been evident in several African countries, such as Burundi, Nigeria, Rwanda and Uganda. To highlight one of these examples, in Burundi, over 100,000 Hutu were killed by Tutsi government forces in 1972. Yet did this not end the Hutu demand for a stake in the polity, unsurprisingly given that they represent 85 per cent of Burundi's population. Further violence, in which 30,000 people were killed, followed in 1988, before a loose power-sharing deal was put in place (Lemarchand 1993).

An alternative approach is to recognize ethnic groups and concede them limited autonomy within state structures, provided that loyalty to the central regime is not undermined. This form of ethnic harnessing is commonly associated with liberal democratic regimes, evident in, for example, Spain's post-1978 constitution which conceded considerable political autonomy to Basques and Catalans. Spain's approach of conceding greater devolution to the Basque region has met with partial success in containing militancy. Basque claims to an ethnic nation are of the type most difficult to accommodate as they straddle two nations, given the claim to part of South-West France. Kurdish claims to their own homeland embracing parts of Turkey, Iraq and Iran are seen by most observers as impossible to reconcile with the integrity of those 'parent' states. Ethnic claims are easiest to contain when lodged within a single territory. Canada's concession of autonomy to French-speaking Quebec has helped preserve the integrity of the state, despite tensions between Anglo and Francophone identities, with the French-speaking sector stressing the need to promote the French language and culture, ambitions which militants claim can only be fully realized via independence. Belgium's accommodation of its Dutch speaking population in Flanders and French Walloons has been problematic, although the country remains united despite its bi-communalism. Ethnic accommodation is not always conceded by liberal democracies. For example, the tradition of centralism in France and the notion of the indivisible republic ensure that little has been done in terms of even partial acknowledgement of the claims of militant Bretons to be a separate Celtic nation. Indeed, greater ethnic accommodation has occasionally been conceded by ostensibly totalitarian regimes. Tito's communist regime in Yugoslavia demanded loyalty to the central government but acknowledged the existence of different ethnic identities within its federal construction, in an elite-level authoritian consociation.

It may also be impossible to achieve political accommodation between rival ethnic groups where there has been domination by one group over another. In Northern Ireland, the domination of the Unionist tradition from 1920 onwards was effectively removed by the introduction of British direct rule from London in 1972, encouraging minority participation in the state and culminating in formal power-sharing from 1998 amid the subsiding of violence. In Afghanistan, however, the continued onslaught by the Taleban, abetted by Pakistan, rendered near-impossible aspirations of stable consociation and the government's remit barely exists in parts of the country. An enduring power-sharing solution would be difficult even in an Afghanistan less riddled with violence, given the previous dominance of the Pashtuns at the expense of the other main ethnic groups, Hazara, Uzbeks and Tadjiks. This raises the question of who is the state being built for? It highlights the difficulties of Western encouragement of state-building in a polity which, in order to survive, has a 'need to give antidemocratic, often anti-Western leaders a stake in the political process' (Sherman 2008: 330).

Separating Peoples: Partition, Secession and Independence

Assertions of nationhood may often take violent forms, particularly in a situation where the dominant country is viewed as a colonial aggressor. Although much of Britain's retreat from its unaffordable Empire after the Second World War was peaceful, anti-colonial struggles for independence were also evident and diminished the desire of the colonial power to remain. The rebellion by the Kenyan Mau Mau during the 1950s was defeated, but nonetheless hastened British withdrawal from the country by 1963. French withdrawal from Algeria was another example of colonial retreat under pressure from insurgents. Although there may be a loss of prestige and resources, the award of independence, if clearly desired by a population, may be a low-cost means of addressing conflict. Often however, the presence of an indigenous group, supportive of the colonial power, complicates matters. France's retreat from Algeria was opposed by settler-colonials but did not prevent withdrawal, unlike in Ireland, where the British government responded to the threat of civil war from nearly one million resolutely pro-British citizens by partitioning the country and retaining part of the territory.

Rather than attempt to reconcile the presence of rival ethno-national groups in a single country, with little chance of healing ethnic divisions, it may be better to partition states. However, this most extreme response to ethnic pluralism risks new inter-state hostilities supplanting intra-state conflict. Partition has the attraction of physically separating combatants, yet has rarely been used, with fewer than 20 cases during the twentieth century (and several of these being the dissolution of the USSR and the emergence of new states). A majority of partitions have struggled to contain ongoing violence, but there are successful examples, more generally those introduced amid an absence of violence. The separation of Slovakia from Czechoslovakia in 1992 gave Slovaks the nation-state they felt they deserved and the partition was peaceful and amicable. Nonetheless, the separation was complex, requiring 30 separate treaties and 12,000 legal agreements. The creation of Bangladesh in 1971, following conflict in East Pakistan, was the first state created by partition since the formation of Pakistan in 1947, after India ended British colonial rule. That partition might be judged a success, but it is worth noting that violence has been attendant, evidenced in the late 1990s in the northern Indian regions of Jammu and Kashmir, following a Pakistan-inspired uprising involving a variety of Islamic militants. Moreover, Bangladesh contains 45 diverse ethnic communities, some of which have been marginalized amid the assertion of dominant Bengali culture (Jeong 2010).

The impact of partition needs to be judged over a long period. India and Pakistan fought a war 18 years after they had divided and India has been subject to challenges from ethnic groups in Kashmir and Punjab, demanding exit from the state. Indeed, Kashmir has been partitioned between three countries, India, which controls the Southern and central regions of the country, Pakistan which controls the North and West, and China, in charge of the North East. Each of these respective claims is contested by the other states and Kashmir remains unstable amid episodic violence, mainly between Islamic militants and Hindus. As another example of instability attendant to partition, the formal separation of Sudan into North and South in 2011, following a 2005 peace treaty and declaration of independence by the South, has not ended violence in the region. Whilst the Sudan People's Liberation Army has transformed from guerrilla irregulars to become the regular army of the southern Sudanese state, it is vulnerable to challenge by other militias, such as the Lord's Resistance Army, bereft of a clear political strategy and committed to the continuing use of violence. Almost half a century had elapsed before the partition of Ireland was to contribute to further conflict between the British state and the IRA. During the twentieth century, almost three-quarters of partitioned countries experienced at least one bout of armed conflict and one-quarter became embroiled in civil war, in some cases amid demands for repartition, with the worst cases being those where small states were formed via partition amid violence, conflict being a more important variable than ethnic unity within newly formed states (Tir 2005: 554). Partition rarely creates ethnic unity within states, due to the impossibility of the population movements required, which is why most scholars rarely endorse its utilization (see, e.g., Horowitz 1985; Kumar 1997).

Despite these concerns, supporters of partition argue that separation can provide the most direct route towards the diminution of antagonism between two rival populations. The chief basis of such contention is that maximum homogeneity within partitioned states offers the most apposite solution (e.g., Kaufmann 1996, 1998) despite the obvious risks of ethnic cleansing associated with forced removals of populations. Ethnic compositional 'purity' does not remove the risk of intra-ethnic division which may emerge within new states if there remain two or more ethnic groups within a new state. Violent separation of states or formation of new ones is fraught with difficulty as it elevates the use of force, consolidates the roles of rival armies and may place military figures at the head of emergent polities. Violence may mean that partition is imposed more than it is agreed. Those displaced or forced into a secessionist state may continue to fight for the return of 'their' land or for the reunification of the two states. Ethnic groups within the rump state may demand their own secessionist state, encouraged by the earlier fracturing of the territory.

Struggles for secession are common, taking place where an ethnic group wishes to establish its own nation, feeling that true nationhood and expression of ethnic identity is achievable only via the establishment of a new, distinctive state and withdrawal from the existing parent entity. When an embryonic 'nation-in-waiting' declares intent to secede, conflict often erupts, as when East Timor declared its intention to quit Indonesia, to offer merely one example (Wolff 2006). Secessionist struggles rarely end in victory for the group desiring breakaway, only 7 per cent of such conflicts ending in triumph, with nearly half witnessing persistent armed conflict and the bulk of the remainder resulting in defeat for the insurgents (Heraclides 1998). However, the figure for success rises when secession for nations from federations, as occurred in the dissolution of Yugoslavia, is also considered. With a median of over 9,000 deaths per conflict, secessionist wars appear to be of similar intensity to non-secessionist wars, for which the median is 10,000 (Lacina 2006).

The grounds for secession may vary. Assertions of self-determination for self-ascribed nations form the bulk of such claims, although the precise basis of claimed nationhood may be a complex mixture of myth, history, geography, language, culture, economics, discriminatory treatment and support from other countries. Moreover, there is no neat equation which indicates whether demands for secession will be peaceful and democratic in nature, or insurrectionary and violent, although ethno-religious struggles for secession can be particularly difficult to contain. Demands for secession may follow its award in neighbouring areas, creating a domino effect.

Consociational Power-Sharing and Conflict Management

One of the most fashionable political frameworks for managing conflicts is consociation – an association of political elites representing different ethnic groups combining to govern a divided society. Consociation is seen as an appropriate means of ensuring adequate representation of all the major ethnic blocs within a polity. Rival groups share power under particular rules and guarantees. There is an ongoing debate over the 'rules' of consociation. The original exponent of consociational theory, Arend Lijphart (1968, 1977) declared that the principal ambition of consociation does not necessarily concern a particular institutional arrangement, but is based upon overarching cooperation at the elite level in a culturally fragmented system. Yet Lijphart (1977) did assert four core aspects of consociation which have come to be seen as the system's essential features: grand coalition government incorporating the political representatives of the main ethnic blocs; proportionality in government and other representative institutions, to ensure fair and adequate representation of majority and minority ethnic blocs; veto rights for minorities, via cross-community consent for legislation to ensure non-dominance by the majority ethnic group; and community autonomy for ethnic blocs, although the extent to which this is a key feature varies considerably according to the nature of the consociational agreement. Communal autonomy may amount to little more than the maintenance of pre-agreement arrangements, such as the facilitation of religious schools, as evident in the pre- and post-Ta'if Accord in Lebanon and the Good Friday Agreement in Northern Ireland. Given that communities are subject to the same policing, judicial, economic and political regulations, to cite four areas, the status of segmental autonomy as an essential, rather than possible, feature of consociation has rightly been questioned (Coakley 2009). Alternatively, the political arrangements of Macedonia and Iraq offer considerable communal self-governance on a territorial basis (Wolff 2009).

In acute cases of conflict, even consociationalists initially urged caution over the utility of power-sharing deals, McGarry and O'Leary (1993: 37) concurring with Horowitz (1985: 571–2) that 'consociationalism may only be practicable in moderately rather than deeply divided societies'. Yet that has not stopped the subsequent application of consociation – and claims made regarding its success – in a variety of difficult conflict arenas, Bosnia and Iraq being two such theatres. Lijphart (1975) was sceptical over the utility of consociation in Northern Ireland during the 1970s, but revised his opinion amid the reduced violence – but not necessarily lessening of division – evident in the 1990s. Consociationalists also stress the need for internal fidelity to state-building. Lijphart emphasized internal solutions to internal problems as the most hopeful scenario for consociational solutions, but Kerr (2009: 219) insists that 'the existence of strong or balanced external powers promoting power sharing and maintaining a stable political environment remain crucial'.

There are two key criticisms of consociation. The first is the empirical verdict that it simply does not work, as there are very few sharply divided societies where it has resolved an internal conflict. Consociation has, to be charitable, a mediocre record. It may aggravate ethnic aggrandisement and consociational agreements are chiselled less from mutuality of interest (although that may exist) than from communal perception of the best deal available for ethnic advancement. This claim of failure is strongly contested by recent empirical research. The study of civil wars by Mattes and Savun (2009) suggests significant reductions in the propensity to re-ignite violence if power-sharing follows conflict, whilst Norris's (2008) analysis of power-sharing institutions indicates that they have a strong record of conflict prevention and political stability (see O'Leary 2013: 41–5).

Others are more sceptical. The (anti-consociationalist) Rupert Taylor (2009a: 6) claims 11 cases of consociational agreements since 1980: three temporary deals, in Zimbabwe, Czechoslovakia and South Africa, and eight enduring pacts, in Lebanon, Bosnia-Herzegovina, Burundi, Northern Ireland, Macedonia, Afghanistan, Iraq and Kenya. Malaysia and South Tyrol are highlighted as other contemporary cases where consociational deals have stuck since the 1970s. Other consociational cases are those applied to countries with ethnic division but bereft of serious conflict, such as the Netherlands, Belgium and Switzerland. Even in these successful cases, there are caveats. Cantonization is at least as important in the Swiss case, whilst in Belgium consociation has contributed to the deepening of the two main communities to the point where 'there is no longer any real political centre within the state and there is no sense of Belgian national solidarity and public opinion' (Deschouwer, 2005: 105).

Of Taylor's list of consociational cases, South Tyrol, Northern Ireland and Bosnia-Herzegovina provide clear examples of success, and Lebanon might possibly be claimed as such (Taylor, 2009b). These consociations have worked on a pragmatic and popular basis, albeit with the rather important qualification that no constitutional alternatives were ever laid before the people in a referendum. Even if naysayers can argue that the worst of the conflict was over some time before the most successful consociational deals, the form of agreement helped secure a fragile peace. Macedonia's claim to be a genuine consociation is somewhat more contentious, although admissible given that power is shared between Macedonian Christian Democrats and ethnic Albanians. Bosnia's confederal principles, developed via the 1995 Dayton Agreement, are of arguably almost as much importance as the consociation. Dixon (2005) has been a lone voice in questioning Northern Ireland's consociational credentials, arguing that consociationalism now so lacks precision, as applied via the 1998 Good Friday and 2006 St Andrews agreements, that it amounts to little more than power-sharing, for which the rules are made ad hoc. The orthodox view is clearly that Bosnia and Northern Ireland are the big success stories. South Tyrol offers a more dated example. Agreement was reached between the Italian and Austrian governments to protect the autonomy of the majority Italian and minority German-speaking populations in 1969, following a decade of low-level conflict. This low-level violence was prompted mainly by the feeling amongst the German-speaking population that their ethnicity and rights were under challenge, fuelling their desire to align with Austria. By the 1990s, over two decades of communal protection had been sufficient for the measures to be put into disuse as divisions had largely biodegraded in the manner which consociationalists insist is possible in the long term.

Macedonia saw a brief conflict between Macedonians and Albanians in 2001. Since then, power-sharing via the Ohrid Agreement, a claimed consociation but, unusually, with a majoritarian government, has been established. There is considerable reliance upon municipal authorities as the guarantors of ethnic autonomy, which begs the question whether this system is an elite-level consociation or a case of devolution. Moreover, there was controversy over the composition of political elites for a time. Although there is a presence within that government for the Albanian minority, its representatives were chosen by the Macedonian-dominated government. Thus the popular Democratic Union for Integration was temporarily overlooked in favour of the less popular Party for Democratic Prosperity as the representatives of the Albanians, based predominantly in the west of the country, within the ruling administration following the 2006 elections, until a more representative coalition emerged after 2008.

Of the other countries cited as consociations, Lebanon's Ta'if Accord has often been usurped by external interference from other countries. Afghanistan has often been a warzone without an effective multi-ethnic power-sharing government. More than 11,000 civilians, 3,000 Afghan policemen and 2,000 Western soldiers were killed between 2001 and 2011 (Burke 2011) with year-on-year increases in the civilian death toll from 2006 to 2011. Stable consociation appears elusive. The fear of Pashtuns, based mainly in the south of the country (and who attract sympathy from Pakistan) is that they would be marginalized by non-Pashtuns, notably the Panjshiri Tajiks (who attract sympathy from India). Pakistani Pashtuns are, to different degrees, sympathetic towards the Taleban, even though most reject the concept of Islamic jihad (Lieven 2011). Amid external interest and an internal failure of state-building, power-sharing between the representatives of each group may remain difficult to build.

Despite strong external mediation from the Organization for African Unity and the United Nations, plus direct input from Nelson Mandela, Burundi's consociational deal, finally agreed in 2000, did not end violence. The agreement was preceded (and followed) by years of violence which included the killing of two Hutu Presidents within one year, as Rwandan Tutsis attempted to regain control. Four years of stop-start negotiations followed a collapsed earlier deal and antagonism between Hutu and Tutsi militants was perpetuated, a number of armed groups remaining outside the process. Given the scale of previous inter-ethnic conflict, the Arusha power-sharing agreement could be claimed to have improved the situation. One of the rebel armed groups, the Palipehutu-FNL, now the FL, abandoned violence in favour of politics and registered as a political party. It may be stretching a point, however, to claim Burundi as a consociational success. Given the country's linkages to regional conflicts in Rwanda and Uganda, there must be some doubt over whether a stable internal consociation can ever be viable.

In Kenya, a grand coalition power sharing deal has been in evidence since 2008, between the Orange Democratic Movement and the Party of National Unity (PNU), following violence in 2007 which saw nearly 1,000 people killed and 600,000 displaced amid ethnic cleansing. Cabinet posts and the two deputy prime ministerial posts are shared evenly between the two parties. There are considerable cross-cutting cleavages, but the PNU is most closely associated with the Kikuyu ethnic group, amounting to one-fifth of Kenya's population, the largest of the country's 40 ethnic groups and seen as the most prosperous. Its prominent position as the main ruling elite since the end of British colonial rule antagonized other groups such as the Luo and Kalenjin. The power-sharing arrangement has attracted much scepticism over its sustainability, and federal structures, or greater local autonomy, may yet displace elite-level consociation.

In Iraq, formal consociational arrangements are undermined because 'there is no spirit of accommodation allowing dialogue among the various groups' (Steiner 2009: 201). Ethno-religious fracture remains acute and Sunnis, one-third of Iraq's population, boycotted the new constitution (from which they were excluded anyway) established in 2005. This exclusion, on the grounds that Sunnis did not want to be part of the settlement, was hardly 'proportionality in government' or 'mutual veto'. The integrity of the state may be called into question, with greater federalism or secession possible. Finally, the Malaysian 'consociation' is unusual in that a single coalition force, the Barisan National, acts as an umbrella organization for racially and religiously divided parties.

Few post-conflict scenarios fit all of Lijphart's (1968, 1969, 1977, 1984) ideal-type criteria for the application of consociation. The checklist of favourable factors has been subject to variation. Bogaards (1998: 476–80) claims that four different sets of conditions for the operation of consociational government were produced by Lijphart between 1968 and 1985, arguing that these modifications and the sheer number of favourable features, indicate a 'lack of theoretical coherence' and 'fickleness', which is 'equalled by the liberty other authors take in selecting their custom-made set of favourable factors for the purpose of a country study or theoretical exercise'. In concentrating upon internal conflict management, consociationalists have struggled to deal with the desire for secession from the state, or allegiance to a different country, when felt as strongly by combatants as a desire for internal power-sharing. Moreover, ethno-national civil wars are rarely purely internal, entirely bereft of external agitators. Similarly, consociationalists have also struggled to regularize how they treat external interventions in a polity (Steiner 2009). Consociation is claimed for Lebanon, but the 'noises off' there in terms of external interference have been loud.

The debate over supposed preconditions, often conflated with ideal-types, is reductionist. Moreover, the argument over most favourable conditions does not clarify for how long each pre-condition ought to have been in place, nor does it clearly distinguish between whether these conditions are appropriate for experimenting with – or sustaining – consociation. There is little predictive capacity offered by dogmatically insisting upon the existence of a definitive set of pre-conditions. The search for a perfect pre-existing set of conditions for consociation is self-defeating. What matters more is whether consociation's four core features hold when power is shared between rival ethnic groups in a state previously marred by conflict. As a communally-based collective, a new power-sharing government established after conflict is likely to include ethnic militants whose previous loyalty to the state may have been questionable. That, after all, is the point of establishing inclusive power-sharing designed to place earlier extremists within the tent, part of what Morrow (2005: 54) labels 'consociationalism's compromise with antagonism'.

Consistent ideal-type criteria for consociation include the need for the conflict to be confined to a small (ideally only two) warring parties, preferably within a small country. Ethnic populations should ideally be fully geographically segregated, but a more common feature is patchwork quilt ethno-geography, the existence of ethnic enclaves amongst a hegemonic or rival larger ethnic group. An optimum history is one of political and economic parity between the rival traditions, but this is rare – hence the existence of conflict. The same pertains to a tradition of elite accommodation between ethnic rivals; had it existed, conflict might not have occurred. More common are majoritarian triumphalism, relative economic disadvantage, second class citizenship and a lack of magnanimity displayed by the dominant ethnic group towards 'inferiors', apartheid South Africa and Unionist Northern Ireland providing two examples of differing degrees of supremacy. Overarching loyalty to the state and rejection of external interference is another preferred condition, but this may be consequential upon substantial change to the internal workings of that state. Lijphart (1977) argued that external threats were beneficial only where they united different ethnic groups against a foreign danger.

More common is that at least one internal group holds allegiance to an external 'parent' state, destabilizing internal relationships with other ethnic groups. Lebanon provides an obvious example of external intervention in the workings of a country's consociational arrangements. A representative party system, based upon moderation and an absence of ultra-nationalism, is ideal, but again rarely evident in conflict arenas. The Cypriot constitution of 1960, established following independence from Britain, facilitated power-sharing, but was beset from the outset by intercommunal strife between those with overarching allegiances to either Greece or Turkey. Civil war in 1963 was followed by attempted union of Cyprus with Greece in 1974 by Greek military nationalists, a move immediately followed by a Turkish invasion and establishment of the Turkish Republic of Northern Cyprus. A further modern difficulty is when one group holds loyalty to a religious 'vision' with scant regard for the integrity of the state. Thus Nigeria is divided between a predominantly Christian South and a Muslim North. The violent actions and Islamic militancy of Boko Haram ('western education is sacrilege') are maintained as part of a campaign to overthrow the existing government (headed by a Christian President) and establish sharia law.

Cross-cutting political cleavages are useful and tend to exist in even the most acutely divided societies, although parties with multi-ethnic support bases tend to be small. Moreover, ethnic accommodation will not necessarily be developed though cross-cutting parties, but instead is achieved via the leaders of ethnic pillar parties. In his various works, Lijphart omits detailed discussion of one crucial pre-requisite for the successful achievement of consociation; the ability of ethnic bloc leaders to 'deliver' their supporters in supporting a power-sharing deal which invariably includes some difficult compromises (Pappalardo 1981). Weak bloc leaders unable to steer their followers will contribute to instability, especially if rival leaders emerge, critical of aspects of a political agreement. Insofar as Lijphart (2002) prescribes in this area, it is to suggest closed party list proportional representation, whereby party leaderships choose the bloc of election candidates fielded by a party, weeding out mavericks, ethnic extremists and destabilizing elements (see also Wolff 2005). Voters choose parties not candidates, an imperfect but pragmatic approach to democracy.

The second major criticism of consociation is theoretical; the argument which suggests that it does not work in solving conflicts, despite the evangelical claims on its behalf, due to its deficiencies as a conflict-solver arising from its crude primordial tendencies. Under this interpretation, consociation exacerbates rather than eradicates ethnic divisions, potentially deepening the causes of conflict supposedly being managed. Even a sympathetic analyst, who argues consociationalism is far more liberal than is usually perceived, acknowledges that it elevates ethnicity to the point where it begins to 'close down the space for other ways of living' (Finlay 2011: 10). Consociation is alleged to rely upon a bleak view of humanity, grounded in Realist notions of the inevitability or normality of conflict if warring parties are not recognized as profoundly different and antagonistic. Even consociationalists acknowledge a degree of separation or segregation may be involved, but argue that 'good fences make good neighbours' (McGarry and O'Leary 1993: 16).

Critics see the excessive importance on group belonging as damaging. It reinforces psychological and in some cases physical senses of separateness from other groups. This notion of inclusion versus exclusion based upon group identity, often bereft of cross-cutting cleavages, breeds intolerance and undermines the positive aspects of elite-level inclusiveness apparent in consociational deals. Integrationist arguments contend that, instead of government by categorization, it is far better to unfreeze ethnic identities in favour of a common humanity or identity and that failure to do so means that conflict could re-ignite, as it has been merely managed, not resolved. The rigid consociations evident in Lebanon and, to a lesser extent, Northern Ireland, are cited as possible examples. It is true that consociationalists are vague over the precise means and timetable for reintegration. However, consociational agreements do not preclude cross-community dialogue or integrationist measures. What such accords do is to acknowledge that different ethnic groups need formal access to decision-making structures as a means of preventing conflict. The best means of guaranteeing such access is through grand coalition.

Consociationalism is accused of fuelling ethnic aggression by encouraging ethnic entrepreneur party leaders to engage in a process of outbidding, designed to bolster electoral popularity. It is assumed that centrifugal political forces will triumph, appealing to popular prejudice and fear, at the expense of centripetal organizations building from the moderate middle. Yet these claims of critics are not necessarily supported by empirical evidence and ignore the tendency of avowedly hardline nationalist parties to moderate their agendas whilst still purporting to act as ethnic tribunes (Mitchell et al. 2009). Where consociationalism is more vulnerable is to the charge of haziness of how and when ethnically-fuelled parties begin to dismantle the communalism that has assisted their rise to power and substitute bi-communalism or bi-nationalism with a 'unity-of-people' (singular) outlook. Consociation reproduces the previous conflict in another setting and reproduction is a poor substitute for dissolution. If ethnic parties can thrive in hermetically sealed ethnic blocs, where is the motivation for dismantling such blocs? The best outcome, according to critics, can be no more than the perpetuation of a benign apartheid, in which separation and segregation are the norm in civic society, thinly veiled by the association of ethnic elites at the summit.

The obvious retort is that by agreeing to share power at the top – a modest form of institutional integration at least – ethnic parties are acting in a non-sectarian manner and that their respective communities will follow that lead. Consociationalists argue that this thawing is possible given the 'anaesthetic effects' (Kerr 2009: 215) upon society wielded by an agreement to end hostilities and share power. Whilst in the short term this power-sharing may constitute more of a division of spoils, growing confidence in the sincerity of inter-communal cordiality, allied to sustained peace, will allow improved relations and fence removal to develop organically. Whilst this is logical sequentially, critics argue that much of this thinking is wishful and unproven, certainly in countries with strong, conflict-causing divides.

Consociation is also criticized for subverting liberal democratic norms, dividing power between ethnic entrepreneurs, who having been rewarded earlier intransigence are then impervious to the normal scrutiny evident in a regular system of government and opposition. The requirements of mandatory cross-community coalition may insulate party leaderships from inspection, as they are sustained in office regardless of performance. Under consociational systems, identity can be licensed, even privileged, as in Lebanon, where parliamentary seats are allocated to representatives from a particular community, at the expense of those who decline to adopt a communal affiliation. Individual identity is subordinate to group belonging. Consociation may also lead to 'political blackmail', 'cold peace' and stagnation through the use of veto rights, creating a system in which immobilism is more evident than progress (Sisk 2003: 140). The inability of ethnic freezing to thaw relations means that more consociations break down than survive, as one or more ethnic group tires of the deal. Consociationalists tend to treat ethnic identity as primordial and assume that only regulation and enforcement can manage a zero-sum game inter-communal dynamic (O'Dowd 2009). Consociation does not offer any obvious means of eradicating contestatory identities, beyond a wishful aspiration that differences may somehow biodegrade as a sustained period of peace elicits greater inter-communal trust. Integrationists argue that a more positive programme of interaction is required to ensure the usurping of difference and to move the sticking plaster of consociational conflict management towards conflict resolution.

A third criticism of consociationalism is rather different, arguing that the concept has come to lack meaning. Dixon's (2011) arguments are not based merely upon opposition to what he alleges is the 'voluntary apartheid' inherent within consociational systems. He also accuses consociationalists of incoherence and lack of rigidity in claiming consociational cases, changing the supposedly fundamental rules of Lijphart's original model to the point where consociationalism is effectively any form of power-sharing which appears to work. Thus he asserts that consociationalism's most prominent current exponents have diluted its rigidity to the point where consociationalism has become so amorphous that it can be 'non-ethnic, democratic, non-democratic, regional, central, weak, ambivalent, pluritarian, traditional, revisionist, corporate, liberal, rigid, concurrent, complete, semi, quasi, formal, informal, and flexible' (Dixon 2011: 318).

Yet this is stretching a point (considerably). Dixon would be correct in questioning whether communal autonomy is an essential aspect of consociation. As Coakley (2009) has argued, there is often nothing new in the communal autonomy pertaining to some consociations which was not previously evident prior to the consociational political agreement. However, the other three Lijphartian pillars – of mutual veto, grand coalition and proportionality, are clearly evident in empirical scrutiny of consociational regimes, so, amid the dancing on the head of a pin, it is unclear how such systems cannot be claimed as consociational.

Integration: Panacea or Utopianism?

Integrationist arguments reject the managed division approach of consociationalism and argue that the mixing of society is a better long-term cure for conflict than the reinforcement or legitimation of ethnic division. Integrationist arguments have antecedents in Allport's (1954) work on intergroup contact. His evidence suggested that regular contact between different groups diminished the scope for conflict and helped ameliorate division. There were important qualifications to this thesis. Contact had to be meaningful, not token; those meeting needed to be of equal status within either community or group and treated as such; clear purposes underpinning the contact should be evident and community leaders needed to support such meetings. Since then, across numerous conflicts, there has been a plethora of peace workshops in which people, especially young persons, from communities estranged from their rival, have met across ethno-sectarian divides. The cordiality of these meetings and recognition of commonalities challenges the negative perceptions of the 'other' brought about by those religious and ethnonational structures which exacerbate communal faultlines. Positive results in terms of understanding, diminished hostility and acknowledgement of hurt inflicted have been reported from numerous contact initiatives, examples being meetings between Israelis and Palestinians (e.g., Ben-Ari and Amir 1986) and between Catholics and Protestants in Northern Ireland (Paolini et al. 2002; Hewstone et al. 2006). Yet the irrelevance of minor contact experiments to the broader conflict scenario is also evident. Malhotra and Liyanage (2005) report favourably on contact initiatives between the Sinhalese and Tamils in Sri Lanka, yet such experiments were swept aside amid the determination of the Sinhalese government to ensure that protracted conflict ended in victory.

Integrationists argue that the positive lessons from contact theory can enjoy a much deeper application. What is required is not merely contact across divides, but a holistic approach containing positive programmes of action requiring different communities to interact on a consistent basis, as the only viable means of diminishing inter-communal difference and achieving social transformation. Healing divisions on a bottom-up basis, beginning in civil society, is more effective than the imposition of new relationships from the top down, via an elite level consociation (see, e.g., Dixon 1997; O'Flynn 2005, 2009). Consociation is, at best, a modest form of integration at the top, whereas what is required is horizontal integration throughout the rest of society.

In developing their thesis that divisions cannot be challenged via their reinforcement, integrationists argue that to view identity as fixed and unyielding is mistaken. Identities are socially constructed, not pre-ordained, making them malleable given appropriate incentives for change. For integrationists, consociation cannot eradicate a division it perpetuates; if you legitimize communalism and build a polity upon ethnic pillars, it is illogical to expect the dissolution of ethnic rivalry. A more appropriate means of tackling conflict is to challenge each 'ethno-centred historical narrative, populated with internal heroes and external villains' and displace this with an inclusive approach (Young 2003: 14). Consociation cannot do this according to integrationists, as it merely replicates the earlier divisions which caused strife. Inter-communal reconciliation cannot be built upon the preservation and reinforcement of 'antagonistic ideologies' (Wilson 2009: 224). The excessive focus upon institutional design within consociational systems, in order to accommodate rival ethnic groups within political structures, has been at the expense of the appraisal of horizontal inter-communal relationships and vertical relations between leaders and led within groups (Morrow 2005: 51–2). Instead, what is required is the cultivation of inter-culturalism, distinct from multicultural-ism which preserves difference in its cherishing of diversity. Inter-culturalism is a process of polity-building, weaving together previously antagonistic grass-roots, on the basis that their identities are not enduring.

To accompany grassroots integration, there needs to be electoral incentives to reward those parties willing to appeal across ethnic divides, preferable to the consolidation of ethnic polarity via the election and subsequent power-sharing of ethnically exclusivist parties (Horowitz 1985, 2001, 2002). These incentives usually incorporate a proportional model of voting (the type of system dependent upon the regional ethnic geography), in which the acquisi-tion of transfer votes may require parties to pitch across a sectarian divide. This requirement marginalizes ethnic extremists, whilst moderates benefit from their cross-community appeal.

Integrationism is criticized as utopian and, for all its advocacy of grassroots reconciliation, appears elitist and patronizing in downplaying the impor-tance of legitimate identities held by communities. Integrationism ignores the difficulty that a peace process has to start from a difficult position, often the existence of inter-communal violence, bitter division rendering integra-tionist strategies a utopian fantasy or, at best, a very long-term project. If rein-tegration is attempted prematurely, it could lead to a resumption of violence. Moreover, the collectivization of identities into a single core begs the question, which core? Integrationists may deny that their project is assimilationist, arguing that a core single national, or post-national identity does not entirely eradicate previously-held identities, but there is a lack of clarity amongst inte-grationists over the extent to which previous identities are indeed removed in favour of what critics label a requirement for 'public homogeneity' (McGarry and O'Leary 2009: 346) and the establishment of a mono-cultural state. What of those who, as examples, reject Belgian, or Northern Irish, or Lebanese iden-tities? A hegemonic identity may displace the sincerely-held belief systems of identities which dare to be different from the dominant constructed identity. This constitutes absorbtion not accommodation. Wilson (2009) appears to adopt strongly single-identity integrative ideas and rejects multi-culturalism, whereas O'Flynn (2009) appears content with the co-existence of an overall loyalty to the state (which is required anyway under consociationalism) and the continuing existence of substantial alternative political, religious and cultural cleavages, merely toned down in terms of the acuteness of their formal recognition within the polity (see also Hadden 2005).

It is not always clear from integrationist approaches whether the unit of analysis is the individual, in which case the logical outworking of the reconstructed society is one of atomized individuals selecting political parties on the basis of non-ethnic, non-religious logic (it is unclear why party choice on the basis of say, economic position, is better) or whether communal affiliations can remain, but should merely be ignored by the state. Integrationists possess a tendency to charge as 'sectarian' (a term never properly defined, as Taylor (2009b) to his credit acknowledges) those who wish to retain and celebrate their communal affiliation.

Integrationists also ignore the capacity for inter-communal reconciliation to occur organically at the same time as an elite-level consociation is in place. Integration may take place through local initiatives, such as contact between former combatants and ex-prisoner groups across the divide, or through global developments. Secularism eroded much of the pillar politics and confessional rivalries of the Netherlands, to cite one example. Integrationists can be accused of elitism. Instead of accepting and cherishing diversity, identity is seen as an affliction held by people, requiring remedial treatment. Integrationists ignore that societies are divided ethnically or multi-nationally for a reason; the people chose – or at least declined to repudiate at adulthood – those identities. Integrationists assume a lack of voluntarism in the formation of such identities, believing that people are 'trapped' via birth, failing to recognize that identity, whilst initially ascribed, may be retained as free choice. To tamper with such choice in coercively integrationist projects is a stance at least as illiberal as the enforcement of the ethnic designs underpinning consociation.

Moreover, enforced integration may remove rights held in liberal, pluralist democracies, such as those of Catholic or Muslim parents to educate their children in the religious faith of their choice. It may also diminish the advancement of a community, where separate, faith-based schools have been successful. Strategies of assimilation or integration cannot wish or enforce away sincerely held beliefs, communal values or sub-national or national identities. Basques and Catalans do not want to be labelled as Spanish and wish to be respected as a distinct people; the same may be said for many Catholic nationalists in Northern Ireland who do not want to be labelled as British or, in many cases, even as Northern Irish. Integrationists risk viewing nationalism as retarded, ignoring its progressive components.

Management via Moderate Constitutionalism: Devolution, Cantonization and Federalism

Where the award of outright independence to an entire country is impossible, constitutional restructuring may maintain peace and political progress. Devolution is the minimum option for a state to exercise, as it comes under internal pressure to concede greater autonomy. It does not require a transfer of sovereignty, as new political institutions are subordinate to the centre. Whilst this holds obvious attraction in terms of the retention of central power, devolution tends to be an incremental process, in which political concessions rarely sate fundamentalist demands for autonomy. Devolution may undermine centrists fearful of the establishment of a 'trojan horse' for independence, whilst doing little to assuage those for whom devolution is a precursor to far greater demands for regional autonomy, the Basque case being an obvious example.

Federalism (normally) allows states or nations a formalized, semi-autonomous relationship with a parent state. Federalism normally offers constitutional guarantees of autonomy beyond those of devolution or cantonization and is thus an attractive option for ethnic groups demanding autonomy. The territorial integrity of a state is preserved, satisfying the dominant group or national government, whilst the statutory basis of the federal arrangement may offer sufficient succour to appease would-be secessionists. Yet federalism has generally failed to appease hardcore secessionists, even in relatively stable entities such as Canada, where Quebec separatist sentiment lingers, occasionally bursting into life. The Soviet Union's federalism could not be sustained without adaptation amid ethnic challenge and the Yugoslav Federation collapsed rapidly with catastrophic consequences in the early 1990s. Arguably, Bosnia-Herzegovina provides an example of a viable federal (or confederal) state as it has begun to embed, albeit not without difficulties (see chapter 7).

In permitting the autonomy of regions, federalism assumes that an overarching loyalty to the state will coexist with strong regional sentiment, allowing a federal government to offer some limited influence over the constituent parts of the federation. Yet federal governments have struggled to be recognized in conflict zones. Somalia has failed to develop a central government since the outbreak of its civil war in 1991. Whilst the transitional federal government, backed by the Haber Gedir clan, has attempted to establish a permanent federal settlement, groups such as the Digil Mirifle desire even greater autonomy than that permitted under the constitution, whilst Islamists in the south of the country wish to topple the regime and replace it with a fundamentalist Islamic regime based on sharia law. There is disagreement over what constitutes a semi-autonomous region and attempts at creating such can 'quickly degenerate into a violent struggle to carve out separate "clanustans"' (Menkhaus 2008: 206).

A variation on the idea of devolved or federal structures is the award of special status to a region. The 2005 peace agreement between the Indonesian government and the Free Aceh Movement created considerable autonomy for Aceh in the north of Indonesia, allowing its elected 'government' to implement sharia law and have few laws imposed from the Jakarta government. Whilst this does not equate to the full independence self-proclaimed in 1976, which led to decades of conflict, it is very much a maximum version of devolved authority.

The creation of ethnic cantons is different from consociationalism, in that the cantonization is a lower-level policy designed to achieve adequate ethnic recognition at grassroots level, whereas consociationalism is operationalized at the level of ethnic bloc elites. As McGarry and O'Leary (1993: 31) stress, cantonization, a process of subsidiarity in ethnic relations, 'must be distinguished from mere administrative decentralisation, common in unitary states: it is built upon the recognition of ethnic difference and allows for asymmetrical relations between different cantons and the central government'. Cantonization has the advantage of preserving the territorial integrity of a state and ostensibly allowing it to flourish as a multi-ethnic entity. More negatively, it runs the risk of particular ethnic cantons attempting to secede from the state where a particular canton's majority ethnic group holds allegiance to a parent state elsewhere. As an explicitly ethnic arrangement, cantonization produces a 'patchwork quilt' state rather than a convincing organic, united polity. Cantonization risks isolating ethnic minorities trapped within a canton dominated by a different ethnic group. For cantonization to be successful, it is helpful for a clear geographical segregation of the populations to pre-exist (this may, of course, be a consequence of previous 'ethnic cleansing'). Cantonization is rare and the Swiss model is the one invariably deployed in the absence of clear empirical successes in conflict zones. It has been mooted as a possible solution to the problem of Palestine (Galtung 1971; Nordquist 1985), although what was considered appeared closer to federalism, and ethnic cantonization of Bosnia-Herzegovina was offered in the short-lived Vance–Owen plan of 1993.

Conclusion

Predicting the onset of peace processes is complex and too much of the conceptual and empirical work on ripeness and mutually hurting stalemate is tautological and reliant upon supposed retrospective vindication, despite protestations to the contrary. Ripeness and mutually hurting stalemates are too indeterminate as concepts to offer predictive value. One could not confidently deploy assessments of ripeness to current global conflicts to determine the likelihood of development of a successful peace process within the next five years. More useful has been the growth of a range of political capacities designed to facilitate and develop peace amid cessations of violence.

Cross-national learning from peace processes ought to facilitate better political arrangements for solving or managing conflict. Ethnic conflict is not impervious to treatment and the range of political prescriptions outlined above offers a comprehensive toolkit for resolving claims to territory and to rectify asymmetrical power relationships which have precipitated violence. The division of states, reconfiguration of existing nations and creation of new countries are all common tools which, if applied with dexterity and sensitivity, can satisfactorily prevent the development or re-ignition of conflict. The sharing of political spoils via consociational political structures allows adequate treatment of different ethnic groups within a polity. That so many of these political remedies are difficult to implement is because they are not accompanied by sufficient desire for immediate peaceful resolution of the problem. The longevity of ethnic conflict, the persistence of 'winner-takes-all' beliefs and zero-sum game virulent assertions of ethnic identities may be more sustained than a desire for the compromises and acknowledgement of the needs of rival ethnic groups required for successful power-sharing arrangements or appropriate territorial divisions.

CHAPTER THREE

Peace: Implementation; Maintenance; Reconciliation

The development of an inclusive peace process may need to be followed by a process of 'forcing' people to be peaceful. The political apparatus outlined in the previous chapter can be accompanied by a range of additional physical measures and external humanitarian assistance. These may include the release of combatants, the physical separation of ethno-national groups, the return of refugees, the stripping of armies and the reintegration of armies into civilian life. Processes of disarmament, demobilization and reintegration may be lengthy and often open-ended, demonstrating that, as the search for a definitive starting point to a peace process is fruitless, the same applies to scouring for a neat conclusion. As military aspects are dealt with, economic recovery becomes perhaps the key aspect of post-conflict reconstruction. The World Bank has recognized this via its provision of earmarked post-conflict funds since 1997 and its maintenance of a Conflict Prevention and Reconstruction Unit (Ramsbotham et al. 2005: 222). Relief agencies such as the Red Cross and Oxfam may assist in the short-term amelioration of humanitarian crises but sustained inward investment to develop a viable economy is also required. This chapter goes beyond the cessations of violence and conclusions of a peace deal upon which so many studies of peace in particular localities are naturally focused, to examine the interplay of military, economic and psychological recovery processes. It explores the physical and psychological aspects of conflict resolution.

Physical and economic aspects of keeping the peace may need to be accompanied by psychological accommodation. The achievement of peace often falls short of the accomplishment of reconciliation, the latter reliant not merely upon physical transition away from violence, but upon accompanying processes of psychological healing which address trauma and grief. Reconciliation involves, as a minimum, perpetrators acknowledging the harm they have caused to others, even if the legitimacy of their actions is still defended, and pledging to take all means necessary to avoid future bloodshed. Reconciliation may require forgiveness from the families of victims towards the perpetrators, an act which may be particularly difficult given that such expectations of forgiveness may follow war crimes. Reconciliation may also require amnesties (such as those offered in Angola, El Salvador and Guatemala) to be offered to those who committed killings. There is also the difficulty of sequencing. As Jeong (2010: 219) notes, 'most people feel uneasy about offering forgiveness

54

prior to satisfying the demands of justice'. For effective peace-building to take place, there may be a need to satisfy demands for justice via war crimes trials, imprisonment or reparations, before a genuine healing and reconciliation can take effect. Regular acts of remembrance associated with conflict contain the potential for healing and may bolster the knowledge of young people of horrors of the past, yet equally contain the possibility of re-opening old wounds.

Getting Rid of Weapons and Keeping the Peace

Whilst political solutions are essential to transform peace processes into permanent peace, physical peacekeeping is often a necessary part of the transition from violence. Peacekeeping forces may be needed to keep rival groups apart, to oversee processes of demilitarization and disbandment and to verify the decommissioning of weapons, although disarmament features in fewer than half of all peace agreements (Harbom et al. 2006). Decommissioning requirements may be blithely ignored; Hezbollah had no intention of getting rid of its weapons despite the strictures of the 1989 Tai'if Agreement in Lebanon and provided an established irregular army (and much more) in the south of the country. However, the sheer scale of decommissioning that has occurred in modern peace processes might be regarded as impressive. Although the process was protracted and sufficiently controversial for it to be barely touched upon in the Good Friday Agreement, the Provisional IRA did eventually dispose of its weapons. To that success can be added decommissioning processes covering over 850,000 ex-combatants in eight African states alone: Ethiopia, Angola, Eritrea, Liberia, Mali, Mozambique, Namibia and Uganda (Mac Ginty 1999; Darby 2003). The re-ignition of conflict in several of those countries is indicative, however, of the fact that decommissioning is no guarantor of a successful peace process, as weapons were re-acquired from new sources.

More common in peace processes is the need for 'on-the-ground' intervention designed to prevent heavily armed former combatants on either side clashing. The need for physical peacekeeping and for the distribution of assistance to conflict societies undergoing reconstruction has seen a rapid growth in the number of deployments by the UN, sometimes merely as observers but more commonly as peacekeepers. During the first half-century after the Second World War, the UN deployed troops on 38 occasions, with almost two-thirds of those deployments taking place in the final seven years of the period (Bertram 1995: 388). African countries have most commonly been the site of UN deployments, whilst the UN has also featured heavily in conflicts in Central America and the Middle East (Bobrow and Boyer 1997).

Although many missions continue to suffer from insufficient resources, the number of countries contributing to UN peacekeeping missions has increased considerably since the 1980s. The UN has been obliged to intervene notwithstanding its proclaimed respect, regardless of regime type, for the territorial integrity and sovereignty of states where its troops are deployed. The principal role of a UN mission may still be, at its core, a simple one: to stop the fighting. Thus in the conflict between Eritrea and Ethiopia, as one example, the primary task of the UN was to create a buffer zone between the warring parties. The costs of such operations and their limited capacity require movement by the sides to accompany the physical prevention of violence. Should the peace hold, disputes may be played out in less threatening diplomatic arenas and it is in this field that the UN has also expanded its orbit. The growth of a range of international decision makers, such as the International Court of Justice and the Permanent Court of Arbitration, testify to continuing disputes over territories and resources. These are abetted by local peace monitoring organizations, created to oversee the full implementation of peace agreements, such as the National Commission for the Consolidation of Peace set up in El Salvador during the 1990s.

Although the nature of peacekeeping operations has changed, the preservation of the integrity of (UN-approved) states (old and new) remains at the core of deployments of international peacekeepers (MacQueen 2006). The political rationale for interventions for peace has been refined in recent decades. The principles of just or liberal intervention in terms of deployment of military action are claimed as based upon the removal of exponents of tyranny or ethnic cleansing, prompting debate over the legitimacy of the export of liberal democratic ideals. Liberal interventionism may be new(ish) as a term, however, but as a basis for action it is hardly novel; Britain's declaration of war upon Germany in 1939 after the latter's invasion of Poland constituted liberal interventionism. What is new is the use of the term, not the action. Supporters of modern liberal interventionism designed to achieve regime change can legitimately argue that liberal democracies do not fight each other; as such, a proliferation of enforced democracies will further reduce the risk of inter-state conflict. Against this lies the uncomfortable fact that liberal democracies are prone to fighting plenty of other regime types. As Mack (2005) and Cochrane (2008) both note, the United States, United Kingdom, France and Russia top the list of countries involved in international wars during the last sixty years. Western liberal democracies have propagated the doctrine of 'responsibility to protect'. Governments are obliged to protect their people and those governments which fail to do so risk intervention from external forces. The outworking of liberal interventionism has been seen in recent times in Libya, Iraq and Afghanistan, although interference has been selective, being absent from Zimbabwe, for example, despite human rights violations.

The principles of liberal interventionism have been extended post-conflict to justify a continued military or economic presence by outside organizations or states, aimed at the consolidation of peace (see Ramsbotham et al. 2005: 282–7). The conditions for extended external intervention are those of capacity to prevent loss of life; to mediate local disputes; to implement a just political settlement; to oversee economic and physical reconstruction; to physically separate communities; and to arrest suspected war criminals. As Wall and Druckman's (2003) multivariate analysis indicates, the range of mediation techniques is strongly related to the severity of a dispute, rather than the rank of UN officials 'on the ground' or the length of a mission. External intervention is not justified in cases where the risk of success is low, but this may be difficult to judge, nor is it necessarily justified in terms of providing a permanent alternative government. However, a new political leadership installed as a consequence of external intervention is often seen as a puppet regime and external intervention is often criticized as more a process of the upholding of dominant external interests than the maintenance of a rigorous ethical framework.

The first priority of peacekeeping missions is to do no harm, ensuring that their presence does not exacerbate an already difficult situation, given that the UN is only deployed in cases of acute difficulty. A typology of ideal-type interventions, some of which state the obvious, but with the following key variables, emerges from the case studies offered in Durch (2006). Firstly, there must be local political support, in that the deal to be policed is not simply an imposed top-down accord, which risks being ignored by grassroots militants. The agreement may require local actions, such as disarmament, which without consent on the ground will not be achievable. Secondly, there needs to be clarity over the remit and purpose of the peacekeeping mission: who is protecting whom, for what reasons, on what conditions and for how long? Thirdly, there must be unity of purpose with the local peacekeeping force and, in certain conditions, local militias, prepared to marginalize ultra groups still committed to violence. Finally, the accountability of peacekeeping forces is desirable, although this is far from fully developed at present, with UN forces immune from local jurisdiction.

The UN has been active as a peacekeeping force in a wide range of conflicts over recent decades including, in a very far from exhaustive list, particularly taxing assignments in Haiti, Nicaragua, Palestine, Namibia, El Salvador, Cambodia, Somalia and Sudan, Angola, Mozambique, Liberia and Rwanda. UN peacekeeping forces have had, at best, mediocre results. Three periods of intervention have not secured permanent peace in Liberia, nor in Sudan, to cite two examples. A large deployment of UN troops in Ivory Coast has not prevented further violence since a 2003 peace agreement ended the state's civil war. Insufficient has been achieved to necessitate rethinking Bertram's (1995: 387) conclusion towards the close of the twentieth century that 'clear successes ... are few and fragile', a consequence of lack of commitment to peace amongst combatants combined with inadequately resourced UN missions bereft of clear objectives and timescales. There is also a lack of enthusiasm for participation in UN peacekeeping missions displayed by some countries. Amongst the 193 member states of the UN (a figure which has risen steadily in recent decades), only a minority have offered their own forces for deployment. The frequency of participation varies considerably, Sweden and Norway, as examples, taking part in more than twice as many operations as Spain and Germany since the late 1980s, whilst China has the lowest rate of participation for a permanent member of the UN Security Council (Bobrow and Boyer 1997: 732). Financial contributions also vary considerably, relative to the GDP of participating nations.

Yet despite numerous setbacks, UN roles have increased numerically and in terms of remit, with 'mission-creep' extending to the point where the organization has often become the key agent of post-conflict reconstruction. The UN's roles may include the creation and upholding of peace lines; demarcation and the establishment of secure zones; monitoring of human rights standards and abuses; assistance to the civil power on issues such as the delivery of food and materials; overseeing the conduct of fair elections; and the protection of officials. The UN cannot address the root causes of conflict, nor by itself create peace. It cannot act as a substitute for the political will of combatants, but its absence, or ineptness and lack of clarity over its mission can contribute to the restoration of hostilities. Where it acts as a moral custodian, helping to broker and defend peace agreements, but without the requisite political will on the ground, the UN is stripped of authority and power. Its political role may be undermined by lack of local backing, evident in the aborted attempt of United States and UN forces to restore the democratically elected President of Haiti to power in 1993, following a military coup (Bertram 1995).

The aims of UN missions have embraced, to differing degrees, physical prevention of violence, restoration of order, return of refugees, monitoring of elections, and assistance in processes of demobilization of armies and decommissioning of weapons. UN forces helped contain violence, although certainly not eradicate it, in Nicaragua (where the UN helped disarm the Contras who had fought the Sandinista government), Cambodia and El Salvador.

The UN was effective in dissuading South Africa from undermining Namibian independence. Yet UN forces proved largely impotent when hugely outnumbered by combatants in Angola (where UNITA guerrillas ignored strictures to disarm), Rwanda, Somalia and Sudan (see Durch and Berkman 2006); and failed to prevent massacres for several years during the Bosnian conflict, most infamously in Srebrenica, although the UN was arguably otherwise effective in that conflict. Too often, UN peacekeepers have relied upon the prior approval of antagonists (for fear of worsening the situation) before intervening directly, even though the UN Charter does not automatically require UN forces to solicit such consent. In 2012, the Syrian regime under Assad denied entry to the UN's humanitarian aid officials who wished merely to assess the extent of need for emergency relief.

UN peacekeeping has been most effective when it has been proactive rather than reactive and when it has operated on a regional rather than single-country basis, a feature which (belatedly) helped end the genocide in Rwanda, with the UN abetted politically by the African Union (Wolff 2006). However, even a more coherent regional policy did not prevent the UN being largely impotent in the neighbouring Democratic Republic of Congo, where genocide became even more evident from the late 1990s.

Spoilers, Ultras, Renegades and Dissidents

Renegade groups who refuse to accept a peace settlement appear to be a predictable feature of peace processes. Opponents of compromise or 'sell-out' are endemic to processes which involve some retreat from original demands. The emergence of spoilers may be inevitable, but their capacity to operate and their willingness to pursue absolutism may vary considerably. Stedman's (1997) typology of spoilers suggests three types: the limited, which are the least dangerous as the peace and political processes can perhaps be adjusted to deal with their additional demands; the greedy, whose demands fluctuate according to circumstance; and the total, those bereft of a capacity to compromise. He suggests that demobilization and disarmament of armies, the reform of policing and judicial systems and the involvement of nongovernmental organizations in civil society are the best means of ensuring effective peace-building.

Yet full disarmament is rare and leakage of weaponry to spoilers is more likely than not. The typology of spoilers is unsatisfactory, as the extent to which groups are 'limited' or 'greedy' is often impossible to assess at the time and the distinction between those two categories is indeterminate. Stedman (2003: 108) attempts to narrow the definition by insisting that 'spoilers can only be defined in relationship to a given peace agreement' and he also acknowledges that the definition of a group as a total spoiler can change, as groups, except the most fundamental, tailor their demands according to circumstance. What matters more than artificial and arbitrary categorizations are the following aspects: the overall willingness of such groups to continue to use violence in pursuit of ends; the capacity and opportunity structures of such groups to perpetuate violence; the perceptions of the utility of continued violence; the extent of unity amongst spoiler groups, which are likely to fragment or dissipate under pressure; the level of outright support or sympathy (the two need disaggregation) for spoiler groups; and the history of a conflict. Does a particular dispute have a sustained history of splits amongst violent groups amid propensity towards compromise? History becomes cyclical, as spoiler groups become part of the mainstream and in turn are outflanked by later spoilers. In this respect, defining a spoiler group by reference to a single peace agreement, as demanded under Stedman's (1997, 2003) original thesis, is irrelevant. Spoilers are part of a historical process which demotes tactics in favour of principle, eschews compromise and relies upon supposed lessons of history to reject all compromise.

Opportunity structures determine the extent of activity of spoilers to a greater degree than the intent of renegades. Greenhill and Major's (2006–7) study of peace processes in Angola, Mozambique and Cambodia indicates that the distribution of power and the opportunities afforded by such distribution are key to the development or squashing of spoilers. UNITA in Angola briefly felt it had little to lose by continuing violence for a period after the settlement. In Cambodia, however, the Khmer Rouge forces were utterly marginalized by a combination of domestic repugnance at its human rights abuses, withdrawal of international 'sponsorship', loss of military capacity and firm UN actions. In Mozambique, the potential spoilers in the Mozambican National Resistance (RENAMO) could gain little by continuing to pursue a military struggle. They lacked political credibility with faltering election performances, contained war-weary troops and had little access to resources. As such, a military campaign was no longer viable. Opportunities for spoilers are determined by a range of factors, which may be divided into the ideological and situational or practical. In respect of the former, the extent of compromise undertaken by combatants is crucial in shaping the perceptions of hardliners, who may have invested much in armed struggle, risking death, injury, arrest or imprisonment. The capacity of leaderships to sell a deal becomes crucial. The situational and practical aspects of spoiler capacity are more agency-driven. They are shaped by the ability of state forces to deal with dissident groups and neuter their potential to derail a settlement. It may also be conditional upon the capacity and willingness of the former allies of dissidents to take action against those refusing to adhere to the settlement. This action may take a variety of forms, from political isolation to more physical means of discouraging those who wish to continue violence – 'internal housekeeping' as it was once infamously described by a former Secretary of State for Northern Ireland, in respect of those 'dissidents' who wished to continue violence.

Key Post-Conflict Issues: Prisoner Releases, Demilitarization, Demobilization, Reintegration and Refugees

Speed, clarity and comprehensiveness are the three most important prerequisites for the release of prisoners after a conflict; all were evident in the Northern Ireland case, but absent after the Oslo Agreement in the Middle East (Shirlow et al. 2010). In cases where the conflict has been one mainly between the state and a terrorist group, the release of 'terrorist' prisoners may be one of the most emotionally (and morally) difficult aspects of any peace process, effectively elevating 'terrorists' to the status of prisoners-of-war. Yet rates of recidivism may be sufficiently low – less than 3 per cent in the Northern Ireland case, for example – to offer succour to the view that prisoner releases are pragmatically justified, regardless of attendant moral issues (Shirlow and McEvoy 2008). Prisoner releases are rarely unconditional, with terms of release directed at the armed group and the individual. For example, FARC prisoners were released from incarceration in Colombia and had their sentences quashed provided that their organization continued its cessation of violence, whilst those individuals benefitting from this scheme were obliged to make some contribution to the reparations of victims. Yet prisoner release schemes need to be comprehensive in scope. A universal release scheme is far easier for the leaders of a warring group to sell to followers than those which create a hierarchy of prisoners, only some of whom qualify for liberation. Attempts to use prisoners as regular bargaining chips after an agreement are likely to derail a deal. The successful reintegration of prisoners is also aided by effective representative groups, such as Coiste, which has aided thousands of former Provisional IRA prisoners.

Demilitarization, demobilization and reintegration (DDR) are central to the achievement of permanent peace. They involve the removal of weapons, the standing down of armies and the movement of combatants into regularized civilian roles. Whilst the 'privileging' of ex-combatants may cause tensions, their successful reintegration into society is crucial for reconstruction (Ozerdem 2002). DDR can be a colossal undertaking. In Sierra Leone, the UN oversaw the 'civilianizing' of over 70,000 combatants (Berman and Labonte 2006). Success may be conditional upon the level of skills held by ex-combatants and the extent of legitimacy within their community, along with state support for reintegration. In Mozambique, for example, the government encouraged AMODEG, the Mozambican Association of the War Demobilized, to engage in programmes of civic education to discourage others from being attracted to violence (Shafer 1998). In Liberia, however, the failure to devise employment schemes for those exiting the conflict left large numbers of former combatants unemployed, disaffected and prepared to countenance a return to violence. The 1993 Cotonou Agreement was not implemented in full, with the majority of combatants remaining in control of their weapons and the groups which had fought the civil war still intact several years after the deal. Failure to deliver on promises of redundancy payments and land redistribution to ex-combatants in El Salvador led to the occupation of parliament and threats to the rebuilding of the polity (Berdal 1996; Rolston 2007).

Failure to achieve demobilization and reintegration and the continuing presence of irregular armies makes state-building acutely difficult. Hezbollah ignored the decommissioning requirements of the 1989 Ta'if Accord and Lebanon has remained insecure. In Afghanistan, Mujahideen retained their weapons and fought each other after Soviet withdrawal, before eventually fighting Western forces. Even in those countries where demilitarization occurs largely successfully, a residual amount of weaponry still in circulation can encourage a crime wave and gangsterism, as evidenced in parts of South Africa. When the state offers financial reward for the surrender of weapons, the arms decommissioned may be obsolete, with useful firearms retained, as occurred in Angola (Gamba 2003). The Liberian 'arms-for-cash' offer during the 1990s saw over 100,000 people 'cashing in' their arms, but the scheme proved costly and short term, diverting money from sustained reintegration projects (McGovern 2008: 344–5).

The focus within peace processes may have been upon the reintegration of former combatants into civilian life, but such processes may also involve the return of thousands of displaced individuals to their homeland. Failure to address the issue of Palestinian refugees has dogged the Middle East peace process for decades. The expenditure of the UN Relief and Works Agency in the West Bank and Gaza amounts to more than 3 per cent of total Palestinian gross domestic product and ought to help many dispossessed Palestinians, but there is no long-term solution, with responsibility for the issue held by the largely impotent Palestinian Authority (Brynen 2008). In contrast, the Dayton Agreement for Bosnia-Herzegovina was explicit on the rights of refugees to return, to the point that, by 2004, 200,000 of 217,000 claims for the return of property had been upheld and it is claimed that 'no other factor has done more to change the environment' (Cox 2008: 257). The success of the refugee provisions has done much to dilute the possible embitterment of those dispossessed during the conflict. Yet even here, refugee returns have been largely to 'safe' areas, those living in (once) ethnically mixed zones more likely to feel permanently ousted.

Dealing with Conflict Legacies: from Truth and Reconciliation Commissions to Remembrance of Victims

Support for the idea of truth and reconciliation commissions has grown in recent decades, although such commissions are only viable in successful peace processes. They are seen as a means of dealing with the recent past which can facilitate 'moral, political and legal disassociation from the crimes of the previous regime' (Dimitrijevic 2006), whilst also contributing to the stabilizing of an incumbent government and allowing former combatants to detail and explain their actions, narratives which may permit understanding. Truth and reconciliation commissions are thus seen as a means of bringing closure to a conflict, allowing a voice to combatants and victims in a non-pejorative arena. Such commissions are a means of averting criminal justice procedures, instead offering a therapeutic staging post towards societal reconstruction.

Truth and reconciliation commissions are normally accompanied by an amnesty for participants, as an obvious incentive towards truth-telling. Amnesties feature in over one-quarter of modern (1989 and beyond) peace agreements (Harbom et al. 2006), although they are not always of the unconditional, blanket variety such as those offered at the end of civil wars in Guatemala and El Salvador during the 1990s. Despite these guarantees, some members of the truth commissions were threatened by the perpetrators of killings merely for asking questions. Normally, repudiation of past deeds is not required; merely non-repetition. The recommendations of truth commissions can be ignored. The UN Commission report on killings in El Salvador recommended the resignation of the most senior members of the judiciary, given their complicity in acts of violence, but this demand was blithely ignored by the relevant judges. Truth and reconciliation commissions are not some secular form of a Catholic confessional, in which absolution from sins is offered in return for genuine contrition and repentance. Instead, the contrition bar is set much lower. Former antagonists may regret the suffering caused by their actions, but expressions of regret are not tantamount to rejecting the validity of the actions perpetrated, which may still receive political justification and validation.

The South African Truth and Reconciliation Commission is seen as an exemplar, one of the largest and most comprehensive processes yet seen. It involved over 20,000 witness statements, 7,000 requests for amnesties (invariably accepted, but formal applications had to be made) and a seven-volume final report. Its proceedings attracted a phenomenal amount of interest, with broadcast 'highlights' being amongst the most watched or listened to items in the South African media (Gibson 2006). The commission's remit was to focus upon gross violations of human rights regardless of perpetrators and justifications, such even-handedness criticized as a failure to link its findings to apartheid structures amid an obvious asymmetry of political evils (Campbell and Connolly 2012).

Backed by religious leaders urging forgiveness and political leaders supporting societal healing, the commission's search for the truth contributed to reconciliation (Gibson 2004). The commission, insofar as it was judgemental, apportioned responsibility to all sides in terms of human rights violations, whilst being condemnatory of the apartheid regime. Thus, for example, 'necklace' killings committed by blacks, whereby a burning tyre was placed around the neck of a victim, were condemned alongside the murders committed by white state forces. Even-handedness and the universal application of standards were crucial to the success of the commission. White South Africans were shocked at the extent to which their government had acted outside the already-weighted law in countering subversion, whilst blacks, utterly opposed to the draconian white supremacist legal framework, nonetheless acknowledged that not all acts of liberation could be regarded as glorious episodes. Given the political change already in evidence, the process was successful, if still infused with controversy over the nature of many of the killings that had occurred.

That the Truth and Reconciliation Commission highlighted the injustices of apartheid reinforced the view of the African National Congress (ANC) that the conflict was a just war of liberation. It may also explain why black South Africans were more positive concerning its deliberations than other racial groups, particularly white Afrikaners. However, the truth and reconciliation process was successful in 'making many South Africans less certain about the purity of their side and forcing people to acknowledge that the "other side" was also unfairly victimized' (Gibson 2006: 414). This acknowledgement of the hurt inflicted upon others was crucial to achieving reconciliation. Whilst political partisanship remained, cognizance of the pain inflicted upon opponents was part of a therapeutic de-blinkering and healing process.

Yet truth and reconciliation commissions are heavily infused with controversy, seen as a means by which the most violent actors can cheat justice. In one of the most notorious instances, the leader of child-soldiers in the Liberian civil war, Joshua Milton Blahyi, was recommended for amnesty. Blahyi was responsible for at least 20,000 killings. His conversion to Christianity and appointment as a pastor preaching forgiveness encouraged him to testify to the Truth and Reconciliation Commission, but his immunity from trial contrasted with the war crimes trials imposed upon other antagonists in different conflicts. Truth and reconciliation commissions thus encourage an inconsistent approach to warlords and may offer hope that antagonists can escape responsibility for their actions at the conclusion of the conflict. Beyond the problem of exoneration of hideous crimes, the chief problem with truth and reconciliation commissions is that they may engage in a fruitless search for an objective, authoritative and decontextualized truth which may not exist. Whilst it is possible to construct an empirical catalogue of *who* killed who (the basic truth), a more subjective perception is needed to explain *why* X killed Y. X may have believed that Y was engaged in a military offensive, but Y, self-evidently unable to testify, may have regarded military operations as essentially defensive. The past is revisited, but the conditions which produced that past are not dwelt upon. Instead, the modus operandi appears to be story-telling. Whilst a truth and reconciliation commission cannot be a forum for dreary ideological monologues, the causes of conflict cannot be detached from what occurred.

There is also the issue of the conditions in which the use of a truth and reconciliation commission is apposite. Snyder and Vinjamuri's (2003) study of reconstruction after 32 civil wars suggests that such commissions are effective mainly where there is a democratic government in place and where the state has some history of stability – in other words, where the political situation is not too grim. This is hardly a ringing endorsement of truth and reconciliation commissions, reducing them to the status of a 'mopping-up' exercise when the hard yards of a peace process have already been travelled. It suggests that political culture may be a more important variable than the intrinsic merits of truth and reconciliation commissions in shaping societal reconstruction. Where commissions do have value is in effectively providing an amnesty for former antagonists via an institutional means more acceptable to the public than a straightforward state pardon, which may be politically difficult. In the South African case, the outgoing apartheid regime demanded an amnesty for its forces in advance of the transition to black majority rule, which might otherwise have been difficult for an incoming black majority rule government to concede other than via the auspices of a commission.

Truth and reconciliation commissions allow recollection of the past. What, though, of remembrance of that past, long after such commissions have deliberated? Dealing with permanent tributes to victims is one of the many contentious aspects of any peace process. Although constructed to prevent more victims, many such processes indulge combatants, bequeathing them, variously, power, territory, aid or amnesties. For the families of those killed or injured, far less may be on offer. Families may benefit from government aid and reparations, but the psychological loss may be of far greater impor-tance. They have the opportunity to articulate their grief through a truth and reconciliation commission, but this is a transient means of dealing with hurt. Regular commemoration of victims has thus become an increasing feature of reconciliation. Remembrance has a strongly political aspect, in reminding communities of the horrors of conflict and the need to strive for inter-communal and inter-state peace. In its apolitical form, remembrance affords space for families of victims to remember their loss, which otherwise might be a largely forgotten aspect of the conflict. With the passing of those families, the historical-political aspect of formal commemoration becomes the dominant form.

Retributive Justice and the Deployment of War Crimes Trials

As part of the healing process, restorative justice of the sort described above may be more important (and common) than retributive justice. Nonetheless, there often remains a strong desire amongst victims and non-victims alike to see the perpetrators of conflicts account for their actions and face conse-quences. An alternative approach to amnesties and truth and reconciliation commissions is to pursue the persecution route. War crimes trials are a device with similar aims – to bring closure to a process – but adopt a different phi-losophy, in which justice is frontloaded as the key aspect. Until recently, war crimes trials arose from ad hoc tribunals, focused upon a single conflict, as was the case for atrocities committed in Rwanda, Sierra Leone and the former Yugoslavia, although activities may involve other states. The Special Court for Sierra Leone, for example, convicted Charles Taylor, Liberia's ruler from 1997 to 2003, for his role in organizing the activities of the Revolutionary United Front (RUF) beyond his own country, the RUF having been the rebel force in Sierra Leone's civil war.

The establishment of the International Criminal Court (ICC) in 2002 has made a major contribution to placing post-conflict justice on a secure and non-arbitrary footing. With over 120 countries ratifying the ICC's charter, the Rome Statute, the body has already investigated killings and other human rights abuses in conflicts in four African states and the extent of its remit is such that no military or political leader is beyond its potential reach. The pace of progress has nonetheless been slow, with only 27 indictments issued in the first decade of the ICC's existence. Moreover, the court is, as Neumayer (2009:

659) notes, 'no substitute for humanitarian intervention and multinational peacekeeping since, at best, it provides ex post justice, together with the hope of deterrence of future crimes, but no immediate relief and assistance to people at risk of becoming the victims of grave offences'.

Indeed Neumayer (2009) wonders whether the belief that the perpetrators of genocide will eventually be brought to justice may actually deter risky humanitarian intervention at the relevant time by the United Nations. Post-conflict trials may achieve justice, but they can also be criticized as partisan. Serb leaders have been far more prone to conviction than Croatian military figures (the most senior Croat figures convicted had their judgements reversed within one year of their sentencing). Trials also allow defendants an opportunity to espouse detailed narrative 'justifications' of their actions which risk inflaming old tensions. The ICC is, of course, dependent upon the successful apprehension of suspected criminals, far from certain in a fevered immediate post-conflict environment and the biggest single barrier to its enforcement capacity. Nonetheless, the Court has demonstrated its willingness to charge senior political and administrative figures regardless of the potential political consequences. In 2012, for example, the ICC charged Kenya's Deputy Prime Minister, the former Education Minister and the Head of the Civil Service with crimes against humanity following 1,200 deaths arising from inter-communal rivalry associated with the 2007 Presidential election.

War crimes trials may be initiated long after the conflict, as was the case in Bosnia. UN-funded, the International Criminal Tribunal for the former Yugoslavia (ICTY) operates as a separate, geographically concentrated jurisdiction, from the broader ICC. The ICTY did not begin its work until after the Dayton Agreement and court appearances of several of the key suspects in the Bosnian conflict, notably those of the Serbian leaders Milosevic, Karadzic and Mladic, did not begin until more than a decade after the 1995 deal. Indeed, Milosevic had been indulged, even courted by the West, beyond Dayton, which made no mention of war crimes. Arrests of those suspected of war crimes in Bangladesh's war of independence in 1971 did not begin in earnest until 40 years after the conflict, accompanying the establishment of a government tribunal.

Conclusion

There has been a welcome focus in recent years upon post-deal aspects of peace processes. How to maintain peace is palpably as important as its clinching, whilst the need to deal with the physical and psychological impacts of conflict has grown in importance. In terms of the UN's peacekeeping missions, successful deployments in countries as diverse and war-torn as East Timor, Sierra Leone and Bosnia indicate how the presence of neutral forces can aid the maintenance of peace and create space for the outworking of political agreements. Provided that UN missions possess clarity of purpose, are even-handed, are time-constrained (usually) and proportionate in size to the problem, they have a reasonable chance of success, one that ought to improve further as best practice is adopted via policy learning.

The removal of weapons via processes of decommissioning is less important than the abandonment of the intent to use armaments, but decommissioning may nonetheless be elevated to a key confidence-building measure. Where this is the case, decommissioning needs to be verifiable, overseen by neutral forces, completed over a short time scale and undertaken by all parties, but the full range of these components is rarely apparent. Demobilization of warring groups will not be effected unless imprisoned combatants are released, but such releases are likely to be infused with controversy. The key requirements of prisoner releases are that they must be universal not selective and completed over a short period, but are conditional upon the prisoner's armed group maintaining a ceasefire and the individual not transgressing and returning to the conflict via a spoiler group. However, in the event of a re-ignition of violence, the state's capacity to return large numbers of combatants to prison may be very limited. The reintegration of former combatants is best implemented when the state does not impose employment barriers and actively encourages those who fought as irregulars to join reconstituted state security services. This, however, is an ambitious project, and the norm is for reintegration to be attempted less satisfactorily through the struggles of voluntary associations of former prisoners to rehabilitate and reintegrate those who fought, the success of the process highly contingent upon the available opportunity structures. Societal reintegration will be conditional upon the nature of the political agreement pertaining to the peace process.

Reconciliation is the ambitious endgame of a peace process and the subject of an ever-growing range of vehicles. Healing through truth-telling, via truth and reconciliation commissions and victims' commissions, offers a therapeutic approach to dealing with the past, one which aspires to psychological repair to the damage of war. Whilst these measures are often laudable, sometimes grassroots-based and a useful means of understanding why conflict occurred, honesty about the past does not necessarily generate forgiveness from the opposing side, nor does it constitute rapprochement. Vehicles of reconciliation constitute 'soft landings' for peace processes as they do not require sanctions or blame to be placed upon former combatants, instead tacitly assuming a symmetry of pain and victimhood. These notions often remain highly contested and many may favour retributive forms of reconciliation, in which the pursuit of justice in respect of the worst perpetrators of violence in a conflict may be paramount. Retributive justice nonetheless is invariably the asymmetrical justice of the victors, in which it is the vanquished who overwhelmingly have to account for their actions.

CHAPTER FOUR

Deadlock: The Palestinian 'Peace Process'

One of the most enduring but seemingly unsuccessful peace processes has pertained to permanent resolution of the Israeli–Palestinian conflict. Episodically, the process appears buried amid the absence of serious dialogue, the elusiveness of the much-vaunted two-state solution, the omnipotent expansion of Israeli settlements on Palestinian territory and the fundamentalist outlooks held by antagonists on both sides of a territorial argument with religious dimensions. Yet, amid the scepticism, there has been fairly regular exploratory dialogue, hints of conciliation and, occasionally, even hope of an enduring peace deal. The violence attendant to the conflict has varied considerably according to the local situation and the same can be said of aspirations for peace. At times, the region has even been cited as a location where stalemate suggests ripeness for peace. More common, though, is a perception that the problem is intractable. Israel's occupation of Palestinian territory will not cease; nor, despite the aspirations held by many, is there a genuine prospect of at least a retreat to the pre-1967 Arab–Israeli war borders. This chapter analyses the foundation of the conflict and peace processes and assesses the proximity to peace reached in the most serious processes to date, those producing the ill-fated 1993 Oslo Agreement and the 2000 Camp David dialogue.

War not Peace: Historical Disputes

Resolution of the Israeli–Palestinian conflict relies upon secular solutions to ethno-religious claims, territorial compromises and recognition of mutual hurt. At the heart of the dispute lies Palestinian resentment of the territorial annexations undertaken in the cause of Zionism, territorial claims justified by religious Jews on the basis of their biblical assertion and by those less religious due to the substantial historical evidence of their persistent maltreatment. The plight of Jews persuaded the 'architect' of modern Zionism, Theodor Herzl, that assimilation of the Jewish population was impossible and as such an independent homeland was the only option. Such historical interpretations have long been contested. Revisionist narratives have, for example, rejected exile-and-return Zionist propositions that Jews were forcibly expelled by the Roman Empire and debunked claims that most of the Jews in Europe descended from those forced from Israel. Instead, Jews were bound by religion not nationhood (Sand 2010). Nonetheless, the impact of the Holocaust ensured that Zionism was turned from an abstract ideology only tentatively indulged by national governments to one which became a serious, expansive political project. Realization of Zionist ambitions advanced the original liberal, humane project, but not always in the directions intended; instead it adopted sectarian feelings of superiority, ironic given the shocking pseudo-scientific anti-semitism which necessitated at least the partial fulfilment of Zionist aspirations.

The creation of the state of Israel was principally via the violence of the Lehi, Irgun and Haganah against British rule, providing a lesson that the use or threat of force pays dividends. The British tired of the violence, passing the issue of a Jewish homeland to the UN, which approved the creation of Israel (Resolution 181) by 33 votes to 13, with ten abstentions, including Britain. Palestinians were forcibly dispossessed, the original works of Benny Morris (1988) (before his political U-turn) illustrating how local Zionist leaderships ousted the indigenous Arab population notwithstanding national leadership pleas for a more moderate approach. Only one-fifth of the 475 Arab villages within the pre-1967 borders of Israel remain.

For Palestinians, the peace process is predicated upon at least a partial reversal of the al-naqba (catastrophe) which saw their displacement by the creation of a Jewish state in 1947–9, with Israeli borders extending well beyond those originally anticipated. For Palestinians, there has been little shift in Israeli attitudes from the desire of Ben-Gurion, Israel's first Prime Minister, to simply displace those inhabitants who got in the way. Israel declined to negotiate with Palestinians at the 1949 Lausanne conference and her borders expanded further via gains in conflicts in 1967 and 1973, the latter achieved after the Israelis were initially surprised by being attacked on Yom Kippur, the Day of Atonement and the holiest in the Jewish calendar. Amid Israeli territorial expansion, Palestinian hopes for rights of return for refugees, the establishment of a significant Palestinian state and the return of Jerusalem as the Palestinian capital have all faded. Palestinians perceive themselves as victims of an unyielding expansionary Zionism, a Jewish colonial project whose inflated territorial aspirations have long eroded sympathy over the historical mistreatment of Jews and their desire to create a safe haven (Pappe 2006; Alexander and Rose 2008).

For Israelis, the concept of Eretz Israel, a homeland extending from the Jordan to the Mediterranean, was a natural and justifiable response to the systematic persecution of Jews in other lands amid rife anti-semitism, with its latest and most grotesque phase, the Holocaust, emphasizing the need to implement the Zionist project. The Jewish narrative stressed that they were once the main population of Palestine, a position usurped by Roman and Crusader invasions. As the Zionist project revived at the end of the nineteenth century, so did anti-Zionism. Britain's Balfour Declaration acknowledged the need for the creation of a Jewish national homeland at the time of the British conquest of Palestine in 1917. Churchill fused altruism with self-interest in declaring that such a homeland would be 'good for the world, good for the Jews and good for the British Empire' (Gilbert 2007: 11). The modest British project, outlined in the 1937 Peel Commission's plan to partition Palestine, differed from the larger Zionist territorial conception, but was accepted by the Jews, whereas the Arabs, with more to lose, rejected the proposals, although there was much intra-Arab division over how to oppose the plan, a recurring feature for subsequent decades. The formation of the Arab League in 1945 nonetheless brought together different shades of opinion in opposition to the formation of a Jewish state.

Following the genocide of Jewish populations across Europe during the Second World War, the establishment of a Jewish homeland was inevitable and the 1947 UN partition plan proposed the formation of Jewish and Arab states in Palestine, linked by an economic union. It provided the first of a series of missed opportunities for compromise. Arab Palestinians rejected this offer of statehood as an unsatisfactory emasculation of their territory and six Arab armies invaded the embryonic entity of Israel in 1948, the first state to be created by the UN. The tactic proved disastrous, with the Israelis triumphing in their war of independence after the deaths of thousands, doubling the size of Israel through territorial seizures, and creating over 700,000 Arab refugees. With the Gaza strip now held by Egypt and the West Bank by Jordan, a substantial state of Palestine was already looking remote. Meanwhile, the Israeli government invited Jewish settlers from across the world to reside in Israel, with nearly 600,000 arriving from Europe alone during the following two decades. Fatah, formed in 1964 and effectively in control of the Palestine Liberation Organization (PLO), attempted to place itself at the head of resistance to Israel, but could achieve little.

The 1967 Arab–Israeli war proved even more disastrous for Arab forces than the 1948 version. Fearing attack from massing armies of hostile neighbouring states and enduring a shipping blockade, Israel attacked, capturing swathes of territory, including Sinai from Egypt and the Golan Heights from Syria. The Israeli occupation of Jerusalem removed Jordanian control of the Old City. The Israeli conquest of East Jerusalem in the 1967 war was followed by the Knesset passing legislation guaranteeing free access to all Holy Places for all religions, a move which did little to assuage Palestinian anger. Israeli narratives point to the effective administration of the city, the continued running of Haram al-Sharif (the Noble Sanctuary) by a Muslim Waqf and the increase in the number of Arab and Jewish citizens in the area since 1967 (Gilbert 2007).

Jordanian control west of the River Jordan was removed. The contours of the Israeli state were hugely expanded, a homeland built, as critics noted, on the ruins of another society (Kimmerling and Migdal 1992). The West Bank became an Israeli-administered area, placing a further 600,000 Arabs under Israeli occupation. The Israeli position was consolidated by Jewish settlements on the West Bank. Arab states, with financial backing from the Soviet Union, sponsored reprisals against a wide range of Israeli targets within and beyond

Israel itself (the nadir arguably the attack upon Israeli athletes at the 1972 Munich Olympics), but were powerless to prevent the 1967 expansion. Israeli retreat to the pre-1967 borders, which themselves were unacceptable to the Arab population at the time, has now assumed totemic status as a panacea for the region's ills. The final effort of that era to drive back Israeli territorial advancement came in the October 1973 war, but after taking the Israelis by surprise and recapturing parts of the Sinai, the initiative ground to a halt. Israel was a state under siege, but one which had survived repeated attempts at its emaciation and had greatly enlarged its territory.

What followed was a succession of peace initiatives, juxtaposed with intifadas, rather than attempted full-scale military incursions by Arab states upon Israeli-held territory. Within six years of the 1973 war, Israel and Egypt had concluded a peace deal, one which held despite the assassination of the Egyptian leader Anwar Sadat in 1981. The Israel–Egypt peace deal of 1978–9 is indicative of the capacity for peace-building in the region. Menachem Begin's acceptance of the need to return the Sinai to Egypt and Egypt's recognition of the futility of strategies designed to obliterate Israel indicated that major compromise is possible.

Palestinian hopes of implementing UN resolution 242, demanding Israeli withdrawal from the territories occupied in the 1967 war (but also requiring acknowledgement of Israeli sovereignty over pre-1967 boundaries) faded with the rise to power of Likud in Israel in 1977, a party committed more explicitly to the concept of Eretz Israel than its main rivals. In terms of the enactment of historical claims, the Israeli occupation of Palestinian land after the 1967 and 1973 wars has blended physical control, coercion and exploitation of resources, humane and punitive 'licensing' of the population, rewards for acquiescence, settler ideologies and strategies of normalization, all classic aspects of colonialism (Finkelstein 2003; Gordon 2008; Makdisi 2008). Israel's permanent insecurity and sense of external threat was a dominant discourse used to justify such tactics. The state remains culturally militaristic, often impervious to criticism amid an uneasy juxtaposition of self-righteousness and fear of a hostile external environment. This siege mentality offers an internal sense of unity of purpose that masked internal urban versus rural and religious versus secular divisions (Jones and Murphy 2001). Israeli govern-ments have often not distinguished between criticism of their actions and the wider critique of Zionism offered by Palestinians as a remorselessly colonial ideology.

Comprehending the Modern Basis of Territorial Conflict

The contemporary basis of conflict has been marked by internal changes amongst Palestinian forces, continued Israeli expansionism and continuity in terms of the deal-breaking territorial aspects which infest the peace and political processes. The rival territorial claims are clear. Palestinians want a viable state which, ideally, would mean the annexation of the state of Israel, a demand which remains in the Hamas Charter, but realistically, involves a retreat by Israel from the West Bank and towards somewhere nearer the pre-1967 Israel border. Israel points to the fundamentalism of the Hamas Charter, which rejects the very existence of Israel, although the extent to which Hamas has any desire, let alone capability, to put into effect its desires is disputed, and formal recognition of states need not be a precondition for progress. Hamas is losing the recognition argument. The number of countries recognizing Israel has more than doubled from the 1980s and non-recognition is now rare.

The immediate short-term aspirations of many Palestinians embrace Israeli acceptance of a viable Palestinian state, with territorial retreats to begin as acts of good faith, rather than demands for outright destruction of Israel. Moreover, harsh economic conditions and low employment prospects in virtually all of Gaza and much of the West Bank (notwithstanding recent economic growth) rank as highly as matters of concern amongst Palestinians as their anger at the ever-expanding Israeli 'security wall', which effectively annexes 10 per cent of the West Bank and was declared illegal by the International Court of Justice in 2004 because of such incursions. Israel's de facto control of the West Bank remains acute and it is the nature of that Israeli occupation, via the wall, checkpoints and settlements, which angers Palestinians on a daily basis as much as the broader issue of territorial reverses they have endured over several decades. Military occupation has been accompanied, in many cases replaced, by 'occupation by bureaucracy' via the need for applications, licences and permits to conduct daily life (Žižek 2009). Israel defends the 'security wall' as necessary on the grounds that a similar encasement around the Gaza Strip appeared effective in preventing suicide bombings.

Palestinians overwhelmingly demand a reversal of the current patterns of settlement and full Israeli withdrawal from the West Bank and Gaza, positions rejected as unacceptable by a majority of Israelis (albeit with a significant conciliatory minority), and seemingly the only possible compromise in terms of a retreat to the pre-1967 war border is the granting of other land by the Israelis to the Palestinians. The particular location of territorial concessions is obviously crucial. East Jerusalem, occupied since the 1967 war by the Israelis, whose patterns of settlement encirclement also threaten Palestinian access, remains the desired capital of the Palestinian state, embracing the old city and Haram al-Sharif, the noble sanctuary and holiest Arab place in the city for the Palestinians, and Temple Mount, with its Wailing Wall, to Jews (see, e.g., Sebag Montefiore 2011). Only some form of shared sovereignty over Jerusalem can resolve this, but the indivisible claims do not lend themselves to such a compromise. It is impossible to contemplate an Israeli or Palestinian leader diluting a sovereign claim over the holiest parts of the city. For Palestinians, Jerusalem has to be part of an Arab state and most would eschew UN control and favour rejection of an agreement which attempted to proceed without such an explicit commitment. Israeli opinion appears more evenly split on whether Jerusalem's status need be a deal-breaker, and both sides show willingness to compromise on the issue of access to holy sites within the city (Irwin 2012: 158–9). Beyond Jerusalem, the need to connect Gaza to West Bank and the linkage of territorial acquisitions to resources, notably water, are perhaps the most important issues which need to be addressed.

The Al-Aqsa Martyrs, the military wing of Fatah, has offered only modest resistance to Israeli occupation since the intifada of the early 2000s. Hamas's military arm, the Al-Qassam Brigades, offered more substantial responses prior to a successful election campaign in 2006, and used suicide bombings as a weapon. Although such tactics may have been useful in enforcing intra-Palestinian supremacy over Fatah, the military effectiveness of suicide bombings remains the subject of considerable debate (see Frisch 2006). Whilst creating fear amongst the Israeli population, they have not reversed the pattern of territorial settlement.

The Illusion of Ripeness: the 1993 and 1995 Oslo Accords

Hopes of a breakthrough rose in the early 1990s, even amid a continuing intifada. The election of a Labour government in Israel in 1992 under Yitzhak Rabin offered prospects that a peace dialogue opened in Madrid in 1991 could be taken forward. The Madrid dialogue extended into 1992 and although little was achieved in real terms, the advantage was that at least the Israelis were 'becoming used to the idea of talking to Palestinians' (Quandt 2005: 21–2), thus preparing the ground for formal recognition of their historical enemy, the PLO. Nonetheless, any optimism had to be tempered, given that the new Israeli government continued to insist that the status of Jerusalem could not be altered. Nonetheless, Israel halted settlement growth and took a more flexible approach to the release of Palestinian detainees, creating a supposed ripeness for peace.

The 1993 Oslo Agreement followed secret dialogue between, initially, a low-level Israeli delegation, accompanied by academics and PLO officials. Seven rounds of negotiations preceded the outcome of Oslo, which did not ultimately offer precise solutions to ongoing problems, but, at the insistence of Arafat, these would supposedly be covered in final status negotiations (Bregman 2003). For the first time, the Israeli government recognized the PLO as the legitimate representatives of the Palestinian people rather than as merely a 'terrorist group'. For its part, the PLO finally dropped its refusal to recognize the state of Israel and acknowledged the need for peaceful co-existence. Yet the PLO obtained remarkably few tangible gains, in return for mere recognition of its negotiating rights. The PLO was already in decline, weakened by the removal of financial support from several Gulf States, angered by the organization's support for Saddam Hussein in the first Gulf War. It was divided over the Oslo Agreement, one-third of its ruling council resigning in protest over the organization's endorsement.

Israel and the PLO agreed a Declaration of Principles on Interim Self-Government Arrangements (the Washington Agreement) to accompany the Oslo Agreement and pledged to work towards a comprehensive peace settlement and historic reconciliation. Insofar as the Oslo process offered tangible proposals, what was envisaged was a staged Israeli withdrawal, involving the transfer of most of the West Bank to the Palestinian Authority, provided that the PLO maintained a ceasefire. Three types of area status were created: Palestinian cities under total Palestinian control (type A); Palestinian towns and villages under Palestinian civil control (B) and areas remaining under total Israeli control (C). It was envisaged that, amid consolidated peace, type C areas would become B category and B areas could become categorized as A class territory.

In May 1994, the Cairo Agreement offered greater detail for the statements of principle in the Oslo and Washington Accords. The Palestinian Authority was to be awarded legislative, executive and judicial responsibilities over parts of the West Bank, presiding over policing, health, education and welfare functions (Gilbert 2007). Although external negotiations with other states on economic matters could be initiated by the Palestinian authority, this still fell considerably short of a sovereign Palestinian state, as the Israeli government retained control of the high politics of foreign policy and defence. Some progress on territory was evident in the first year after Oslo, however, with Israel withdrawing direct administration over the Gaza Strip and Jericho. Israel and Jordan concluded a peace deal in October 1994, further raising expectations of the Oslo process, given that this bilateral deal had followed the same trajectory of an outline declaration of principles, the Common Agenda, in 1993. The Cairo Agreement was followed one year later by an interim Israeli–Palestinian Agreement which agreed the areas of Palestinian Authority control, amounting to 80 per cent of the West Bank, subject to final status confirmation scheduled for the end of the decade – a position never reached.

The Oslo process began unravelling at the same time as progress was supposedly evident. The PLO's ceasefire, ignored by some renegades, became irrelevant, given that Hamas stepped up its armed campaign, killing over 100 Israelis within 18 months of the Oslo Agreement, some via suicide bombings. A Jewish settler killed 29 Arabs in a single attack upon a mosque in Hebron. Internal Israeli bitterness over the recognition of the PLO mounted, culminating in the assassination of Yitzhak Rabin in 1995 by a Jewish ultra. Many in the Knesset, which had only backed the Oslo process by a slender 61–59 majority, denounced the accords. From the onset of Oslo to the next serious attempt at conflict resolution at Camp David in 2000, the population of Israeli settlers doubled in size in the West Bank and Gaza (Alexander and Rose 2008: 22). The Palestinian economy worsened and the numbers of Palestinians permitted to cross into Israel for work was more than halved. By the end of the 1990s, hopes of implementation of the Oslo deal had been abandoned. Many Palestinians were unimpressed with the agreement, which did not mention, let alone guarantee, a Palestinian state.

In skirting rather than confronting the key issues which needed to be addressed, the Oslo Accords exacerbated the problems. Oslo was never extended from a Declaration of Principles, which itself fell far short of outlining what a settlement might eventually entail, into a credible set of proposals. There were no commitments offered by the Israeli government in respect of prohibitions upon settlements, refugee rights of return, or of Palestinian statehood, whilst issues of detail in respect of Jerusalem were never addressed. Thus, for critics, the Oslo deals 'changed the modalities of the occupation but not the basic concept' in that the colonizer recognized the legitimacy of the representatives of the colonized and moved a step closer towards the establishment of a 'Bantustan' – a Palestinian homeland equivalent to that 'awarded' to black South Africans during the apartheid era (Chomsky 2003: 227–8).

The Israeli recognition of the PLO was premised upon the belief that it could rein in more militant Palestinians, but delivery of this was only remotely possible in the event of serious territorial movement by Israel to demonstrate the value of dialogue. The value of the Oslo Accords was that they indicated that peace and political processes might be constructed. Indeed, it was perhaps absurdly ambitious to expect the first serious attempt at rapprochement to be successful. Dialogue continued intermittently between 1995 and 2000, before the next serious piece of peace process 'grandstanding' at Camp David. The PLO signatory to the September 1993 recognition agreement, Mahmoud Abbas, conducted bilateral talks which offered to recognize West Jerusalem as the undisputed Israeli capital in return for further negotiations on East Jerusalem, a declaration of Palestinian statehood and compensation (but not automatic rights of return) for refugees (Beilin 2004; Quandt 2005). Such a deal would have been difficult for Abbas to sell. The two sides did conclude the Hebron Agreement in 1997 and met again at President Clinton's Wye River Summit in 1998, but the main significance of both lay more in the Israeli Prime Minister Netanyahu's recognition of the PLO, in contrast to his stance whilst in opposition, than in tangible territorial progress.

Closeness to a Territorial Deal: the 2000 Camp David Talks

Perhaps the moment closest to a resolution of the rival territorial claims came at the Camp David negotiations in summer 2000. Approaching the end of his Presidency and flushed by successful (if minor) input to Northern Ireland's Good Friday Agreement, Bill Clinton was determined to attempt one final brokerage of the problem. Fearing a further intifada in the absence of dialogue, Clinton drew together the Israeli and Palestinian leaderships in a bid to secure sufficient territorial compromises to produce an agreement which would create a viable Palestinian state and secure peace. Two months of preliminary dialogue were followed by serious negotiation at Camp David.

The supposed ripeness for peace immediately prior to Camp David stemmed from several factors. The resumption of hostilities post-Oslo Agreement had achieved little; war-weariness was evident on the Palestinian side and the mood in Israel appeared to have softened; Labour's Ehud Barak had been elected Prime Minister pledging to bring peace to the region. Prior to Camp David, Barak engaged in bilateral discussions with Clinton and tentatively sought peace with Syria, a process which quickly collapsed amid a lack of territorial compromise from Barak or the Syrian President Assad.

Barak was sceptical over the intentions of Arafat, although the two did negotiate directly, Arafat comparing his own position to that of a trapeze artist about to let go of the bar, unsure whether his partner was ready to catch. Barak had continued to expand Israeli settlements around Jerusalem and had reneged on promises to release 350 Palestinian prisoners. Nonetheless, he felt that it might be possible to offer sufficient (over 90 per cent) return of the West Bank and all of Gaza to interest the Palestinians. Barak's domestic position did not shore up his offers. Whilst he could rely on backing from Israeli Arab parties and Meretz to support peace negotiations, the National Religious Party, Shas and the Yisrael B'Aliyah were all far less enamoured and began to detach themselves from the fragile coalition assembled by Labour (Lesch 2008). The lack of rigidity in terms of the principle of collective cabinet responsibility – minor parties in government often feel disobliged – has been a persistent problem. Oslo and Camp David saw persistent criticism from governing 'colleagues' of the Prime Minister (Arian 2005). Barak lost a no-confidence vote in the Knesset by 54 votes to 52 on the eve of his Camp David mission, but the lack of an overall parliamentary majority (of 61) amongst the naysayers meant his government survived. Public opinion was only narrowly in favour of his mission (Bregman 2003).

In exploratory dialogue in advance of the Camp David talks, the Israelis formulated a position on refugees in which the Palestinians expressed some interest. In return for Israeli retreat from the vast bulk of the West Bank and Gaza, Palestinian refugees would be offered the 'options' of resettlement in a newly-created Palestinian state; to emigrate or to remain where they were, with a token number of 10,000 allowed to return to Israel proper. The sweetener was a $20 billion compensation package for their dislocation (Bregman 2002). Initial Palestinian interest was displaced by a reversion to a more traditional position of full rights of return during the eventual full negotiations.

At the outset of the Camp David talks, Arafat made clear that the most important item was the most difficult: that of Jerusalem, with the Palestinians demanding a minimum of half of the city as the Palestinian capital. Barak's opening position was that no part of Jerusalem would be surrendered: it must under Jewish sovereignty. Yet some within Barak's team of 12 negotiators urged concessions. Clinton was enraged by the tokenism of Barak's opening offer of surrender of minor Israeli-held villages at the outset of the talks, informing the Israeli leader that he had no intention of selling Barak's opening concessions (of minor Palestinian territorial gains) to Arafat. Barak's second offer was much more serious: that of a shared Jerusalem. Half of the city would be placed under Arab sovereignty, much more than had been anticipated and close to what Arafat had demanded. However, Haram al-Sharif would remain under Israeli sovereignty given their own preoccupation with Temple Mount, with mere Palestinian custodianship offered. Clinton sold it to Arafat as his own proposal, but the Palestinian chief negotiator, Saeb Erekat, was fully aware of its source. Mohammed Rashid, Arafat's economic advisor, acknowledged that Arafat feared for his own life, arguing, in respect of control over Haram al-Sharif, that what belonged to the Islamic world could not be given away; to do so would be to sign his own death warrant. Arafat could also highlight the requirement for Israel to withdraw from East Jerusalem under UN resolution 242. A retreat by Israel to its pre-1967 war borders would still have given the Palestinians only 22 per cent of the land of the original Palestine. This might have been 'sellable' to Palestinians if a clear victory on Jerusalem was the accompaniment.

In the absence of a deal, Arafat returned to popular acclaim from Palestinians, his uncompromising insistence that Jerusalem is the capital of the Palestinian state having played well. Meanwhile, Barak was denounced in the Knesset for the concessions he had offered during the Camp David talks. Clearly the respective leaderships were constrained more by internal considerations; the fear of being seen as a betrayer stalked Arafat in particular, whilst Barak faced continual domestic criticism for his 'concessions'. Barak's chief critic, Ariel Sharon, decided to 'assert' Israeli claims to Temple Mount by engaging in a public walk around the site. Whilst 'proclaiming peace', Sharon's provocative arrival at the al-Aqsa mosque contributed to the onset of a new intifada, derailing any lingering hopes of a Barak–Arafat deal. Although unilateral attempts to revive the process were undertaken later in 2000 by French President, Jacques Chirac, sympathetic to the Palestinian cause, they failed to come to fruition.

Clinton's final proposal, in winter 2000, attempted further compromise on the vexed issue of Jerusalem, a variant of the Camp David proposals. A Palestinian state with a capital of East Jerusalem would be established and Palestinians would hold sovereignty over Haram al-Sharif, but Israel would retain control over the Western and Wailing Wall and all other parts of the city. It was a 'top-down' solution of a different kind. The Palestinians would have sovereignty of the top of the Haram al-Sharif; the Israelis would have sovereignty over other holy space below. Such a compromise was unacceptable to Barak or Arafat. In total, the Palestinians were offered over 90 per cent of the West Bank at the 2000 Camp David talks, as they were in the previous Oslo Accords and in the 2001 Taba Plan. Arafat still declined the offer, arguably a failure of leadership and an abdication of the need for Arafat to lead rather than follow his people (Morris 2010). Domestic politics had become the 'larger part of each side's decision-making equation' (Wittes 2005: 135). Arafat insisted: 'I can't betray my people. Do you want to come to my funeral? I'd rather die than agree to Israeli sovereignty over the Haram al-Sharif . . . I won't go down in Arab history as a traitor' (Dajani 2005: 64).

Partial Peace; Partial Process; Initiatives and Failures since 2000

Failure at Camp David did not end peace initiatives, but any early hopes for peace appeared remote. Clinton's Presidential replacement, George Bush, had quipped sympathetically to the American Israel Public Affairs Committee during his election campaign that 'in Texas, there are driveways that are longer than that', in acknowledging Israeli concerns that a retreat to pre-1967 borders would leave Israel less than nine miles wide at one point (cited in Smith 2007: 501). Barak was replaced by Sharon, who authorized the targeting of Palestinian leaders by the Israelis. The construction of an Israeli 'security wall' and indiscriminate suicide bombings by Hamas did not provide an aus-picious backdrop for political negotiations. Israeli forces laid siege to Arafat's base, the Muqata, rendering him powerless. Almost 1,800 attacks were made upon Israel in 2001, mainly via crude rockets, but the bulk of conflict victims continued to be Palestinian.

Intra-Palestinian competition for supremacy intensified following the death of Arafat, who had acted as a unifying force, in 2004. The Al-Aqsa intifada may have symbolized Palestinian frustration, but was counter-productive in terms of its death toll, with 4,000 Palestinians killed compared to 1,000 Israelis, from 2000 to 2005, a ratio which worsened for the Palestinians in the remainder of the decade. This second intifada was wider in scope. The intifada of the late 1980s and early 1990s mainly targeted the Israeli security forces; the post-2000 version involved rocket attacks on civilian areas, some targeting of settlers and rioting in Arab parts of northern Israel (Bregman 2002).

The collapse of the Camp David talks had been followed by a determined Israeli effort to isolate Arafat, backed by hawkish elements within the United States administration. This isolation strategy was accompanied by the target-ing of leaders of Arafat's movement and those of Hamas. Yet innocent civilians were the main casualties on both sides, whether from Israel's supposedly 'sur-gical' strikes or Hamas's suicide bombings. The election victory of Hamas in 2006 owed perhaps as much to frustration with the perceived complicit, cor-rupt and complacent Fatah regime, which it felt had become too comfortable with Israeli occupation, as it did to the particular appeal of political Islam. Yet, as Dajani (2005) argues, one could hardly blame the Fatah leadership for partial disintegration. Years of occupation had wearied and demoralized the PLO and rendered it vulnerable to ethnic outbidding once the era of Arafat, the solitary unifying figure, had passed. Arafat had managed to dominate the

PLO and marginalize its more extreme wings or rival leaders, such as the neo-Marxist Popular Front for the Liberation of Palestine under George Habash. Despite the internal friction amongst Palestinian groups, there remained a semblance of pan-Arab unity. In 2002, the Arab League offered Israel recognition from all 22 Arab states in return for a retreat to the 1948–67 borders and the establishment of an independent Palestinian state. This offer highlighted the lack of trust at the heart of the process. Ostensibly the deal offered Israel peace and security, but Israel perceived the powerful Palestinian state as a threat to its borders and doubted the capacity of the Arab League or individual states to move decisively against renegade Islamic militants still committed to Israel's destruction by force.

Internal political developments within Israel took a surprising turn in 2005 with the formation of Kadima (Forward), an avowedly centrist and secular political party, headed by the hitherto uncompromising Ariel Sharon. Given his military credentials and persistent denunciations of Arafat as a terrorist, the new moderation of Sharon surprised many. Sharon's authorization of Israeli withdrawal from Gaza in 2005 constituted the first significant Israeli territorial retreat since withdrawal from Sinai. Kadima, under the post-Sharon leaderships of Ehud Olmert and Tzipi Livni, led the coalition government from 2006 to 2009, capturing backing and members from Likud. As Prime Minister, Olmert offered much of the West Bank to Palestinians and pledged to uproot Israeli settlers, but the offer was declined due to Israel's desire to formally annexe 6 per cent of the territory. Yet amid the rise of Hamas and the attempt to isolate the organization by Israel and the Bush Presidency in the United States, there was little real prospect of progress. By the 2009 election it was evident that Likud was responding successfully to the threat posed by Kadima. In coalition alongside other rightist groups such as Yisrael Beitenu (Israel Our Home), which has sought to deny citizenship to 'collaborator' 'disloyal' Arabs, and the orthodox Shas Party, Likud could continue to dominate Israeli politics, with the Labour Party struggling to offer a consistent line on the Palestinian issue. Likud and the Israeli Right more broadly does particularly well when Israel appears under threat from Palestinian violence (Berrebi and Klor 2008).

From Spoilers to Representatives of the Palestinians: the Role of Hamas

Amid frustration at the territorial impasse, Hamas has shifted from spoiler group status to the mainstream of Palestinian resistance since its 2006 election victory. Central to any peace settlement will be compromises by Hamas which move its realpolitik far from its charter, which rejects the right of Israel to exist, and repudiates 'bogus' peace processes. Israel's current stance is to ask why it should negotiate with an organization formally committed to its destruction. Hamas remains committed to its charter's demand to raise 'the banner of Allah over every inch of Palestine'. Overt movement towards recognition of Israel appears unlikely due to the difficulty for the organization of accepting the confiscation of Palestinian land. For Hamas, Israel and Israeli occupation are not entities which can be disaggregated.

Hamas has correctly been described as 'Islamist and nationalist . . . as much a movement against Palestinian secularism as against Israeli occupation' (Milton-Edwards 2006: 154). In being as much concerned with the nature of the state after the end of occupation, it is arguable that Hamas downplays Palestinian nationalism to the point where it is largely subordinate to wider Islamic concerns, seeing Palestine merely as part of the ummah, the community of believers. This distinction from Fatah's nationalist concerns has led to assertions of a 'great divide between the two competing movements, the nationalist and the Islamic, over the character of the future entity' (Frisch 2005: 403).

Yet Hamas may contain a more pragmatic wing, which amid avowed religious zeal, deals with the world as it exists. A compromise position of long-term truce, *hudnah*, may be a realistic prospect given the lack of opportunity to advance Hamas's ultimate goal (Alexander and Rose 2008; Tamimi 2006). Moreover, although created in 1987 as an Islamic resistance movement, Hamas's promotion of Islamism is somewhat distant from the fundamentalist outlook that was once originally conceived. Hroub (2006: 120) plays down the extent of Islamism as the driving force of Hamas:

> The vague idea of establishing an Islamic state in Palestine as mentioned in the early statements of the movement was quickly sidelined and surpassed. Even when it was repeated by members of Hamas it never amounted to any really serious proposal with thoughtfully considered details. If anything, its early reluctant existence, followed by almost complete disappearance in Hamas's documentation and discourse, reflected the tension in the minds of Hamas's leaders between the political and the religious.

Having emerged as a spoiler group, suspicious of moves towards compromise undertaken by the PLO, Hamas had moved within two decades to becoming the electorally dominant arm of the Palestinian movement. The movement used a combination of resistance via its al-Qassam Brigades, which emerged in 1992, and development of political Islam, enforced by the Executive Force (in effect a Hamas police force) to offer radical popular appeal to the most dispossessed Palestinians. Although its appeal is to the particularly disadvantaged, the leadership of Hamas is highly (often western) educated. Its founder, Sheikh Yassin, was killed by the Israelis in 2004 and other prominent officials have also been targeted.

Hamas's election victory in 2006, on a Change and Reform label, saw the organization win 42 per cent of the vote. It was a success achieved partly due to the inadequacies of Fatah and criticism of the Palestinian Authority, seen as an accoutrement of Israeli occupation. The vote for Hamas and Fatah in 2006 was fairly evenly divided in both Gaza and West Bank, but control of the two Palestinian territories was split after the 2007 intra-Palestinian conflict.

The Palestinian Authority accepted financial assistance from the United States to tackle Hamas in the 1998 Wye Agreement and almost accepted Israeli terms in the 2000 Camp David summit; as such it was regarded with suspicion or even contempt by many Palestinian militants. Even some Palestinian members of Fatah were dismissive of those Palestinian Authority senior officials who they dismissed as 'the "Tunisians", i.e. Palestinian exiles who had lived a comparatively luxurious existence in Tunis and elsewhere whilst they suffered under Israeli occupation' (Lesch 2008: 378). A considerable amount of cooperation between the Israelis and the Palestinian Authority against the common 'enemy' of Hamas was revealed in a variety of documents leaked in 2011 (*The Guardian* 2011). For Hamas, the leakage of the 'Palestine papers' merely publicized what they had long contended: that Palestinian Authority 'negotiators' had abandoned antagonism to become quasi partners with Israel, their main aims being 'to remain in power, preserve their role in the process and maintain the special status and privileges accorded to them as individuals in exchange for collaborating with the occupiers' (Hamdan 2011: 30).

Election success for Hamas was also due to the organization's anti-corruption drive and sympathy for the plight of its officials, with, at one point, dozens of the organization's elected representatives held in Israeli prisons. Hamas fuse welfare and warfare and have eschewed peace initiatives, from which the organization was excluded anyway, such as the fruitless Annapolis peace conference in 2007. Hamas's triumph led to a short-lived national unity government in 2007 following the Mecca intra-Palestinian deal, before Hamas seized control over Gaza's 1.5 million inhabitants, arguably preventing a preemptive Fatah coup (Shlaim 2010) amid much conflict, with over 100 deaths in one week in June 2007. There is considerable evidence that the United States, British and Israeli intelligence agencies encouraged a Fatah uprising against Hamas.

In Gaza, Hamas found itself besieged by Israeli forces and episodic attacks from both sides were evident (incursions and air strikes from Israeli forces and rocket attacks from the al-Qassam Brigades), in addition to a concerted three-week attack on Gaza by the Israeli Defence Force in Operation Cast Lead in 2008–9, killing hundreds. Elements within Israel's governing coalition, notably the Shas Party, wanted the entire 'removal' of the Hamas regime. The impact of the attacks was to eventually encourage reconciliation between Hamas and Fatah, which arrived in 2011 following a Cairo deal between Mahmoud Abbas, the Palestinian President and Khaled Meshaal, the Hamas leader. Israel responded to the accord with financial sanctions against the Palestinian Authority. Palestinian unity remained fragile and the fracture between groups a further barrier to assertions of statehood.

During its period in control in Gaza, Hamas has been obliged to recalibrate its position, the defence of that area replacing suicide attacks upon Israel, although some rocket attacks continued. Yet any moves towards explicit compromise by Hamas, or even a semi-permanent *hudna* (ceasefire) may be exploited by more militant groups. The Al-Quds Brigades, the armed wing of Islamic Jihad, would be likely to act as one spoiler group. Salafist Islamic militants in groups such as Tawheed and Jihad believe that Hamas, reliant upon secular support, has been insufficiently Islamist in its governance of Gaza, even though Hamas has moved against 'decadent' aspects of society, banned alcohol, ordered the wearing of the hijab and enforced sharia law. Such groups are likely to oppose any peace deal. Yet the links between Hamas's armed wing and Iran, which, with its growing nuclear capabilities and avowed aspiration of President Ahmadinejad to remove Israel, is the current main concern for Israel and the West more broadly, mean that an enduring Israeli–Hamas deal remains in any event a most unlikely prospect (Taheri 2010).

The Israeli government remains unconvinced that demands for a Palestinian state are mere expressions of Palestinian nationalism, believing instead that they form part of a broader pan-Islamic axis committed to the destruction of Israel. Indeed the Hamas Prime Minister, Ismail Haniyeh, has cautioned against the 'trap of nationalism' which he argued was a 'Zionist-Crusader conspiracy to divide Muslims across national lines' (Taheri 2007: 23). This position could shift, in the same way that Israel's fears of pan-Arabism were replaced by individual peace deals with neighbouring states. Moreover, the extent of unity between predominantly Sunni organizations such as Hamas and Shi'a groups, such as Hezbollah, might be questioned. The withholding of EU and US funding following Hamas's election victory exacerbated already poor economic conditions and seemed likely to increase rather than dilute militancy amongst Hamas supporters.

Yet following Hamas's 2006 victory and amid little public optimism for peace, the Annapolis peace process, from 2007 to 2009, again came close to agreeing the territorial formula for a two-state solution. Given the absence of Hamas, it is questionable whether the Palestinian negotiators under the leadership of Saeb Erekat had the capacity to deliver, but it is evidence that there were serious and realistic appraisals of what might constitute a settlement. Under quiet pressure from the US administration, the Israelis engaged in a temporary reversal of the policy of settlement, whilst the Palestinians allowed some Israeli expansionism around Jerusalem, the largest Jewish control of Jerusalem to date. Erekat also appeared to go beyond Arafat in accepting the Barak/Clinton Camp David formula for dividing Jerusalem, based upon shared sovereignty, the Israelis controlling the Jewish Quarter of the Old City. However, the desire of the Israelis to annexe settlements south of Jerusalem as permanent Israeli territory proved a stumbling block, whilst the issue of control of the Haram al-Sharif/Temple Mount was not resolved. Erekat made conciliatory noises, in contrast to Arafat's rejection of loss of control of the Dome of the Rock and al-Aqsa mosques, but the issue was merely parked.

Is a Solution Possible? The Two-State Orthodoxy

As Dowty (2008: 207–8) argues, 'Arab-Israel conflict will not be solved by argu-ments over historical rights or claims of victimhood', yet it is precisely such insistences, the clinging to 'outdated fantasies', which permeate the peace process in the region. A two-state solution remains (just) the most realistic outline of what is attainable (Smith 2007). However, it makes assumptions which draw upon insufficient empirical evidence, which somehow lead to a conclusion that the actuality and contours of the two states can be agreed.

Firstly, the avowed willingness of Israel to accept a two-state solution ignores the 'facts on the ground' of regular patterns of settlement in an emaciated Palestine. Surrounded or breached by an ever-growing 'separation fence' and host to thousands of settlers, the West Bank is surely 'so fragmented and debilitated that it is almost inconceivable that it could function as an independent state' (Cohn-Sherbok and El-Alami 2008: 240). The economic asymmetry of Israeli and Palestinian states would be stark. Secondly, two-state mantras assume that 'historical rights' do not infuse contemporary claims, when the converse is true. In terms of realpolitik, the ostensibly secular form of Zionism offered by Likud has not differed markedly from the religiously-derived demands of the party's coalition partners such as Shas. Thirdly, in terms of intra-Palestinian agreement, two-state solution mantras assume a more hegemonic role for the more secular Fatah organization, which indeed would probably accept such a deal given (and it is far from a given) substan-tial Israeli territorial retreat. Yet Hamas's avowed willingness for a long-term truce has been too readily conflated with acceptance of a two-state solution by optimists. No such acceptance is forthcoming. Islamic Jihad and other Islamic groups would be unlikely to cease violence. Internal division between Palestinians, allied to lack of confidence, has dogged the negotiating power of those within Fatah willing to negotiate with Israel (Dajani 2005).

Unsurprisingly, opinions on optimum solutions are divided between Israelis and Palestinians. The favoured option for Palestinians, supported by approximately four-fifths, is that of a historic Palestinian state extending from the Jordanian river to the sea, with a majority (but not an overwhelming one) of those supporters arguing for an Islamic Waqf, whilst fewer than one-third of Palestinians would support a shared Israeli–Palestinian state (Irwin 2012: 155). Amongst Israelis, only a minority (27 per cent in the Irwin (2012) poll) believe that a Greater Israel is essential or desirable and no solution commands majority support. Opinion is evenly divided between a two-state solution and the political status quo, a substantial minority supporting con-federations between the West Bank and Jordan and between Gaza and Egypt (Irwin 2012: 156). Overall amongst Israelis and Palestinians combined, the two-state solution has the most support and the fewest outright opponents, but it is far from overwhelming backing – and obviously does not resolve the issue of the contours of the two states.

A two-state solution remains the form of conflict management most commonly advocated. It is the avowed policy of the US and the UN, the latter confirming backing for the concept in Resolution 1397 in 2002. The core Israeli demands, if a two-state solution is to be accepted, are retention of the Israeli West Bank settlements; an Israeli military force on the eastern border of the West Bank, in the Jordan Valley; and the retention of Jerusalem as Israel's indivisible capital. The Camp David negotiations in 2000 indicated that flexibility on (parts of) Jerusalem might be possible and the removal of settlers from Gaza could conceivably be replicated on the West Bank, but appears less likely. A two-state solution based upon a Palestinian state of the West Bank and Gaza would comprise only 5,000 km^2 of the 22,000 km^2 of the 1947 British Palestine. A larger two-state solution would be that of a Palestinian–Jordanian confederation to Israel's East, a loose amalgamation of the West Bank, Gaza and Jordan, palpably a more viable Arab entity, but one which does not disguise the erosion of old Palestine.

The Israeli tendency remains that of referring to a Palestinian 'entity' rather than a state. Israelis demand Palestinian recognition of Israel as a Jewish state, Palestinians demand full UN recognition of a Palestinian state. Observer status for Palestinian officials had been awarded by the UN in 1974. Partial statehood for Palestine was agreed (with more than 100 votes in favour) by the UN General Assembly (but not the UN Security Council, for which Palestine remained a mere 'entity') following the urgings of the Palestinian National Council way back in 1988, via adoption of Resolution 43/177. As such, there was little new in the Palestinian return to the issue at the UN over two decades later, amid little prospect of the 15-member UN Council backing the measure. Article 4 of the UN constitution declares that the admission of full new members 'will be effected by a decision of the General Assembly upon the recommendation of the Security Council', such an endorsement vulnerable to veto. The US veto, as one of the five permanent members of Council, remained in place, contrasting with its ready acceptance of Israel's status in 1948. Article 18 of the UN constitution requires a two-thirds majority in favour of admission of new states. In 2012, the UN's members voted 138 to 9 (with 41 abstentions) to award Palestine the status of non-member observer state, short of full statehood.

If awarded full state status, Palestinians could then increase the pressure upon Israel to end the occupation of that state, given that Israel controls 60 per cent of the West Bank and all of Jerusalem. Yet the statehood route appeared a cul-de-sac without a change in US attitudes. In 2008, the US and Israel opposed a UN resolution supporting the 'right of the Palestinian report to self determination' which nonetheless was passed by 173 votes to 5. Full statehood would permit direct elections to the Palestinian National Council, the parliament in exile which could conceivably unite disparate Palestinian factions. An interim Palestinian Authority was established under the Oslo Agreement and a Palestinian Legislative Council was formed in 1996. Yet elections to legislative bodies covering the West Bank and Gaza exclude the huge number of Palestinian refugees.

The revival of the statehood approach by the Palestinian Authority was part of a constitutional programme initiated by the leader of Fatah and President of the Palestinian Authority, Mahmoud Abbas, designed to pressure Israel, via use of the International Criminal Court. Conceivably, Palestinians, or sympathetic states, could threaten the arrest of Israeli politicians for 'war crimes'. However, Israel is not a signatory to the Rome Statutes by which the Court operates. The new(ish) constitutionalism and moderation rebuts those who seek to present a future Palestinian state as the antithesis of a liberal, secular democracy and fronts the Palestinian cause with officials from middle-class areas (e.g., Ramallah) far distant ideologically from religiously militant Islamists. The Palestinian National Authority Prime Minister, Salam Fayyad, embarked on a strategy of economic development of the West Bank, attracting substantial inward investment and facilitating rapid economic growth, reversing years of diminishing Palestinian GDP, as part of an effort to demonstrate sound governance and show the Palestinian Authority as a government-in-waiting, presiding over an embryonic state. Economic growth on the West Bank from 2006 onwards deepened the argument concerning the viability of a Palestinian state. Israelis claimed the credit, whilst Palestinians pointed to the continuing high levels of unemployment and poverty as evidence of colonial mismanagement which would be rectified by self-determination.

Could a Single Bi-National State Work?

Despite the modern movement towards physical separation of Palestinians and Israelis via 'security walls' and amid endless mantras of 'two-state solutions', there remain advocates of a one-state solution in which Arabs and Jews co-exist within a single political entity. The argument for a unitary state ought to be couched in positive language of shared nationhood and amiable co-existence, but instead tend to be grounded, firstly, on the contemporary incapacity of the Palestinian state to exist amid erosion by Israel and secondly, because the tactics of separation, security and encasement pursued by Israel will merely exacerbate insecurities and instability within the region (Tilley 2005).

There are three broad forms of one-state solution. The first is a unitary state in which party politics is exercised in accordance with the usual democratic norms of majority rule, human rights and fair treatment for minorities. Differences are not institutionalized; places in the legislature are not 'reserved' or allocated on the basis of ethno-national or ethno-religious difference and the power is shared, not divided. Disputes over territorial boundaries and who controls Jerusalem are ended. The obvious criticism of such a 'solution' is that it makes utopianism look cautious. Whilst secular and moderate political forces are certainly evident in Israel and Palestine, there are also sizeable political organizations whose existence is a derivative of religious Zionist or Islamic projects, visions which do not coincide and may be impervious to integrationist projects.

The second model is a consociation, in which Palestinians and Jews would share power with the usual safeguards of proportionality in government, mutual veto and communal autonomy. If attainable, such a state ought to satisfy the historical claims of Arabs and Jews to the land of Palestine. It would allow free return for refugees and whilst a bi-national state would not be an exercise in full self-determination for either population, there could be considerable communal autonomy, which might be assisted by the 'transfer' eastwards of Arabs within Israel, as proposed by the Israeli Foreign Minister, Tzipi Livni, in 2008, in return for partial withdrawal by the Israelis from West Bank settlements. This new bi-national state would no longer be the Jewish homeland long treasured by Israelis and it is difficult to conceive it ever being agreed. If the West Bank is wholly absorbed into Israel, such a bi-national venture risks creating a future Palestinian majority, or a more immediate one if refugees were permitted rights of return. Low Jewish birthrates and the limited attractions of a Jewish state for many Jews (especially secular western ones) remain a concern for Israelis (Fraser 2008) and the proposition of emigration to Israel might be yet more unattractive if the country amounted to a fragile bi-national consociation. Alternatively, Israelis might continue to encourage mass immigration of Jews to the area, heightening tensions. Consociations have a poor international record of success and this would be one of the riskiest ever attempted. It would, at best, probably produce benign apartheid between two populations still possessing a competitive mindset and could dissolve into civil war. The practical difficulties of unitary or consociational models are evident. Is it possible to visualize Hamas, Islamic Jihad and the Israeli Defence Force merged into a single entity in defence of a nation which fails to realize the vision of any of those organizations?

The alternative third model would be a confederation, in which Israel and Palestine would be nominally joined, presumably with joint elections to a ruling body drawn from both states and with an economic union, but would operate effectively as two largely autonomous, self-governing states with only a weak central unit. This has the advantages of self-determination (to a considerable degree) and communal autonomy, offering a less risky enterprise than attempting to construct an elite-level consociation. It also avoids the need for reintegration. However, the issues of the contours of the Israeli and Palestinian states within the confederation, the control of Jerusalem (presumably co-sovereignty would be less sensitive?) and the return of refugees (to the Palestinian state only?) would still be difficult to revolve. If the two entities retain separate armed forces, there is a risk of armed struggle re-erupting.

Is there any evidence that peaceful co-existence within the same umbrella state could be viable? Bi-nationalism has a poor historical record; even benign

Belgium has struggled to remain united in recent years, so attempts to forge a new 'Palrael' or Israstine' seem extraordinarily ambitious. Advocates point to the representation of Arabs within parties in the Knesset; the near-doubling of the Arab population within Israel within the first two decades of the state's existence; the joint status of Hebrew and Arabic as the state's official languages and the award of civil and democratic rights to all Arab citizens within Israel. Yet this co-existence may be evident because the modest Arab population in Israel, mainly confined to the North and living largely separate lives, does not constitute a threat to the Jewish nature of the state. A broader Palestinian confederation, embracing the reduced Palestine, Jordan and possibly other surrounding Arab states would be an alternative option with a bi-national entity. However, this removes the distinctive Palestinian claim to a state, effectively making Palestine an adjunct of Jordan (which Jordan's political leadership would not welcome). It would leave Palestinians in Gaza potentially cut off from their parent state.

Exogenous Assistance

Although negotiations between the Israeli government and Palestinian representatives have become routine in recent decades, there remain strong cultural differences in addition to the obvious territorial points of dispute, further diminishing the prospects for a breakthrough and necessitating external mediation and brokerage. A security mindset drives Israel's negotiators, who are accused of having attitudes towards Palestinian officials which 'still tend to fall somewhere between condescension and poorly concealed contempt for low levels of professionalism' (Klieman 2005: 93). Given this, the brokerage role of the United States may yet be crucial and neither Israel nor Fatah (but not Hamas) is particularly hostile to the idea of external mediation. The criticism offered by Palestinians is that the primary role of the Washington administration has been to uphold an Israeli veto of a political settlement and reject Palestinian assertions of statehood, against an international consensus. The Israeli narrative suggests international lack of understanding of the vulnerability of Israel's position, but given the widespread contemporary international acceptance of Israel – but not at its current borders – this has been a more difficult argument to sustain in recent times.

As demonstrated by Mearsheimer and Walt (2008), the Jewish lobby in Congress remains very powerful. This notwithstanding, the United States administration is hardly monolithic in its approach to Israel. During the Bush Presidency in the 2000s, the Secretary of State, Condoleeza Rice, perceived the Israeli occupation as one comparable to the South African apartheid regime (Landau 2007). The Bush government, along with the EU, UN and Russia, asserted its support for a two-state solution and pledged to 'end the occupation that began in 1967, based on the foundations of the Madrid Conference, the principle of land for peace, UNSCRs [United Nations Security Council

Resolutions] 242, 338 and 1397, agreements previously reached by the parties and . . . acceptance of Israel as a neighbour living in peace and security, in the context of an overall settlement' (see Lesch 2008). The difficulty is that 'the overall settlement' can probably not occur without prior adherence to the UN resolutions cited and the US administration has rarely been seen as even-handed given the lack of pressure upon Israel to adhere to those US stipulations.

President Obama's frustrations with the Israeli leader Netanyahu did not lead him to push Israel towards an unfavourable settlement and the US peace envoy George Mitchell resigned in 2011 amid a widespread belief that his peacemaking efforts were not fully backed by the US administration. Despite the obvious limitations of the US in the arena, alternative brokers with the clout to shift policy are not easily found. Whilst some commentators (e.g., Andrew Sullivan in the *Sunday Times*) placed faith in the capacity of Barack Obama to rein in the wilder settlement aspirations of Prime Minister Netanyahu, there was little empirical evidence to sustain this argument. The Israeli leader categorically refused a moratorium on settlements during negotiations in 2010, his government announcing the building of new developments on the West Bank and East Jerusalem and arguing that Jerusalem was not a settlement but the Israeli capital.

Obama's avowed preference was for a contiguous, functioning and effective Palestinian state with an Israeli retreat to somewhere approaching its pre-1967 border, but there was little prospect of any Israel administration converting this wish. The infamous words of President Truman that 'Jesus Christ couldn't please them [the Jews] when he was on earth so how on earth could anyone expect that I would have any luck?' might be recalled (cited in Sebag Montefiore 2011). Truman's sentiments found an echo in Bill Clinton in 1996 with his frustrated utterance in response to Netanyahu's intransigence: 'Who the **** does he think he is? Who's the ******* superpower here'? (Cornwell 2010). A 'special relationship' exists between the US and Israel, but based more upon the pragmatic interests of both rather than deep love.

Meanwhile, the Republican Right has long been overtly pro-Israel, stances which appeal to its Christian Right potential vote, far more important than the much-vaunted Jewish vote, which forms only 2 per cent of the US electorate (although Jewish donations to US political parties are sizeable). The American Israeli Public Affairs Committee (AIPAC) continues to punch above its (Jewish) vote weight in Congress, albeit with slightly less direct influence within the White House, although the influence of lobbying has been challenged; Lieberman (2009) suggests that US foreign policy would in all likelihood be pro-Israel anyway, given the threats to US interests posed by the other forces in the region. AIPAC conferences attract extraordinary levels of Congressional interest; 67 senators and 286 members of the House of Representatives attended the 2011 event. In contrast, Arab lobbying has always appeared amateurish.

Beyond Territory: the Other Current Key Issues

Three key issues beyond territorial spoils remain evident: those of prisoners, refugees and settlers. There are more than 6,000 Palestinian prisoners in Israeli jails. Prisoner exchanges between the Israelis and Palestinians have been commonplace, but a systematic means of dealing with prisoner releases has remained elusive. Instead, piecemeal releases and exchanges have been the norm (Fraser 2008). The release of prisoners by the Israeli government is invariably linked to ceasefires by Palestinian armed groups, but as a confidence-building rather than conflict-ending measure, and the treatment of the prisoners' issue in isolation from territorial questions achieves little. The number of Palestinians jailed by the Israelis since the 1967 war exceeds 500,000, including scores of parliamentarians.

Given the lack of consensus on how to deal with the issue, the Oslo Agreement avoided the sensitive issue of prisoner releases. However, the 1994 Cairo Agreement made provision for the release of 5,000 prisoners, although this meant that over 7,000 would remain imprisoned (McEvoy 1998). Prisoner releases were made explicitly and individually conditional upon support for the promised new political dispensation, a premature demand. Individual prisoners were obliged to sign a declaration of support for the peace process to obtain release, a difficult condition for those objecting to various political aspects of the Oslo Accord. Article 16 of the 1995 Israeli–Palestinian interim agreement on the West Bank and the Gaza Strip, which updated and extended the Oslo Agreement, offered further clarification on prisoner releases. It stated that Israel would release in three stages. For the first stage, Israel offered to free all women prisoners, along with men who had served more than two-thirds of their sentence, or who had not caused fatal or serious injury, or were not held on security matters. These releases were to be followed by a second stage incorporating all prisoners less than 18 years of age and those over 50. In addition, those who had already served sentences of ten years were to be released at the second stage. The final stage merely promised examination of whether more categories could be released, meaning that for some prisoners, incarceration remained indeterminate – a move hardly designed to endear them to the process.

Although the scale of prisoner releases was considerable, not least given the hostile reaction from several political groups and families of victims in Israel, the political conditionality and phased nature of the process, along with the lack of precision for its completion, was bound to cause difficulty. The Israeli–Palestinian deal demanded support for the Oslo process, but failed to distinguish between organizations maintaining or fracturing ceasefires. It offered the prospect of some prisoners languishing in jail indefinitely, if not covered by the first and second stages, given the vagueness of the third stage. The desire of Palestinian prisoners for release did not dilute the overarching territorial dispute which prevailed and the Oslo Accord collapsed because of mutual mistrust over the desire of Israel and Palestine for peaceful co-existence (Dowty 2008).

Despite the failings of the Cairo Agreement, Palestinian prisoners offered more progressive positions than some of their political and military associates outside jail. Greater political progress might have been made if those incarcer-ated had assumed primary negotiating positions. The essence of the 'prison-ers' plan' remained the establishment of a Palestinian state in the West Bank, Gaza Strip and East Jerusalem, the right of return for refugees and reform of the Palestinian Authority, demands far less radical than the posturings of mili-tants. Yet mistrust over prisoner releases continues to hamper peace efforts. The Cairo Agreement timetable was replaced by new sets of arrangements agreed at Wye in 1998 (102 prisoners to be released in the first wave) and at Sharm-el-Sheikh in 1999 (350 prisoners in two groups to be released), but such programmes have remained piecemeal and hundreds of 'administrative detainees', processed by Israeli military courts but often not subject to trial, remain held in Israel's prisons.

The refugee issue appears unsolvable, given the demand by Palestinians for absolute rights of return to their previous locations and compensation for those dispossessed by Israeli conquest. There are over 4 million refugees registered with the United Nations Relief Welfare Agency (Dowty 2008: 194) with the largest percentage having moved to Jordan, but with huge numbers in Gaza (where they form by far the bulk of the population); and the West Bank, along with Syria and Lebanon. UN resolution 194 offers rights of return to refugees and the UN has asserted these rights in the Palestinian context, but to little avail. Ostensibly there appears little room for full refugee returns (the US administration in 2008 at one point even floated the idea of Palestinian resettlements in South America, an idea quickly quashed), and Fatah appeared to acknowledge this in discussing the option of a token return of approxi-mately 10,000 refugees during private negotiations with the Israelis. Given the number of potential refugees, the scale of recompense would deter magnani-mous Israeli gestures, which would instead amount, at most, to the low-cost 'apology' type, although the costs of resettlement might in any case deter many Palestinians from returning. The return of Palestinian refugees into a broader bi-national or federal shared state could make them the larger popula-tion within such a construction, another reason why the idea has few takers amongst Israelis. Although the Camp David talks floundered principally on the issue of Jerusalem, the issue of refugees was not resolved and subsequent efforts to address the question have failed. Palestinians continue to demand the right of return to pre-1967 borders for millions of dispossessed citizens.

The problem of settlements becomes more vexed each year. In 1987 the 128 Israeli settlements on the West Bank covered 4,000 hectares of land. By 2005, the settlements had not increased markedly in number (to 149) but had expanded hugely in volume, to over 16,000 hectares. Some settlers argue that they are fulfilling a biblical prophecy in occupying Judaea and

Samaria (the term West Bank is not used), although the majority are political rather than religious zealots. The ever-expanding number of settlements, with 300,000 Israeli settlers now residing on the West Bank and 200,000 in East Jerusalem, where settlers have become increasingly ultra-orthodox in contrast to far more secular parts of Israel, create 'facts on the ground' which surely now prevent the construction of a viable Palestinian state. Only once, with the 2005 removal of 7,500 settlers from the Gaza Strip by Sharon, has the process been seriously reversed, despite a freeze, then reverse, of settlements, being supposedly central to the peace strategy of the quartet of the US, EU, UN and Russia. Settlements do not merely fulfil a political role; they also maintain a presence on the West Bank which Israel sees as useful to the securing of access to natural resources, most notably water, one-third of the supply coming from West Bank aquifers (Tilley 2005: 63). For most Jewish settlers, the heartland of the national claim and the essence of Zionism is 'the return to the heartland'. This return is 'acknowledgement of the truth of the prophesy of the Bible' (Ha'ivri 2010: 1). Many believe that Israel can never accept an additional state west of the Jordan River. The Law of God thus outweighs the niceties of international law. The settlers are aided by an ideologically sympathetic Likud party and a religiously supportive Shas party. The Israeli Foreign Minister from 2009–12, Avigdor Lieberman, was located in one of the West Bank settlements.

Conclusion

In the absence of any serious alternative, such as a single state consociation or 'two states but one' confederation, the two-state solution remains the orthodoxy in the Israel–Palestine peace process. The contours of those states remain strongly contested, seemingly in perpetuity and with rapidly diminishing prospects for the construction of a viable Palestinian state to house a stateless people, in the absence of Israeli retreat from its settlements policy. Permanent ceasefires, greater international monitoring and free movement of peoples need to be a prelude to a political agreement. A contiguous Palestinian state linking West Bank and Gaza remains possible (just) and is a much more viable option than a cantonized West Bank. Most of the West Bank was 'offered' by the Israelis at Camp David in 2000 and the Israeli government and the Palestinian Authority differ mildly over the percentage withdrawal (93 per cent offered by Israel; 98 per cent demanded by Palestinians). A deal based upon Camp David and restated in the 2003 Geneva Accord remains the outline least bad option. In the event of a two-state solution, compromises on issues beyond state borders are possible. Refugees could be given automatic rights of return to the West Bank and Gaza, annual quotas for return into Israel, and compensation for those permanently dispossessed. Jerusalem could be an area of shared sovereignty, with access to the holy sites overseen by the UN. Settlements could eventually be removed, as occurred in Gaza under Sharon's edict. A single-state option can surely be ruled out. The growth in the Arab population means that they could form a majority within a combined state by 2035. It is almost impossible to envisage an Israeli accommodation of such a possibility, or the development of a consociational deal within a shared polity.

Evidence of peace-building capacity exists in the willingness of Arab states to do deals with Israel. Yet, in terms of Israel–Palestine, there is insufficient evidence that the territorial aspirations of Zionist or Islamic-inspired 'totaldom' have been sufficiently downgraded by a section of the political leaderships on either side, nor is there much tangible belief that diplomacy is necessarily a better conduit of business than militarism or territorial assertion. Greater Israel, established gradually via settlement 'facts on the ground', remains an aspiration for several of the significant political parties in Israel, even though successive opinion polls have indicated a greater propensity towards compromise amongst the electorate. Hamas remains desirous of an Islamic state, but Islamification divides Palestinians. The downgrading of such claims is not assisted by the nature of intra-ethnic competition. A Knesset with a dozen parties, including several of the right and/or orthodox variety who may require accommodation within a governing coalition, does not assist moderation, whilst fears of displacement by more militant groups dogged Palestinian approaches to negotiations under Arafat and remain a concern for both Fatah and even Hamas, particularly as the Palestinian to Israeli casualty rate has remained at 6 to 1 throughout the 2000s.

The situation in the Israel–Palestine conflict has altered continually and perceptions of a stalemate, mutually hurting or asymmetrical, are one-dimensional. Clearly the 15,000 strong forces of Hamas are incapable of defeating the 600,000 plus Israeli Defence Forces, a position which does not alter even if Hamas's potential allies in the region are added to its side. Equally, Israel's brief war with Hezbollah in 2006 indicated its diminished capacity to inflict outright territorial defeats or retreats. However, the nature of conditioning Palestinian ideology has altered markedly. Pan-Arabism and conventional warfare from the 1940s until the 1970s was displaced by Palestinian nationalism during the 1980s and 1990s, which offered greater prospects for a deal. Pan-Islamism in the 2000s has diminished prospects for a deal, which in any case remain low due to continuing Israeli expansionism. Israel cannot expect to ever be recognized by Islamic forces, but a cold peace could exist. The patterns of settlement emasculate realistic prospects for a two-state deal. The lack of United States pressure upon Israel and the regional interests of Jordan, Syria and Egypt, doing little to reshape the status quo whatever the rhetoric to the contrary, means there is little shift in policy.

CHAPTER FIVE

Conflict and Confessionalism in Lebanon

Since the end of the 14-year long conflict in 1989, there has been relative peace in Lebanon. However, the political process has been characterized by instability and punctuated by episodic violence, accompanied also by reconstruction and the recasting of political alignments. The 1989 Ta'if Agreement managed and reinforced the country's Christian Western-oriented versus Muslim Arab-oriented confessional divide, whilst re-negotiating the terms more favourably for Lebanese Muslims, compared to the pre-civil war era. Lebanon's traditional faultline has thus been consolidated, but the cross-cutting religious and political cleavages, which have been evident since the Ta'if deal, have also blurred Lebanon's sectarianism. There have been tensions between pro- and anti-Syrian forces, Arab versus Lebanese and, to a lesser degree, Left versus Right. External military and political interference in Lebanon's political arrangements, overtly from Syria (which, via 'Pax Syriana' acted as the 'guarantor' of the Tai'if Accord) and from Israel and indirectly from Iran and the United States, alongside questionable loyalty to the state from some of the internal political actors, has begged the question as to whether a consocation is the most appropriate means of stabilizing and maintaining peace in the country. This chapter analyses the conflict of the 1970s and 1980s, explores subsequent eruptions of violence, and assesses the utility of consociationalism as the mode of conflict management. It analyses the extent to which the Ta'if Agreement has contained conflict against a difficult background, given that 'intercommunal tension has been a feature of the modern state of Lebanon since its creation' (Abul-Husn 1998: 2). The chapter examines why the Lebanese peace process remains fragile amid shifts in the nature of its consocation, changes in the nature of external involvement and amid weak central authority. It explores how sectarianism and shifting alliances, rather than stability, have characterized the post civil war polity.

Unripe for Consocation? How Lebanon's Civil Wars were really Broader Conflicts

The emergence of Lebanon as a sovereign country in 1943, following independence from France, led to the establishment of an unwritten national pact and a consociational political formation, in which Christians and Muslims shared power. Electoral seats were divided between Christians and Muslims, producing a 6:5 proportional Christian:Muslim ratio of elected representatives, with similar proportionality evident in Cabinet posts. The most senior post, that of President, was held by a Christian Maronite, the Prime Minister was a Sunni Muslim, with a Greek Othodox Deputy, whilst the Speaker was a Shi'ite.

Such an ambitious consociation was dependent upon parity of esteem, a condition not felt by Shi'ites, who tended to be poorer and were underrepresented in political structures relative to their size. Indeed, Lebanon was an imperfect consociation, one in which Maronite (and to a lesser extent, Sunni Muslim) elite cartel government was at times as important as power-sharing (Dekmejian 1978). Maronites formed only 29 per cent of the population, albeit as part of a 58 per cent Christian majority in the 1932 census, after which no further official population counts were undertaken (Zisser 2000: 5). There was a 'monopolization of power by a leading elite of 40 to 50 Christian and Muslim families which had existed since the end of the French mandate' (Corm 1988: 263). Maronite hegemony was criticized not merely by many Arabs and Muslims, but also some Christians. Moreover, as Hudson (1988: 238) argues, power-sharing, Lebanese-style, lacked 'the accommodative intra-elite behaviour or the elite-mass discipline that defines consociationalism, nor was there the practice of representation, participation and accountability that is required for democracy, either between or within communal segments'.

The tensions precipitated mainly by Shi'ite disadvantage contributed to a brief civil war in 1958, in a struggle for greater political recognition and better social conditions than those that had been evident under the pro-Western Maronite Presidency of Camille Chamoun. Although the rifts of 1958 temporarily subsided, the continuing grievances of the Shi'ites and the growth of Arab nationalism within the region, which led to Palestinian forces using Lebanon as a base, re-ignited conflict by 1975, as Christian, Muslim and Leftist parties developed militias. Christian Maronites contemplated the partition of Lebanon, but such an entity was rejected by Arabs as tantamount to the creation of another pro-Western Israel within the Middle East. The 1969 Cairo Agreement attempted to regulate between the Lebanese Army and the growing Palestinian forces in the country, but proved ineffective as communal Christian or Arab allegiances were more important than those to the state.

At its outset, the 1970s Lebanese conflict was mainly an internal conflict between the Lebanese Front versus Arab and other forces. The Lebanese Front was strongest in the north of the country and comprised various Christian Maronite forces, including the Phalange, under Pierre al-Jumayil and the National Liberal Party's armed wing, The Tigers, along with the pro-Maronite Guardians of the Cedar militia, all keen to preserve the political status quo. They were pitted against the National Movement, later the National Resistance Front, comprising a variety of leftist forces, embracing the Progressive Socialist Party, the Organization for Communist Action, the Communist Party, the

Movement of Independent Nasserists, the Syrian National Social Party and the Baath Party, alongside Sunni, Shi'ite and Druze religious groups, plus the PLO. Although often portrayed as a conflict between Christian Right and Socialist and Arab Left, this is somewhat reductionist. The most important political parties within the Lebanese Front, the Kataeb and the National Liberal Party, claimed to be socialist and centrist, respectively, and the civil war originated via far more of an inter-communal and identity-based struggle than a Right–Left ideological battle (Vocke 1978). Insofar as the conflict was ideological, it was a struggle between the innate conservatism of the Lebanese Forces and the radicalism of their opponents.

The Druze, under Kamal, then Walid, Jumblatt, protested loyalty only to the Lebanese state and argued for replacement of the confessional political system with integrationist socialism, declining to align formally to the National Movement (Abul Husn 1998: 3–4). The Movement desired political change and offered support for the Palestinian cause. Amid shifting alliances and rivalries, the Lebanese Front fractured in 1980 as its Tigers from thereon operated as a separate group. The Front comprised an eclectic mixture of militias, political parties and intellectual figures, such as Charles Malik, a former President of the UN General Assembly.

Each side committed atrocities and used conscription, extortion, taxation and propaganda in prosecuting the conflict, often oppressing the populations they purported to defend. Lebanese Front militias were responsible for massacres in Palestinian refugee camps, most notably at Shabra and Shatila (actions in which Israeli forces acquiesced, as did members of Amal opposed to the PLO) following the killing of the Phalange leader, Bashir Gemayel. Palestinian and National Movement forces slaughtered hundreds of Christians in Damour. Intra-bloc killings were also common. On the Christian side, there were clashes between the Lebanese forces and the militia associated with the National Liberal Party, the Tigers. However, the internal conflict broadened during the 1980s to the point where 'civil war' was perhaps a misleading title for a conflict in which over 100,000 died (Milton-Edwards 2006) and which saw considerable foreign interference.

Israel's invasion of south Lebanon in 1982, under 'Operation Peace for Galilee', took place after a one year lull in the fighting. The largest Christian militia, the Phalange, had formed an alliance with Israel following clashes between Christian and Syrian forces, which provided a pretext for Israeli incursion. The Israeli government blithely ignored UN resolutions demanding it end its occupation of southern parts of the country. A proxy pro-Israeli force, the South Lebanon Army, emerged. Lebanon's official state policy was neutrality on the Arab–Israeli conflict, but neither set of antagonists adhered to such an approach. The Israeli invasion was initially welcomed by some non-Christian Lebanese, including a small minority of Shi'a Muslims who had co-existed uneasily with more secular PLO groups, but the subsequent siege of Beirut and continuing occupation alienated the indigenous population (Milton-Edwards

2006). Israel's invasion, initially supposedly a 25-mile incursion to safeguard its southern border, finally ended in withdrawal in 2000, 17 years after 'agreement' on withdrawal. The Israelis were largely successful in removing the PLO from Lebanon, demoralizing the organization, as the Lebanese conflict became part of the larger Arab–Israeli problem. The PLO's presence had been seen as one of the catalysts for conflict, as the Palestinians had no reason to offer loyalty to the Lebanese state. The overspill of the Palestinian cause into Lebanon was an inevitable development to which the state should have adjusted – but the state was collapsing (Gordon 1980). The PLO was struggling to mount an effective campaign against Israel and, beset by internal friction, it 'came to depend on operations launched through Lebanon to preserve its character as a fighting movement' (Rabinovich 1985: 103). Defeat in Lebanon represented another stage in the organization's decline.

However, the PLO was to be replaced by a more formidable enemy, as Hezbollah began to embed in the south of the country as an Islamic military and welfare movement. Iran and Syria offered support for Hezbollah as it emerged from a split in Amal. Sunni Muslim groups tended to look elsewhere for assistance, mainly to Libya and Iraq, although their interference was very minor compared to Syrian involvement. External intervention extended to the United States, which deployed its troops amid revulsion at the massacres taking place, but retreated after 241 of its forces were killed in a bombing at their Beirut base in 1983.

The National Movement was divided between Arab nationalists and socialists and between those willing to accept Syrian control of the movement and those preferring greater autonomy. Ironically, Syria's interference grew initially on the basis of invitation from Maronite forces fearful of civil war defeat in 1976. However, the civil war merely transferred into a broader theatre of conflict, involving other countries anxious to exert influence in Lebanon. Syria retained a broader ideological belief in Bilad al-Sham, the formation of a single Arab unit embracing Syria, Jordan, Palestine and Lebanon, with its capital in Damascus and viewing Israel as a potential security threat. Syria supported the National Movement, invaded parts of Lebanon and used South Lebanon as a base to launch raids on Israel. Lebanese forces operated in a semi-covert, fluctuating alliance with Israel.

The outcome of the war was a lack of a clear victory for any side. Peace talks, attended by the leaders of all sides, were held in Geneva in 1983–4, but failed amid disagreement over whether to reconstitute Lebanon on the basis of a federal system, desired by the Lebanese Front, or via abolishing confessionalism, as desired by others. Agreement was reached on the removal of sectarianism at a peace conference in Damascus in 1985, but this was usurped by a change of leadership within the Lebanese forces. Only by 1989 were the rival forces sufficiently exhausted from conflict to sign an enduring deal. Yet, although not entirely defeated, Christians had been weakened by the war, not only by the 1975–89 conflict, but also through the impact of General Aoun's determination to fight on against Syria and oppose the Ta'if deal, due to its consolidation of Syrian interests.

Rigid Consociation: the Ta'if Agreement and Beyond

The shift towards peace merely deepened faultlines, which political institutions, reconstituted via the Ta'if Agreement in 1989, have attempted to bridge but not repair. Beydoun (2004) identifies several consolidations of confessionalism arising from the 1975–90 era, notably an increase in the number of religious figures assuming senior political positions; a reduction in the number of mixed residential areas and the growth of communal ceremonies and anniversaries, exclusive in nature and with a tendency to alienate other communities. This confessionalism has been accompanied by the entrenchment of clientelism, with parties based around the cult of leaders controlling the local state, seemingly immune from serious scrutiny of their actions.

The demise of National Pact consociation amid civil war did not mean the death of the idea. The Ta'if Agreement, the National Reconciliation Accord, reconstructed consociational ideas on a politically redistributive basis (Kerr 2005). The Ta'if Agreement was National Pact Mark II, an attempt to rebuild power-sharing on a more equitable basis. The National Pact consociation failed for a combination of reasons; the lack of capacity for adjustment to demographic change; attempts by political elites to engage in control and communal aggrandisement rather than the basic sharing of power needed for consociation; and external destabilization. No suitable replacement was seriously sought or found, as the lack of clear territorial delineation of the rival populations made alternative political arrangements difficult to contemplate (Oren 1992). The Ta'if Accord, whilst acknowledging demographic change and improving upon previous immobilism, added to the problems confronting consociation, via a more explicit bilateral set of arrangements with Syria. This folly was accompanied by myopia in dealing with an apparent 'enemy within' in the form of Hezbollah, whilst the debilitating regional spillover effects of Israel's occupation of Palestine were always likely to impinge upon internal political developments.

The Ta'if Accord was devised mainly by the Arab League and agreed after an intense three weeks of negotiations, before being ratified by the overwhelming majority of Lebanese parliamentarians. It was reached after 22 days of direct negotiations and was agreed against a backdrop of a final, unsuccessful effort by General Aoun's Lebanese ultras to remove Syrian troops from the country. Aoun argued that the exceptionalism regarding Syria doomed the agreement to failure and he was especially critical of Christian backers of the deal. His forces were blamed for the assassination of the first post-Ta'if President, the Christian Maronite, Rene Moawad, within weeks of the accord being signed. Acting as a spoiler group, Aoun's forces of the rearguard contributed to over 800 deaths in the first year following the Ta'if Agreement. Amid anxiety over the possible collapse of Ta'if, and reassured by Syria's supposed guarantees at assisting Lebanese national reconstruction, the deal held and the Lebanese Army defeated Aoun's spoilers, Aoun obliged to seek asylum in the French Embassy in Beirut. The civil war had cost Lebanon $18 billion in damage and a deal which allowed the formation of a viable Executive and Parliament over-rode other considerations (Blanford 2009).

Judged solely on a core aim of reconstructing the country, the Ta'if Agreement could broadly be considered a success. Economic growth, albeit financed by debt and external investment, were soon evident under Prime Minister Hariri's 'government of national salvation'. Hariri's executive mobi-lized economic revival under the Horizon 2000 programme, a multi-billion pound rebuilding aimed at addressing a grim conflict legacy of 20 per cent displacement; 55 per cent housing overcrowding; 35 per cent unemployment; falling wages and a GNP way below pre-conflict levels (Najem 2012: 84–5). It was political unity that the Lebanese peace process found more difficult to create.

The ethos of the Ta'if document was that of 'no victor and no vanquished' (Khalaf 2002: 290), but rather a return to the power-sharing past, but with modifications in favour of Muslims. It declared Lebanon a sovereign unitary state, to be governed by a 'strong central authority', asserted its Arab identity and re-institutionalized religious faultlines, but on a basis more favourable to Shi'as. For a document which declared a wish to abolish sectarianism, the Ta'if Agreement was remarkable in its institutionalization of that very thing. Although the deal promised to abolish religious identification on identity cards, political structures consolidated ethno-religious identification. It con-tained the classical features of power-sharing at executive and legislative level; veto rights; proportionality in government and representative institu-tions; and communal autonomy, the latter exercised to such an extent that the centre's writ has never run deep. Proportional Christian, Sunni and Shi'a Muslim representation was enforced in key executive positions, whilst in the legislature this was extended to proportionality between denominations of each sect. Ta'if enshrined religious freedom, whilst placing religious identifi-cation as the key construct of the institutional apparatus. Christians, Shi'ites and Sunnis were not to be reconciled; differences were to be contained not overcome.

The Lebanese Parliament was increased in size to 128 members, constructed from 26 regions. It was now divided 50:50 between Christians and Muslims rather than the 6:5 Christian to Muslim seat ratio previously in evidence. This may still have over-represented Christians in the legislature, as, although reliable census data does not exist, it was estimated that by the early 1980s, the Muslim population had grown over the previous five decades from two-fifths of the population to three-fifths (Kliot 1987). The seats for each 'side' are allocated proportionately according to denomination. Lebanon's 'seats for sects' is the most rigid in the world, 18 Muslim and Christian groups enjoying parliamentary representation. The 64 Muslim seats are earmarked as follows: Shi'a 27, Sunni 27, Druze 8 and Alawite 2. More than half (34) of the 64 Christian seats 'belong' to Maronites, with the remainder shared between Greek Orthodox (14), Greek Catholic (8), Armenian Orthodox (5), and others (3). Equal representation for Shi'as, Sunnis and Christians was also institution-alized via the Executive, amid the sharing of ministerial posts. Power shifted from the presidency to the cabinet to diminish Maronite power. The Sunni Prime Minister, Rafik Hariri, rather than a Maronite President, became the most important elite figure, although both had to agree the cabinet, headed by the Prime Minister, whilst the President remained the head of the Lebanese defence forces. The Speaker was to always be a Shi'a Muslim. Moderates tended to be elected to these positions given the requirement for cross-community parliamentary support. Mutual bloc vetoes were built into the workings of the cabinet, where a two-thirds majority was required for major issues, such as international treaties, the budget and key appointments, and for the removal of cabinet members. Constitutional amendments required two-thirds parlia-mentary support.

A return to the consociationalism which dissolved in violence in 1958 and again in 1975 was not ideal, but few viable alternatives existed. The acknowledgement of division was unavoidable and its consolidation within a single entity on the basis of communal coexistence, whilst offering little prospect of integration or full reconciliation, was seen as better than the alternatives. There have been efforts to construct a common civic identity via shared schooling, but cross-community appeal has been a diminishing basis of election for many parliamentary candidates. Under the majoritar-ian electoral system, the percentage of votes required to elect a deputy fell sharply, from 80 per cent in 1947 to 50 per cent by 2000, as swathes of votes were wasted, amid a preponderance of 'almost guaranteed victory lists' (Salam 2004: 5). What may be needed is a de-sectarianized, proportional representa-tion system of multi-member constituencies in which parties have to maxi-mize their cross-communal appeal to increase their elected returns in each district.

Patchwork quilt territorial ethno-religious geography, the largely Shi'ite south aside, meant that partition, or even federalism, were not viable options, even if there had been the desire to break up the Lebanese state (Oren 1992). For Christians, parity was an absolute minimum requirement in the state, given their perception of beleaguered status, constituting only 2 per cent of the overall population in the Middle East and surrounded by predominantly Muslim countries other than Israel, but majoritarian government would have been entirely unacceptable to Muslims. Integrationist political projects at local level could have been attempted, but the question of 'who governs?' would have remained at elite level. Moreover, adequate legislative representa-tion at least partly defused tensions between Muslims, such as the friction between secular Amal and religious Hezbollah and between Shi'ites and

Sunnis in west Beirut. Consociation thus remained the only political show in the country. The Ta'if deal allowed 'communal pluralism to maintain its legitimacy in the face of federalist desires, cantonisation and irredentist pan-Arab ideologies' (Abul-Husn 1998: 5).

Beyond political structures, the Ta'if Agreement was ambitious in its demili-tarization programme. The Accord insisted that ceasefires be sustained, that all militias, domestic and non-domestic, be disarmed, with decommissioning to be completed within six months of the deal and that these processes were accompanied by disbandment of armed groups (with some militia leaders heading into parliament or cabinet) and the reunification of the Lebanese Army. That Army forcibly disarmed the remnants of the PLO in 1991, allow-ing their continuing presence in the country, but retaining only sufficient small arms to keep order in their camps. However, this move did not indicate that the reconstituted Lebanese Army had established itself as the dominant force. Rather, it reflected Syria's backing for an action designed to neuter the Palestinians within the state (Winslow 1996).

A glaring exception to the comprehensive provisions of Ta'if lay in respect of the Syrian army, permitted to 'assist' the Lebanese government during the implementation of the Ta'if Accord. Another was in respect of Hezbollah, which simply ignored the decommissioning edict, rebranding itself as a resistance to occupation in a way that other militias could not. Amnesties were offered to ex-combatants. Prison sentences from five years upwards were introduced for individuals refusing to hand over weapons and the legisla-tion threatened prosecution of political parties retaining armed wings, but Hezbollah, backed by significant support, was impervious to such pressure. The disbandment process was successful otherwise; the combined militias of the Lebanese forces, Amal and Socialist groups amounted to over 35,000 per-sonnel, although only a small minority of these joined the regular Lebanese Army. Decommissioning of weapons did not involve the handing over of armaments to the reformed Lebanese government, but instead involved their dumping, or transfer to the Lebanese Army and, in some instances, to Syrian and Israeli forces.

Full rights of return were offered to Lebanese refugees, over 800,000 having been displaced, with more than half returning to their original area of residence. Yet there was an asymmetry of displacement. Of those forced to quit their homes, 670,000 were Christians and 157,500 were Muslims, whilst of those who had not returned 70 per cent were Christians, displaced from swathes of Beirut and its surrounds in particular (Khalaf 2002: 301). The displacement figures illuminate the modern vulnerability felt by Christians, a feeling of dispossession exacerbated by their once superior status. For Christians, there is little incentive to de-confessionalize Lebanon, as the system now protects their minority position with equal status in representa-tive institutions. Christians formed only 22.1 per cent of registered voters in 2005, compared to 26.5 per cent Sunnis and 26.2 per cent Shi'ites (Farha 2009:

87). A further recalibration of power can only damage Christians given their shrinking proportion within the Lebanese polity.

Lebanon's Christian leadership sacrificed the idea of separation from the state amid (inaccurate) charges that the new entity would represent a form of 'Christian Zionism'. In opting for Lebanon's continuing unification, they effectively endorsed internal ethnic tensions in perpetuity and limited external support for their identity within Lebanon, albeit buttressed by sympathy from the United States. Moreover, the desire for a united Lebanon via Ta'if came at a time when secession was about to become more commonplace in Europe. As Phares' (1995: 201) sympathetic analysis of Lebanese Christian nationalism puts it: 'The Christian leadership led its community to partition when international thought was opposed to the idea and they conceded the return to unification theories when world politics favoured separatist claims for ethnic groups.' This leadership struggled to adapt to reduced circumstances. Having been the dominant ethno-religious group, Lebanese Christians now had to adapt to being a defensive ethnic resistance movement.

Christians remained suspicious of Arab and Muslim demands to remove sectarian structures, viewing them as a covert attempt to achieve a takeover, leading to the removal of Christian identity and autonomy and replacement by Arab nationalism or, more likely, an Islamic state. Christians fear that they will be relegated to the status of *dhimmi* under Islamic law, in which they are a protected people, but a group without access to power and status (Helmick 1998). These fears have been heightened by recent events in Syria. The Assad regime, as Alawites, were seen as protective towards Christians, being described disparagingly as Little Christians by critics and even celebrating some Christian feasts as holidays. The potential negative impact of regime change (however desirable on other grounds) in Lebanon's neighbour has added to concerns amongst Maronites in particular.

Druze socialists contend that such sectarianism will permanently prevent the development of a Lebanese national identity, arguing instead for governance by normal party structures and the fostering of internal allegiances. The mere modification of sectarianism put in place by the Ta'if Agreement allowed two nationalisms, Lebanese Christian Maronite (but with Maronite communalism more evident than fidelity to the Lebanese state) and Arab Islamist, to remain the dominant forces to the exclusion of cross-cutting identities. Society has oscillated between conflict and accommodation, given that much political activity has long been conducted on the basis of pragmatic communal self-interest rather than the greater good of the Lebanese state (Barakat 1988). Individual identity remains subordinate to communal affiliation and as such Ta'if has been heavily criticized as offering anti-democratic and unaccountable government, based upon identities mistakenly construed as permanent.

Opponents of change have conflated efforts to de-confessionalize the system with the introduction of secularism, yet the right to worship would not be threatened by a change in political structures (el-Hoss 1994; Khairallah 1994). Khairallah (1994) also criticizes the manner in which the Ta'if Accord allowed religious authorities the right to petition the constitutional council on a range of policy matters, including religious education. Winslow (1996: 295) bolsters the critique, arguing that what he provocatively terms 'the religion disease' reinforces class divisions, as sectarianism inhibits cross-class action. This approach contains its own elitist and patronizing view of humanity, however, in assuming that individuals are mere sectarian dupes, helpless amid manipulation by sectarian masters. Sectarianism and religious observance are too often misleadingly entangled by those who oppose both. What *does* need to be tackled is perhaps best outlined by Makdisi (2007: 24): 'Sectarianism as a culture, therefore, is more than simply mindless religious violence: it is the historically contingent moment when religious difference becomes accepted and imagined as the bedrock of a modern politics of equal representation'. The resilience of the politicization of religious difference shows only modest signs of dissipation, as this forms the basis of power brokerage, even though cross-religious alliances have also long been evident.

Whilst critics of confessionalism are often accused of naive utopianism, there is a pathway for a staged phasing out of sectarian aspects of the system. This would involve making Lebanon a single electoral district; allowing only political parties to nominate election candidates and removing religious weightings to administrative, judicial and military appointments, prior to tackling political posts. A combination of stronger local government, the growth of secularism; the rise of civil society and the importance of non-governmental organizations can combine to move Lebanon progressively from unstable, elite-driven consociation towards a still-inclusive but more functioning polity (Collings 1994). Of course, confessionalism is not the only problem evident amid Lebanon's unstable peace. Pork-barrel politics and clientelism have proved difficult to tackle, both connected to the sectarian construction of the state, which remains bloated and impervious to reform. Thus, as one example, the first post Ta'if Cabinet set a trend for over-large government in containing a preposterously large number (30) of ministers, as sectional interests and personal favours were rewarded (Knudsen 2010).

Exogenous Impediments to Internal Consociation

The Ta'if Agreement demanded the implementation of UN resolution 425, first passed in 1978, requiring foreign forces to withdraw from the country. Yet Lebanon's post-war reconstruction was beset by external interference. The supposedly internal consociation of the Ta'if Agreement recognized the 'special interest' of Syria in Lebanese affairs and Syria was supposed to assist in the decommissioning of armed groups. The requirement for 40,000 Syrian troops to withdraw by the end of the two-year timetable for transition to reintegrated democracy was ignored (Harik 2005). Ta'if was explicit in pronouncing Lebanon an Arab country, 'tied to all the Arab countries by true fraternal relations', but with a special relationship between Lebanon and Syria 'that derives its strength from the roots of blood relationships, history and joint fraternal interests' and which would be 'embodied by the agreements between the two countries in all areas' (Ta'if Accord 1989). Syria viewed the Lebanese and Syrian peoples as 'one and the same' and would not tolerate a partitioned Lebanon (Saliba 1988: 156). Lebanon's peace 'was achieved at the price of its independence', being followed by a succession of unstable governments skewed in Syria's interests, with Lebanese reconstruction subordinate to the desires of its neighbour (Malia 1994: 41–2).

In the run-up to the signing of the accord, the Tripartite High Commission, comprising Algeria, Morocco and Saudi Arabia, working with the Arab League, had criticized Syrian interference as an infringement upon Lebanese sovereignty. Yet, post-Ta'if, Syria was directly involved in designing electoral laws, supervised the contests, increased the size of the parliament, helped compose some of the election candidate lists and encouraged voters to support pro-Syrian candidates – a formidable collection of influences (Frangieh 2004; Kerr 2005). Since devising the rules of the game, Syria has used its influence to attempt to indirectly control cabinet appointments and confine key decision making to those appointments and the President-Prime Minister-Speaker troika (Frangieh 2004).

The Ta'if Agreement was followed in 1991 by the Treaty of Brotherhood, Cooperation and Co-ordination with Syria, legitimizing the perception of Lebanon as part of a 'Greater Syria'. For critics, the 1989 and 1991 deals ensured that Syria 'gained full command of Lebanon' amid a process of 'stagnation and humiliation' for the Lebanese, as their country's government was seen as incapable of governing alone and was 'warped to suit Syrian Ba'thist interests' (Harris 1997: 279). The bilateral 1991 Treaty referred to the common destiny of Lebanon and Syria and effectively conceded a permanent place in Lebanese political and security arrangements to Syria, whose troops remained in Lebanon until 2005. The Treaty established permanent interstate committees, formalizing Syria's role in Lebanon in foreign, defence and economic policy; in other words most aspects of 'high' politics. Article 5 effectively intertwined Lebanon and Syria in a common foreign policy. A Higher Council of the Presidents, Prime Ministers and Speakers of both states was established as a further bonding agency. Additionally, ten bilateral agreements were signed in 1993–4 (Harris 1997: 294). Concurrently, Syria has exerted its influence via the training of the Lebanese Army. It ignored UN resolution 520 demanding withdrawal of its own forces. Syria assisted in the gerrymandering of electoral boundaries to produce favourable results for parties most sympathetic to its involvement, resulting in a Christian boycott of the 1992 elections, which were supposed to restore full democracy after almost two decades of conflict. Christians driven from the country during the conflict were denied a vote and only 5 per cent of Christians in Beirut and 20 per cent elsewhere bothered to cast a ballot, although the net effect was merely to deny support for some moderate Muslims and allow Hezbollah and Amal to perform better than expected (Kerr 2005: 174). Syrian influence was consolidated in 2000, via a restructuring of electoral districts which merged some anti-Syrian areas into pro-Syrian constituencies (Shields 2008).

By the 2000s, even some erstwhile sympathizers with Syria, such as the Druze leader, Walid Jumblatt, were questioning the value of external interference, as pro- versus anti-Syria sentiment deepened as a faultline. Whilst those anti-Syria were mainly Christian and Druze, some Sunni and Shi'a groups also expressed disquiet over the special relationship, and cross-sectarian alliances emerged. In 2004, UN Resolution 1559 demanded the removal of all foreign forces from Lebanon. The killing of the former Prime Minister, Rafik Hariri in 2005, blamed at the time upon Syria, created a wave of protest against external interference in Lebanon. Hariri's murder was followed in 2006 by that of the Industry Minister and critic of Syria, Pierre Gamayel. The Cedar Revolution swept Syrian forces from the country. Yet, as Blanford (2009: 159) argues, 'while the independence intifada was a truly historical event, it was not the demonstration of national unity that its organisers claimed'. Rather, it highlighted the modern political fissure within Lebanon. Whilst Syria had few diehard advocates inside Lebanon in the immediate aftermath of the Hariri assassination, its role in Lebanon was seen by Hezbollah and its sympathizers as a useful counterweight to the risk of United States' influence in the country. The Special Tribunal established in 2009 to investigate the Hariri murder added to the instability by appearing to implicate Hezbollah, whereas the earlier Mehlis Report of the UN had suggested that Lebanese and Syrian government officials were responsible (United Nations 2005).

The other main exogenous actor, Israel, took 18 years to withdraw from Lebanon and retained the Shebaa Farms, captured from Syria during the 1967 Six Day War but claimed by Lebanon as part of its territory. Israel continued to apply pressure by bombing claimed Hezbollah militia and rocket-launching bases episodically from 1991 until 2006. The most sustained clashes included Operation Accountability in 1993 and the 16-day Operation Grapes of Wrath in 1996, before a 33-day conflict erupted in 2006 after Hezbollah captured two Israeli soldiers and Israel responded with sustained bombardment. Hezbollah claimed victory, having demonstrated its capacity to attack Israeli towns with rockets and to operate in a manner which made it difficult for the Israelis to target the organization. Yet the outcome of the short war was 1,100 Lebanese dead (of whom over 1,000 were civilians and one-third were children), almost ten times the number of Israeli victims, whilst nearly one million citizens were temporarily obliged to move and over 100,000 homes were damaged or destroyed (Sayed and Tzannatos 2007). A ceasefire, via UN resolution 1701, followed by re-implementation of the United Nations Interim Force (UNIFIL) buffer zone between Israel and Hezbollah's forces, restored an uneasy peace. That the UNIFIL force was increased hugely, from

2,000 to 15,000 soldiers, spoke volumes concerning the fragility of the peace.

The Winograd Committee of Inquiry in Israel acknowledged that Hezbollah's quasi-military force had been successful in resisting Israeli bombing. Israel hoped Hezbollah would waste most of its weaponry, but acknowledged that within two years of the 2006 conflict, the organization had replaced the missiles lost and increased their number (Spyer 2009). The Winograd Committee concluded that Israel's campaign had lacked a clear strategic rationale and had not yielded victory. Hezbollah appeared securely embedded in southern Lebanon in perpetuity, its credibility relative to Amal (which had retained much support in the area) enhanced and its image as communal defenders (and to some extent Lebanese patriots) bolstered. Yet claims of 'divine victory' for Hezbollah were misleading. Its leader, Hasan Nasrallah, admitted that had Hezbollah been aware that Israel would respond so robustly to the kidnapping of its soldiers, his organization might not have acted in the same way, a pronouncement influenced by serious financial damage caused to Hezbollah's enterprises in the region. An undoubted temporary surge of support for Hezbollah was followed by a more circumspect analysis of its role relative to the regular army within a supposedly sovereign Lebanese state.

As a strategy designed to secure its northern flank, Israel's occupation of Lebanon had failed. It had quickly routed the PLO, but succeeded only in facilitating the PLO's replacement by a more militant and Islamist organization. Yet the strategy of containing Hezbollah, an organization seemingly sufficiently embedded to be incapable of removal, is a crucial aspect of Israel's regional strategy (Tilley 2007). Dealing with Hezbollah is one aspect of facing down Palestinian resistance and securing an insecure Jewish state with permanent borders. UN Resolution 1701 is useful for Israel, given that it explicitly requires Hezbollah to remove its armed forces from south of the Litani River, with only the Lebanese Army and UNIFIL permitted to operate in this region, whilst ignoring the build-up of Israeli weapons at the border (Falk and Bali 2007). Given the history of Israeli non-compliance with resolutions in respect of its borders, it is unsurprising that Hezbollah treats such stipulations with similar insouciance. Israel demands that the Lebanese Army disarms Hezbollah knowing that this is now an impossible task and would risk precipitating a civil war, although the Lebanese Prime Minister Siniora did briefly consider attempting forcible dismemberment prior to the 2006 Hezbollah conflict with Israel. The 2006 conflict merely made the Lebanese administration somewhat more sympathetic to Hezbollah. Any Lebanese attempt to remove Hezbollah would be very risky. Polling evidence suggests that a majority of Shi'ites support the retention of arms by Hezbollah (although a sizeable minority are not in favour), whereas overwhelming majorities in other countries believed that only the Lebanese Army should be armed (Harris 2007: 72). Yet these figures can fluctuate at times of crisis, Hezbollah's support rising during its 2006 conflict with Israel. In that confrontation, Hezbollah and its allies played down the organization's autonomous existence, Syria applauding the 'Lebanese resistance'.

Endogenous Impediments to Consociation: Hezbollah

Post-Ta'if politics were 'seriously infected by a militaristic spirit' from the outset (Picard 1996: 162). Sect aggrandisement remained amid the removal of paramilitaries. Whilst most political organizations and militias were disentangled, the fusion remained in the case of Hezbollah. As a Shi'a Muslim organization, Hezbollah, the Party of God, is often viewed as part of a broader movement, linked to Shi'a movements in Syria and Iran and inspired by the Iranian Islamic revolution. Shi'ite radicalism rose as a consequence of a split in Amal (the main Shi'ite representatives until this point) after Israel's invasions of Lebanon in 1978 and 1982. In addition to causing thousands of deaths, those invasions resulted in the imprisonment of 10,000 Lebanese and Palestinians, many of whom became increasingly radicalized (Mowles 1986). The growing fundamentalism of Shi'ites was evident in the Iranian revolution of 1979 and Hezbollah is committed to the promotion of Islamism, although the extent of this commitment in terms of its activities in Lebanon is contested. Hezbollah is opposed to the existence of Israel and has been accused of promoting anti-semitism via its television station, Al-Manar. Although often seen as a part-Iranian, part-Syrian-backed organization, Hezbollah was not Syria's original 'agent' of choice, that country backing Amal against Hezbollah in the late 1980s and demanding that Hezbollah join the Amal electoral ticket in the 1992 and 1996 elections. Indeed, Syria at times appeared more interested in brokering deals between Amal and Hezbollah than actively supporting the latter and there is greater warmth and ideological convergence in Hezbollah's Iranian relationship (Husseini 2010), even though Hezbollah strove to preserve Assad's Syrian regime in his country's civil war.´

Hezbollah's credibility developed from two sources in its quest to displace the secular Left with political Islam. Its military arm, Al-Muqawama al-Islamiyya (Islamic Resistance) emerged as a serious fighting force, using rocket attacks, local resistance and suicide bombings as tactics. The worst atrocities commonly associated with Hezbollah, such as the 1983 bombing of the US Marines base in Beirut, were claimed by Islamic Jihad, widely seen as a flag of convenience. Large arms shipments from Iran, imported via Syria, allowed Hezbollah to develop into 'one of the best-equipped paramilitary forces in the world' (Gambill 2009: 134).

The political arm of Hezbollah developed as a coalition of structured political party and resistance movement, one which combined continuing commitment to armed resistance to Israel with welfare provision for Shi'ites in southern Lebanon and, eventually, found a role in government. The strength of Hezbollah acted as a corrective to any continued weighting in favour of Christian Maronites in the Ta'if Agreement. As Hiro (1993: 217–18) opined in the Accord's aftermath: 'one can only wonder how long the Muslim community, which forms 60 per cent of the total population, in a country with a multi-party democracy, can be content with a 50 per cent share of the political pie and deny itself the office of President: and how long the Shi'as, constituting the single largest sect, will tag along as junior partners in the Muslim camp'. The answer for militant Shi'as was simply to cherry-pick the Ta'if Agreement, achieving sect strength by selectivity. Thus Hezbollah participated in political structures, but ignored the military edicts of Ta'if, instead maintaining its self-appointed vanguard role in opposition to Israel.

The Ta'if Agreement was ignored by Hezbollah in respect of the decommissioning of weapons, but the deal produced a change in the organization's political approach. Notwithstanding its criticism of the deal as inadequate for Shi'as, the accord marked the moment when Hezbollah 'metamorphosed from a revolutionary "total refusal" anti-system party, into a "protest" anti-system party', still ambivalent over its attitude to the Lebanese state but no longer demanding the overthrow of its leaders (Saad-Ghorayeb 2002: 26–7). Hezbollah declined to confer legitimacy on the Ta'if Agreement and condemned its sectarianism (although it was hardly immune from sectarianism itself), but took a pragmatic approach that attempted to change the political system via participation within its framework.

Hezbollah's more constructive political approach post-Ta'if brought electoral reward. Indeed, its representational expansion might have been more rapid had it not been for Syrian pressure for electoral alliances with Amal, which arguably limited Hezbollah's own advance in the 1992 and 1996 elections. Hezbollah adapted quickly to the parliamentary arena and offered voice on a range of issues well beyond the purely religious, arguing for social justice (its support remains predominantly amongst poorer Shi'ites) and launching populist anti-corruption drives. This has produced a degree of internal political moderation, even nods towards acceptance of Lebanon as a multicultural and multifaith entity, juxtaposed with sustained anti-Israel venom. Its Islamism has been fused with Lebanese nationalism and a desire to establish an Islamic state by popular will rather than force (Deeb 2007). Attacks from Israel merely extended Hezbollah's backing, with even Christians and Sunni Muslims temporarily offering support amid the 2006 conflict (Zunes 2007). The brief war confirmed Hezbollah as a 'full-fledged army', capable of confronting Israel without battlefield support from Iranian or Syrian personnel (Harik 2010: 148).

Hezbollah's integration into Lebanon's political system has led the organization to condemn the activities of Sunni Islamic militants in the north of the country, such as Takfir-wal-Hijra, which attacked the Lebanese Army in 2000. These and other loose affiliates of Al-Qaeda are seen as a threat to the stability of the Lebanese state, bereft of national concerns and interested only in jihad. Hezbollah maintains its close relationship with Iran, but many of the Shi'ites supporting Hezbollah are not overtly religious, with little interest in

Iranian theocracy. Hezbollah has adopted much of Amal's political platform to become more acceptable to the broad Shi'ite community. This has down-graded much of the internal fear of Hezbollah once held by opponents.

Whilst the institutionalization of Hezbollah has correctly been read as a long-term process of Lebanonization, it has also formed part of Lebanon's Hezbollization (Nir 2009). Despite operating its own internal semi-autonomous entity, Hezbollah's presence in national Lebanese politics means that it is accepted as a legitimate political player by most others, its right to exist no longer questioned. Yet Hezbollah does not fully accept the boundaries of Lebanon, viewing Israel's place on its border as an encroachment upon Islamic land. Moreover, Hezbollah's discourse has still been reluctant to identify as Lebanese, one of the organization's more militant leaders arguing: 'Some say we are Lebanese Muslims . . . No! We are Muslims of the world and we have close links with other Muslims' (cited in Saad-Ghorayeb 2002: 77). Where it is convenient for Lebanese national interests and Muslim actions to coincide, Hezbollah is happy to promote both, but nationalism and patriotism are not the conditioning forces of the organization. It remains an organization com-mitted to Islamic revolution, but one sufficiently attuned to political realities to recognize the limits to which people can be coerced in that direction. Hezbollah's election manifestoes have dropped any reference to an Islamic republic in Lebanon (Husseini 2010).

Hezbollah's broad social roles across one-quarter of the Lebanese state have ensured that the EU rejects Israel's request to declare it a terrorist organiza-tion (Livni 2012). It has nonetheless long been designated as such by the United States, which named three of its leaders in a '22 Most Wanted Terrorists' list issued in 2001. Successive US administrations have regarded Hezbollah as an unreconstructed terrorist organization, high on the list of groupings to be targeted. Israel has continued to target the organization's leaders for assas-sination (an example was the killing of Imad Mugnieh in Syria in 2008), yet simultaneously has engaged in some pragmatic indirect negotiations with Hezbollah, via mediators (German brokers were used in 2004, for example) on issues such as prisoner releases. Hezbollah portrays itself as a resistance movement, countering Israeli expansionism. Although there may be private acceptance of the Jewish state as a de facto reality, Hezbollah rejects Israel as an entity, denouncing Jewish settlement on Islamic land. It also sees Israel as a war society in which the distinction between its armed forces and civilians cannot be absolute during conflict, although Hezbollah has usually taken care, at least prior to the 2006 conflict, to avoid counter-productive attacks upon Israeli civilians (Harik 2005). Hezbollah distinguishes between ordinary Jews (Judaism is recognized as a legitimate religion and its adherents deserv-ing of protection) and 'colonial' Zionists (Saad-Ghorayeb 2002). For its part, Israel views Hezbollah's social roles as a veneer for what is primarily a heavily armed Jihadist and anti-semitic organization, pointing out (correctly) that some of its leadership have engaged in Holocaust denial (Saad-Ghorayeb 2002).

Although calls for the de-confessionalization of Lebanon from some of Hezbollah's allies have been often targeted at Christian Maronites, the promotion of Islamic (sharia) law by Hezbollah represents 'a system of communal exclusion more virulent than that of institutionalised communitarianism because it escapes constitutional regulation' (Picard 1996: 163). Hezbollah's Islamism has been accompanied by radical local state-building, including water and electricity construction projects part-funded by Iran; provision of sporting facilities; schooling; and development of a range of media outlets. In effect, Hezbollah-controlled areas amount to an autonomous Islamic republic, a 'state within a non-state' (Deeb 2007: 68). 'Hezbollahland' of rural southern Lebanon and poorer parts of South Beirut co-exists with the remainder of the country, Islamification juxtaposed with growing secular tendencies in nominally Christian parts of the country.

Shifting Alliances and Blocs since Syrian Withdrawal

The outcry over the 2005 Hariri assassination led to huge street protests and reconfigured the political forces in the Lebanese peace process. Syrian military forces finally withdrew and pro-Syrian ministers were ousted from the government in 2006. The anti-Syrian March 14th (Cedar Revolution) Alliance, named after the date of the largest ever anti-Syrian demonstration (in 2005) and backed by the United States, has been particularly strong in Beirut, but predictably weak in the south of the country. It embraced a rainbow coalition of the Future Movement, Progressive Socialists, Lebanese Forces, Social Democrats, the Armenian Democratic Liberal Party, Jamaa-al-Islamiya, Democratic Left, the National Liberal Party and, waveringly, Druze, along with a large number of independent parliamentarians. The pro- and anti-Syrian forces cut across some of the vertical, sectarian-based cleavages, although the fracture mainly united Sunnis and Christians against Shi'ites.

The March 14th Alliance stressed the importance of the establishment of an independent and sovereign Lebanon, free from external interference. For critics, this was myopia, the Alliance only opposing selective interference, namely from Syria and Iran, whilst endorsing influence from the United States, France, Israel and moderate Arab neighbours (Abukhalil 2007). The weight of support for Hezbollah from its external allies exceeded that from Western forces for the March 14th Alliance, not least because of the volatility of that alliance. The US government offered substantial financial assistance to the Cedar Revolution government which emerged in the immediate post-Hariri phase, yet this did little to improve its effectiveness (Schenker 2009). US government backing for the March 14th Alliance was intended to curb Hezbollah's political advances,

The pro-Syrian (and largely anti-Western) March 8th Alliance (Shi'ites had demonstrated on this date in 2005, stressing their alienation from the political system) spanned the Free Patriotic Movement, Amal and Hezbollah, alongside smaller parties including the Lebanese Democratic Party, Marada, the Armenian Revolutionary Federation, the Syrian National Social Party, the Arab Socialist Baath Party and Solidarity. Marada and Solidarity are both essentially Maronite Christian organizations, pitted against fellow Maronites in the Lebanese Social Democratic Party and the National Liberal Party, emphasizing how the new alliances have straddled the confessional divide. Michel Aoun returned from exile to lead the Free Patriotic Movement but then undertook a U-turn, abandoning his one-time visceral hatred of all things Syrian by withdrawing from the March 14th Alliance and then concluding a memorandum of understanding with Hezbollah in 2006 and supporting rapprochement with Syria. Aoun's move effectively cost the March 14th Alliance a working majority and the initiative passed to its opponents (Najem 2012). A unity Cabinet was established, including two ministers from Hezbollah's political arm, Loyalty to the Resistance.

As Lebanon attempted to recover from the 2006 Hezbollah–Israel conflict, it was plunged into acute political crisis, with the National Dialogue Process instigated following Syrian withdrawal soon unravelling. Shi'a Cabinet ministers resigned, President Lahoud refused to recognize the legitimacy of the government, and a successor President could not be elected. There were assassinations of anti-Syrian MPs, strikes, delays in electing a new President, and outbreaks of inter-communal violence in 2008, including clashes between Sunni and Shi'ite forces in West Beirut. Hezbollah objected to attempts to disrupt its telecommunications network, which included surveillance equipment at Beirut Airport. The 2008 Doha Agreement restored a measure of political stability (temporarily), but effectively allowed Hezbollah a veto within a new government misleadingly labelled one of national unity (Najem 2012).

The aftermath of the 2009 elections saw Aoun and his allies form one-third of the government (and part of a successor government in 2011) amid considerable instability and continuing argument over responsibility for the 2005 Rafik Hariri killing. Hariri's son, Saad, who became Prime Minister in 2009, appeared to exonerate Syria, an approach which merely served to increase arguments that Hezbollah was culpable. Such claims were met by ferocious denials, with Hezbollah denying the legitimacy of the Hague-based tribunal of inquiry. A fairly chaotic system of alliances within the government was evident, comprising the Change and Reform bloc, dominated by the Free Patriotic Movement, the March 8th Alliance, straddling Maronite Christians, secular groups and mainly Shi'ite Muslims (although the Glory Movement within the Alliance is mainly Sunni) and a mixture of Independents and Progressive Socialists. It was opposed by the March 14th Alliance, dominated by the Future Movement which held nearly half (26) of the bloc's 60 parliamentary seats. The March 14th Alliance bonded Sunni Muslims, Druze and Christians in loose coalitional opposition to Hezbollah and Syrian influence. This involved some strange bedfellows, moderate anti-Syrian forces at one stage courting Salafist

Islamic militants in the 2005 parliamentary elections and even at one point turning a blind eye to the activities of Salafist-Jihadists, before the activities of armed Islamists began to spiral out of control (Gambill 2009).

The March 8th and March 14th alliances potentially represented a new order in Lebanon, but still based upon a confessional troika and political patronage perhaps no more capable of securing its peace and political processes. The demise of Lebanese Christians, politically and numerically, may have finally led to the diminution of the salience of the old Muslim–Christian faultline. Its replacement is the Sunni–Shi'ite divide, a 'raging conflict' which 'supersedes all others', one which has effectively obliged Christian political elites to decide whether they are on the side of Shi'ites or Sunnis, most, but not all, siding with the latter (Abukhalil 2007). Christians straddled the March 8th and March 14th alliances more than Sunnis. A new overarching axis of a Shi'te versus Sunni divide is evident within and beyond Lebanon, even if talk of a Shi'ite regional crescent is exaggerated (Blanford 2009). There remains considerable intra-communal jostling for supremacy. Whilst much Shi'ite support is offered to Hezbollah, Amal remains a significant force. Many Shi'ites prefer to support the regular Lebanese Army rather than back factionalism, evidenced in the sizeable numbers killed as part of the regular state forces when taking on the Sunni militants of Fatah-al-Islam in 2008 (Zisser 2009). The new sectarianism is not an improvement on the old. Rather, it rearranges the political pieces on the basis of which external countries are seen as broadly sympathetic to the interests of their sect, an approach that does not secure Lebanon's long-term viability as an independent nation. Modern political arrangements have not displaced the Shi'ite sense of injustice and relative disadvantage. They merely shift perceptions that Christian Maronites remain key beneficiaries.

Conclusion

Peace-building in Lebanon has been reasonably successful, in that widespread political violence since the Ta'if Agreement, whilst far from exceptional, has tended to be short-lived and containable. However, senior political figures have continued to be 'killed with impunity' in crimes the state appears incapable of adequately investigating (Knudsen 2010: 18) and a culture of political violence has not been exorcized, with the risk of a return to large-scale conflict still possible.

Lebanon has been re-established as a viable polity and there is no longer the risk of annexation (by Syria or Israel) that seemed conceivable during the 1970s and 1980s. However, the political process accompanying partial peace remains unsatisfactory and the conditions which created collapse and conflict from 1975 to 1989 have not been removed. The historical faultline between Christians and Muslims has to some extent been replaced by new fractures, between pro- and anti-Syrian forces and between Shi'ite and Sunni Muslims. Stable governance has remained elusive amid shifting alliances and weak party systems (no party has ever won more than 15 per cent of the parliamentary seats).

Yet the alternatives to the uneasy consociation currently in existence remain difficult to envisage. Partition of the country into Christian and Muslim entities would not work, given the presence of large minority populations. Crude dismemberment of the country would fail to take account of the cross-cutting cleavages and divisions within each bloc, notably Sunni versus Shi'ite and secular versus religious tensions, which have been of greater import than Lebanon's historical faultline in recent times. Cantonization would formalize divisions, but the geography of Lebanon's divisions, Beirut providing an obvious example, inhibits such a solution. Thus confessional consociation remains the only show at elite level in Lebanon, even though Ta'if desired the demise of confessionalism. The question begged is how does the process of de-confessionalizing Lebanon begin? It will require a major and very risky overhaul of political institutions and the electoral system which might further destabilize the country, and the clamour for reform amongst the ordinary populace, let alone political elites benefitting from the system, has not been deafening. Secession and the establishment of an independent Christian state would further destabilize the region and would be impossible to implement without 'ethno-religious cleansing'.

Lebanon has been beset by external interference. Eight countries had some involvement in the 1975–89 conflict. Syria's direct involvement remained the most enduring, the consociation of the Ta'if Accord part-regulated in its own interests, with influence consolidated by the 1991 Treaty of Brotherhood. Amid the severe challenges to the Syrian regime as the 'Arab Spring' extended its span, Syrian–Lebanon relations remained uncertain, but for a successful internal consociation, the role of external actors needed to be diminished. Lebanon's consociation-based peace process has only been a partial success in state-building due to external loyalties or interferences, and due to the manner in which allegiance to sect remains greater than that to state. Confessionalism and sectarianism remain as important as fidelity to the Lebanese state and communal autonomy is profound. The lack of central state direction is compounded by a predominantly liberal, free-market economy. Hezbollah's governance of the south of the country provides a state within a state. The absence of any prospect of a settlement of the Israeli–Palestinian conflict continues to have the capacity to destabilize Lebanon, southern border skirmishes between Israeli forces and Hezbollah being an endemic feature.

There has been a 'Lebanonization' of Hezbollah, which can no longer be seen simply as a surrogate of Iran or Syria. It would continue its operations, regardless of regime change in either one-time parent. Hezbollah's political functions have grown to equate in importance to its religious mission, and its military arm has been happy to assist regular Lebanese forces in dealing with Sunni Muslim militants. Nonetheless, it remains part of the broader pan-Islamic revolutionary-exporting movement, which facilitated the organization's development. Hezbollah's discourse oscillates between that of Jihadist rejection of Israel's incursion upon Muslim territory, when Shi'ites are being addressed, to nationalistic Lebanese, condemning Israel only in the sense of the threat to Lebanese national territory, when a multi-faith audience is the subject of appeal (Whittaker 2007). Without a resolution of the Israeli–Palestinian conflict and a healing of Israeli–Syrian relations, Hezbollah's military arm is unlikely to decommission any of its weapons, which, as recent conflicts with Israel indicated, have become more potent and exceed the capabilities of the Lebanese Army, which has instead concentrated in recent years on dealing with isolated Sunni Islamist groups.

CHAPTER SIX

Consociational Triumph: Northern Ireland's Peace Process

The Northern Ireland peace process is often viewed as a rare triumph of con-sociationalism. Since the 1998 Good Friday Agreement (GFA) (the term 'Belfast Agreement' tends to be used by unionists), there has been power-sharing between Protestant British unionists, committed to the retention of Northern Ireland's place in the UK and Catholic Irish nationalists, desirous of an ultimate switch in Northern Ireland's status to inclusion in a unitary independent Irish state. After an uncertain start, with power-sharing institutions collapsing by 2002, the power-sharing deal was revived with slight modification in the 2006 St Andrews Agreement. Since 2007, unionists, mainly represented by the Democratic Unionist Party (DUP) and nationalists, mainly represented by Sinn Féin, one-time associates of the Provisional IRA, have shared power pragmati-cally, if not always cordially, in a devolved Northern Ireland governing execu-tive within the UK. This chapter assesses how consociation came to replace conflict, and analyses the extent to which a deal based on the equal legitimacy of two rival political traditions can continue to accommodate differences. The chapter also assesses those aspects which have somewhat tainted the successes; mainly low-level spoiler violence and the persistence of sectarianism.

The Peace Deals: the 1998 Good Friday Agreement and the 2006 St Andrews Agreement

The GFA promised to end a phase of conflict which, between 1970 and 1997, had cost more than 3,500 lives. Of these killings, almost three-fifths were com-mitted by republican armed groups, mainly the IRA, fighting for British with-drawal from Northern Ireland and the establishment of a united, independent Ireland. Almost half of IRA killings were of civilians; the remainder were what the IRA labelled 'Crown forces': British Army and Ulster Defence Regiment soldiers, Royal Ulster Constabulary (RUC) police officers and prison officers. Loyalist paramilitaries killed nearly one-third of the total number of victims in their self-ascribed ultra role, supposedly protecting Northern Ireland's place in the UK. Although loyalists claimed to take the war to the IRA, the vast bulk of their killings were of Catholics unconnected to republican paramilitaries. British security forces were responsible for ten per cent of killings, a majority of these of civilians rather than paramilitaries.

Northern Ireland's peace deal followed IRA and loyalist ceasefires called in

1994 (fractured briefly by the IRA in 1996–7) and was achieved after multi-party – but never all-party (the DUP walked out when Sinn Féin entered) talks and intergovernmental negotiations. It enjoyed external brokerage, via the US Senator George Mitchell, who set time constraints on the political negotiations in order to ensure a deal was completed. The 1993 Downing Street Declaration outlined the principles upon which a deal would be based. The principles included co-determination: the people of the island of Ireland would determine their own future, but on a North and South basis (i.e. separately); there would be parity of esteem for the two traditions within Northern Ireland; and there would be an all-island dimension to political arrangements. The GFA provided the details for the principles, creating a cross-community power-sharing Executive and Assembly. Executive places were dependent upon the size of party representation in the Assembly using the d'Hondt formula, but with the key stipulation that the Executive had to be cross-community or it collapsed. The Irish government relinquished its constitutional claim to Northern Ireland, downgrading Irish unity to a mere aspiration. The 'trade-off' was that the British government amended the Government of Ireland Act to confirm that it would legislate for a united Ireland in the (most unlikely) event of there being a majority within Northern Ireland in favour (O'Donnell 2007).

Northern Ireland's prospects for successful consociation were written off during the 1970s, even though devolved power-sharing, with the other consociational pillars of mutual veto, proportionality in government and community autonomy, appeared as British government policy from the time of the Sunningdale Agreement in 1973. The power-sharing executive created under that deal lasted a mere five months. It required compromises too great for the unionist political elite immersed in majoritarian one-party government for the previous 50 years (Gillespie 1998) and made no attempt to incorporate the forces of republican paramilitarism, at that time bereft of a serious political outlet. Attempts to revive power-sharing, via the 1975 Constitutional Convention, or to roll devolution back to Northern Ireland, with the hope for cross-community compromise, were equally unsuccessful.

That the Good Friday Agreement worked owed as much to a changed context as it did to a fundamental reshaping of the 1973 Sunningdale deal. Republicans were weakened and unwilling to countenance an interminable prolonging of the 'armed struggle'. Unionists were keen for a return of a least of modicum of local power rather than endure further direct British rule from Westminster and feared Anglo-Irish lawmaking. The British acknowledged the need for political inclusion, even of paramilitaries, having failed to entirely quell the IRA. The Irish government was comfortable in ditching its constitutional claim to Northern Ireland, cognizant that the coercion of unionists into a united Ireland was neither politically possible nor desirable from its point of view. Several of these positions were indeed hinted at in the Downing Street Declaration, a statement of principles which foretold their detailed outworking in the political deal climaxing the process. That Declaration and the Good Friday Agreement which followed were also the culmination of much-improved relationships between the British and Irish governments. The former had developed a more nuanced approach to Northern Ireland, less colonial in tone and no longer merely security-oriented. The latter had divested itself of residual nationalistic impulses. Beyond these paradigm changes, O'Kane's (2007: 191) analysis of increasingly cooperative intergovernmentalism highlights 'institutional structures, personal relationships and accumulated intellectual capital' as the crucial elements in the development of a strong axis.

Given the obvious similarities between the 1973 and 1998 deals, the Deputy Leader of the nationalist Social Democratic and Labour Party (SDLP), Seamus Mallon, uttered his famous comment that the Good Friday Agreement was merely 'Sunningdale for slow learners' (cited in Tonge 2000: 39). Each deal required unionists and nationalists to share power in an executive, with proportionality in government, minority vetoes and, to a lesser extent communal autonomy, all present. A very modest set of all-island arrangements was attached and overarching Anglo-Irish cooperation continued. Thus Mallon was not wrong, even if his aside ignored the greater nuance of the 1998 version of consociation. The most obvious differences between the 1973 deal, which Dixon (2008) argues was part of a 'peace process', even though there was neither peace, nor a process involving the paramilitary actors, were those of inclusivity and conflict-ending measures. Sinn Féin, as the political alter ego of the IRA, was included in the dialogue and offered a place in a newly-formed government of Northern Ireland, whilst there were contentious releases of all paramilitary prisoners whose groups remained on ceasefire, along with changes to policing following the establishment of the Patten Commission.

The 1998 deal also enjoyed a popular legitimacy not afforded its 1973 predecessor. Staging a referendum on the GFA was a risky enterprise, but necessary to secure its legitimacy. The lack of support for the Sunningdale Agreement had been starkly illustrated after a mere two months of the deal's operation, when the unionist community overwhelmingly elected anti-Sunningdale MPs. Unionist unease in 1998 was concentrated particularly upon the impending 'terrorists in government', the release of paramilitary prisoners and the changes to 'their' police force, the RUC. Only 57 per cent of Protestants voted in favour of the GFA, whereas Catholics, content with their first-ever stake in the state offered by the deal, voted overwhelmingly in support (Hayes and McAllister 2001) to produce an overall yes vote of 71 per cent, on an 81 per cent turnout. Combined with huge (94 per cent) support in the Irish Republic in its simultaneous referendum to remove the constitutional claim to Northern Ireland (albeit on a low turnout of only half of the Irish Republic's electors), the 1998 deal enjoyed a mandate. Nonetheless, unionist unease was not assuaged for several years, as the painful medicine of prisoner releases and policing changes were swallowed. The DUP prospered in opposition to changes, until becoming the largest party within unionism and negotiating a slightly modified deal, which forced Sinn Féin to become fully constitutional.

Implementation of the Good Friday Agreement proved protracted. Paramilitary prisoner releases, changes to policing and the slow pace of IRA decommissioning of weapons in the immediate post-Agreement years ensured that the Democratic Unionist Party's (DUP) opposition to the deal gathered majority support amongst unionists. In November 1999, the Ulster Unionist Party (UUP) agreed to enter government with Sinn Féin in advance of IRA decommissioning, the requirement for which had been fudged in the Agreement. Despite claims from unionists to the contrary, there was no requirement for the IRA to decommission any weapons, nor was Sinn Féin's participation in government conditional upon IRA disarmament. As the Head of the International Commission on Disarmament, General John de Chastelain (2004: 161), acknowledged: 'Republicans and nationalists pointed out that the agreement's statement on decommissioning talked in terms of it taking place in the "context of the implementation of the overall settlement"', which for them meant the establishment of a viable devolved power-sharing executive'. Whilst two acts of IRA decommissioning did take place in the early years of devolution, in 2001 and 2002 respectively, this was not enough to assuage unionists. UUP support for the Good Friday Agreement was predicated upon a 'no guns, no government' policy, and the party was bleeding support to the DUP, which promised a better deal. Limited continuing IRA violence, an alleged spying ring and the organization's alleged involvement in the £26.5m Northern Bank robbery in 2004 all contributed to the mothballing of the Northern Ireland Assembly from September 2002 until 2007.

Re-implementation of the Agreement followed a renegotiated deal at St Andrews in Scotland in 2006. Crucially, the Provisional IRA finally called off its campaign in 2005, moving into an entirely political mode and decommissioning its weapons. At St Andrews, Sinn Féin's leadership pledged to support the Police Service of Northern Ireland, ratified at a special party conference in January 2007, ending the untenable position of a party of government refusing to endorse the state's police force. Alongside decommissioning and prisoner releases, policing had been amongst the biggest controversies associated with the GFA. Following the 1999 Patten Commission report (Independent Commission on Policing 1999), the RUC, 88 per cent Protestant (and, in republican belief, 100 per cent unionist in outlook), was replaced by the Police Service of Northern Ireland (PSNI), which for a decade recruited on a 50:50 Catholic and non-Catholic basis. Policing changes were aimed at altering the culture, ethos and composition of the police, seen by Catholic Nationalists as intrinsically Protestant and Unionist. As McGarry (2004: 388–9) commented, the Patten Report 'represented an imaginative compromise between those Unionists who, remarkably, maintained that the existing RUC already met the terms of reference the [Good Friday] Agreement and those nationalists, especially republicans, who maintained that the RUC's record mandated its immediate disbanding'. The 50:50 recruitment quota policy was designed to rectify the stark imbalance in composition and address the antipathy towards the police service amongst nationalists, which, combined with the threat from the IRA, had deterred Catholics from joining. The quota policy succeeded in raising the percentage of Catholics in the force to 30 per cent by 2011 (Police Service of Northern Ireland 2012a) compared to only 8 per cent at the time of the Patten Report. However, the sectarian basis of selection was opposed by many unionists and by the avowedly non-sectarian Alliance Party and was ended in 2011.

The PSNI remained heavily armed, owning over 5,000 firearms, with a further 2,000 'loaned' by the Department of Justice, the new ministry created when powers over policing were finally devolved in 2010. Responsibilities for the overseeing of intelligence – which remained a significant aspect of policing and security – were not transferred. MI5 was not to suddenly become accountable to local politicians. Moreover, despite the decommissioning processes, over 146,000 firearms remained legally held (by almost 60,000 members of the public) in addition to those retained by the police.

With the DUP and Sinn Féin now the dominant parties, elections were agreed to further strengthen their respective communal mandates and the power-sharing Executive was restored in May 2007, headed by the DUP's Reverend Ian Paisley and Sinn Féin's Martin McGuinness. The DUP could (accurately) claim that they had shifted Sinn Féin towards true establishment of constitutional *bona fides*. The earlier hard yards – there were, after all, very few returns of prisoners to jail and the RUC did not reappear as the local police force – had been undertaken by the UUP and the constitutional nationalists of the Social Democratic and Labour Party (SDLP), to the ultimate detriment of both parties. The DUP, which had hitherto rotated its ministers on the North-South Ministerial Council in an attempt to undermine the all-Ireland aspects of the deal, now took a more cooperative approach. By 2012, the DUP was even inviting ministers from the Irish government to attend its party conference.

That a consociation was built across such a chasm between the two traditions remains remarkable. It was beset by difficulties as the centrifugal forces of the DUP and Sinn Féin emerged as the dominant electoral forces of their respective ethnic blocs, acting as tribunes for their communities (Mitchell et al. 2009). These newly hegemonic forces within unionism and nationalism were the dominant axis of the revised Agreement when Paisley, hitherto regarded as a rejectionist Protestant fundamentalist, astonished a large section of the population (and angered some members of his Free Presbyterian Church) in concluding a deal with Sinn Féin's leaders. The DUP had not fully prepared its base for the deal and one-third of its supporters were reportedly against the St Andrews Agreement, with less than half (42 per cent) in favour (Dixon and O'Kane 2011: 108). A section of the Protestant electorate briefly flirted with the rejectionist hardline Traditional Unionist Voice party, opposed to power-sharing with Irish republicans, but this proved a temporary departure. Most unionist electors and politicians realised there was no longer much room for manoeuvre. By 2006, the Secretary of State for Northern Ireland, Peter Hain, had wearied of the phantom Assembly, which had not sat since 2002 and yet whose members continued to be paid. Whilst no obvious Plan B existed, Hain had become serious in threatening a permanent abolition of the Assembly, removing livelihoods for some of its members and introducing a form of direct rule which would surely increase the extent of influence for the Irish government (Hain 2012).

The Dynamics of the Peace Process

Much of the dynamic for peace came from those who had inflicted the highest number of casualties during the conflict, republican paramilitaries. From its foundation in 1970 (although it claimed to be the continuation of the IRA dating back to the early twentieth century), the Provisional IRA had insisted that it would not cease its armed campaign until in receipt of a declaration of British intent to withdraw from Northern Ireland. Retreat from that position was the single most important feature of the peace process. In 1994, the Provisional IRA called a ceasefire without any accompanying indication of British withdrawal from Northern Ireland. Loyalist paramilitaries reciprocated, calling their own ceasefire six weeks later. The 1994–5 IRA ceasefire was a fragile entity. During the first part of the 1990s, the IRA displayed sufficient strength, notably via huge bombs in London and Belfast, to indicate that any settlement without their political associates in Sinn Féin would be pointless. As Patterson (1997: 285) explains, even the most politically oriented section of the republican movement, based around the Sinn Féin President Gerry Adams, had 'still seen a use for a refined and more carefully directed violence as a way of influencing debates on Irish policy in Whitehall'.

The republican ceasefire was thus predicated upon the assumption of a smooth entry for Sinn Féin into negotiations with the British government and other political parties. When this did not arrive, amid wrangling over decommissioning and demands for a period of quarantine, the IRA called off its ceasefire with a huge bombing at Canary Wharf in London, followed a few months later by the organization's biggest bombing ever, flattening swathes of Manchester city centre. The IRA was incapable of achieving a united Ireland, but it did appear to have a veto on negotiations. The arrival of a Labour government under Tony Blair in May 1997 changed the dynamic. Labour enjoyed a huge majority and was not hidebound by parliamentary arithmetic reliant upon unionist votes. This led to a renewal of the IRA's ceasefire, amid a promise to include Sinn Féin in negotiations. Sinn Féin was a signatory to the Mitchell Principles of non-violence, repudiating the use of force and agreeing to accept the outcome of negotiations.

The reasons for the changing nature of republican paramilitarism which facilitated much of the peace process are contested. The ideological basis of republicanism which inspired its supposed adherents to take up arms has been challenged as threadbare, its basis requiring 'categorical delegitimization' and its outcome an 'abject failure' (Alonso 2003: 194). However, outcomes are not always predictable at outsets. McIntyre's (1995, 2001, 2008) own 'insider' analysis, as a former IRA member and from a very different ideological perspective from that held by Alonso, also suggests a lack of ideological sustenance underpinning the Provisional IRA's campaign, republicans instead being forced continually to adapt to British state strategies. On this reading, republicanism was shallower and more situational than ideational, developing primarily in response to local oppression from the British Army and police, rather than amounting to a deeper belief in undiluted Irish territorial sovereignty. Amelioration of the worst aspects of oppression has thus diluted the limited republicanism which emerged at the beginning of the 1970s, which had only tenuous links to the Irish rebellion against British rule of the early twentieth century. This supposed shallowness made easier the political contortions of the republican leadership during the peace process, amid the steering of non-negotiable republican principles on sovereignty and territory into an indeterminate identity politics in which the recognition and promotion of Irishness appears sufficient to satisfy all bar the most irreconcilable.

However, the sceptical accounts underplay the durability of militant republicanism, the Provisional IRA forcing the British Army to conduct the longest campaign, Operation Banner, in its history. Moreover, republicans, of the Sinn Féin and Provisional IRA variety, continued to protest fidelity to the concept of the indivisible Irish Republic for which they fought or agitated. The constructive ambiguities (Dixon 2008) which accompanied the peace process for years allowed the Sinn Féin leadership to impart reassuring messages to the grassroots before each compromise. Others have claimed that Sinn Féin's transformation has not been a process of dilution, but has been enacted by 'a leadership that remains unswerving in its dedication to its principal ideological objective' (Frampton 2009: 192).

The inability of the IRA to win its 'war' also contributed greatly to the transformation of republican methodologies (see, e.g., English 2004). It was clear from the 1970s that the IRA could not win a united Ireland by military means and in the 2000s it had been unclear whether this objective could be won by political methods either. Republican tactics have thus shifted regularly, belying the orthodoxy that the peace process was simply a product of a stalemate (Tonge et al. 2011). Although still popular in explaining peace processes, explanations of the Northern Ireland peace process which rely on ideas of stalemate that tend to be grounded in military considerations of the conflict have been contested (Shirlow et al. 2010). Republican tactics have always shifted and the republican military campaign had also struggled at previous times, evidenced in the reduction in violence under the British government's criminalization strategy of the mid-1970s (treating the IRA like common criminals and handing out huge prison sentences). However, fortunes had ebbed and flowed and stalemate theories do not satisfactorily explain why the gestation of the peace process did not occur until much later.

Loyalist paramilitarism also contributed to the IRA's realization that it could not win its war. Loyalists in the Ulster Volunteer Force (UVF) and Ulster Freedom Fighters (UFF) (the latter the killing wing of the Ulster Defence Association, which, remarkably, remained legal until the 1990s) had played a significant role in the conflict. The UVF's 1966 killings of two innocent Catholics were a common tactic repeated throughout the main phase of the conflict. Via a considerable degree of collusion with elements of the British security forces, most notably the Force Research Unit within the British Army, Loyalist paramilitaries had upped their campaign from the mid-1980s. Although Catholics unconnected to the IRA, or even Sinn Féin, remained the majority of their victims, there was greater targeting of republicans. Amid an upsurge of violence, Loyalists killed more than the IRA in the first three years of the 1990s. The extent of collusion was documented in three reports by the Commissioner of the Metropolitan Police (Stevens Reports, 1990, 1994, 2003) which depicted the manner in which parts of the British security forces, via the running of agents within the Loyalist paramilitary groups, acted beyond the law and beyond any form of accountability or scrutiny. The de Silva Report (2012) on the killing of Pat Finucane, a Catholic solicitor, asserted that 85 per cent of the UDA's intelligence was gleaned from collusion with the state's security forces. The IRA responded to the upsurge in Loyalist violence by attempting to kill the UVF and UFF leadership in the Shankill Road bombing in 1993, but the operation was a disaster; the only victims were eight civilians, a UDA member and one of the two bombers.

Beyond endogenous explanations of change, international influences also weighed upon republicans. The African National Congress (ANC) encouraged Sinn Féin's leaders in the arts of negotiation and compromise (skills later transferred by Sinn Féin to Basque nationalist political leaders). ANC support also gave political cover to Sinn Féin, whose leaders were doing far more compromising on traditional goals than the ANC would ever have contemplated in respect of their own historical objectives (Guelke 2001; Tonge 2005). The republican desire to leave the political wilderness was also assisted by American intervention. Amid a more propitious climate, the US President Bill Clinton was more proactive than his predecessors on Northern Ireland, sending Senator George Mitchell to broker the Good Friday Agreement negotiations and acting as an honest broker on areas of dispute. The other key international agent was the EU, whose peace programmes have contributed almost £1,500 million worth of aid since 1995 via a vast range of cross-community projects. With a further £1,000 million received from other agencies (80 per cent of peace funding for Northern Ireland comes from outside the region),

Nolan (2012: 172) notes that 'nowhere in the world has enjoyed such largesse in relation to population size'.

The Impact of Electoralism upon Republicans

The explanation of the shift from militarism to politics amongst mainstream republicans is grounded in electoral logic. Downsian logic indicates the need for any political party to chase the median voter within its ethnic bloc (Downs 1957). This position was articulated altruistically by John Hume, the leader of Sinn Féin's main political rival, the SDLP, in the formative years of the peace process. Hume's pan-nationalism, abetted also by the Irish government eventually cost his party dear, as Sinn Féin moderated its stance and transformed its version of republicanism (Arthur 2002; O'Donnell 2007). Aware from an early stage of the conflict that the IRA could not win (but could not easily be defeated), Sinn Féin's leaders, notably its President from 1983 Gerry Adams, set about the task of alignment with that median voter (Murray and Tonge 2005; Tonge 2006).

The Provisional IRA formally announced the end of its armed campaign in 2005 and completed the decommissioning of weapons later that year. Whilst their exit from the stage was accompanied by Sinn Féin's insistence that a democratic route now existed to a united Ireland, the ending of partition could only be achieved with the consent of a majority in Northern Ireland, a stipulation dismissed throughout the conflict by the IRA as a 'unionist veto'. An overall majority on the island appeared to support Irish unity as an aspiration, but it was clear from the 1998 Good Friday Agreement referendum that the vast bulk of citizens did not want the *enforcement* of territorial unification.

Sinn Féin hoped for a rise in the Catholic population, an increase which was forthcoming. As a percentage of the population, Catholics rose from 35 per cent in the 1960s to 45 per cent by the 2011 census, the latter figure only 3 per cent below that recorded for the Protestant population, the first time the Protestant percentage had dropped below 50 per cent. In the first four elections following the Good Friday Agreement, the Nationalist bloc vote share rose modestly, from 36.9 to 41.4 per cent. Offsetting the growth in the Catholic population, however, was evidence that Catholic attachment to the dream of a united Ireland was waning. By 2010 it was reported that only one-third of northern Catholics now preferred this as their constitutional option (Northern Ireland Life and Times Survey 2010a) with 13 per cent more claiming to favour devolved government within the UK. The Life and Times Surveys have a tendency to under-report republican sentiment, but it should be noted that Hayes and McAllister's (2013) examination of longitudinal data suggests few Catholics thought a united Ireland was workable even during the 1970s. By 2012, the First Minister of Northern Ireland confidently claimed that a 'majority of Catholics now support the Union' [of Great Britain and Northern Ireland] (Robinson 2012).

Sinn Féin's original peace process strategy, to assist the British government to become persuaders for Irish unity, failed to yield anything tangible, whilst the party's outreach to unionists, whilst genuine, will not shift constitutional attitudes. The party's support for a border poll thus appeared surprising given that it seemed most unlikely that one conducted only in Northern Ireland would yield a majority in favour of dismembering partition. Forty per cent of Northern Ireland's population designated themselves as British only in the 2011 census, compared to 25 per cent self-identifying as Irish only and 21 per cent as Northern Irish only. An all-Ireland poll, not on the table, might be rather different. Whilst it is often claimed (with some truth in terms of the acceptability of the prospect if it caused trouble – which it would) that the 'South does not want the North', sentiment remains in favour of a united Ireland. An IPSOS-MRBI survey in 2012 indicated that 69 per cent of the population of the Irish Republic favours a united Ireland (*Irish Times* 2012) even if it meant increased taxes, with 20 per cent opposed. Such an option was, of course, not laid before the electors in the 1998 Good Friday Agreement referendum (the voters might, after all, have said yes, a risk too great for the British and Irish governments) and contentment or acquiescence with that deal is juxtaposed with lingering nationalism and perceptions that the Irish nation is a 32-county, all-island entity. These nationalist sympathies offer succour to Sinn Féin in their avowed pursuit of Irish unity; there is no particular incentive to abandon the ideal given that it chimes with the ultimate aspirations of many Irish voters, North and South.

However, the desire for a united Ireland is tempered by ready acceptance to participate in the northern state rather than reject its institutions. In 1998, even a majority of Sinn Féin supporters backed devolved power-sharing in a Northern Ireland Executive and by 2011, Sinn Féin's supporters were the most satisfied (more than any other set of party supporters) with the performance of a Northern Ireland government they would have once seen as illegitimate in a state they would have once refused to recognize (Evans and Tonge 2013a). It was claimed in a 2012 survey of Northern Irish Catholic opinion (*Belfast Telegraph* 2012a) that a majority would no longer vote for a united Ireland, now or in 20 years, in the border poll which could be called under the terms of the GFA. Much debate remains over whether the pursuit of votes was a mere poor substitute for republicans for the inability of the IRA to achieve republican goals.

Fighting for the IRA's Title Deeds: the Emergence and Development of Spoiler Groups

There has been an imperfect peace in Northern Ireland. There was an average of 262 shooting and bombing incidents per year in the period 1998–2011 (Police Service of Northern Ireland 2012b). This compared favourably to the annual average of 527 shooting and bombing incidents in the eight years prior to the GFA, but indicated a residual armed threat. The severity of shooting and bombing incidents diminished markedly in the post-1998 period (and the 1990s also saw huge IRA bombings in England, not shown in the figures). Deaths attributable to the security situation dropped markedly, from an average of 56 per year in the 1990–7 period to 10 per year thereafter (Police Service of Northern Ireland 2012b). Most of the shootings and bombings from 2006 onwards (660 from 2006 to 2011) could be attributed to dissident republican groups, following the exit of the Provisional IRA in 2005. The persistence of such activity, albeit mostly minor, indicated the tenacity of commitment to 'armed struggle' amongst a small group of irreconcilables, with the British government's official definition of the level of threat defined as 'severe' in this ostensibly post-conflict period.

Much of the existing literature on spoiler groups (e.g., Stedman 1997, 2003; Darby 2001; Newman and Richmond 2006) tends to analyse them as new groups dedicated to the reviving of the armed conflict supposedly contained or resolved by the peace deal. In the Northern Irish case, the spoiler groups, to different degrees, were anxious to emphasize their historical antecedents rather than their novelty. Thus the Continuity IRA (CIRA); the Real IRA (RIRA) and Óglaigh na hÉireann all laid claim to the title deeds of the historical brand name of the Irish Republican Army. The emergence of two of those three republican groups, CIRA and RIRA, preceded the Good Friday Agreement, in 1996 (although CIRA nominally existed from 1986) and 1997 respectively, as the direction of travel towards moderation, or as ultras believed, a 'sell-out', by the 'mainstream' republicans of Sinn Féin and the PIRA gradually became apparent. In 2012, several armed groups, with the exception of the Continuity IRA, merged to form a single unit under the IRA label. The (very small) political associates of these armed groups tend to divide over arcane historical issues. Republican Sinn Féin, linked to the Continuity IRA, still refuses to recognize the Irish Parliament, let alone the Northern Ireland Assembly, seeking refuge in a historical 'mandate' arising from Sinn Féin's victory in the last all-Ireland elections in 1918 (Whiting 2012). The 32 County Sovereignty Movement, linked to the Real IRA, is less interested in historical republican 'purity' and adopts a militarist 'Brits Out' stance.

There is a demographic tendency towards young(ish) males amongst membership of the dissident armed groups, although the average age of those convicted – 35 – suggests membership is not confined to the very young (Horgan and Gill 2011). Membership is also a consequence of regionalism, local contexts and family tradition (Morrison 2011) and is amorphous, with groups prone to splintering. The 'mandate' claimed by dissidents is that of the right to resist British 'occupation'. Clearly a contemporary electoral mandate eludes them and they will not be incorporated into processes of electoralism and compromise (Tonge 2004, 2011, 2012; Evans and Tonge 2012). Support for dissidents would be useful to the groups only in sustaining 'resistance' and such groups at present appear impervious to incorporation within a peace process, given the absolutism of their demands, in common with Stedman's (1997) total spoilers category.

An appeal on military terms to republican groups, asking what they can possibly achieve given that the Provisional IRA's much larger campaign did not succeed, may have greater resonance than debates and counter-narratives over mandates. Majority support for violence against British rule in Ireland has never been clearly evident, but has subsequently been legitimized and celebrated, by all the main parties in the Irish Republic, for its contribution to the formation of the Irish state in the early twentieth century. Sinn Féin lauds the 1970–97 violence as necessary for what it achieved for northern nationalists. Thus dissidents highlight the supposed chutzpah of constitutional republicans for lauding the 'good old' IRA, equally, if not more violent, in their day. Dissident republican strategies and tactics have no chance of yielding the end goal of a united Ireland, but such groups appear to exist to prevent Northern Ireland fully normalizing, with the maintenance of 'armed resistance' also an end in itself. Republican armed groups may be militarist in outlook and unsophisticated in tactics, but their capacity to endure has perhaps been demonstrated, Patterson (2011: 89) concluding that their activities are 'not a passing hiccup in the peace process. It will be more like the nagging but only occasionally chronic IRA challenge that faced both states [Northern Ireland and the Irish Republic] between 1923 and the 1950s'. Indeed the then Head of MI5, Jonathan Evans, acknowledged in 2010:

> Our working assumption was that the residual threat from terrorism was low and likely to decline further as time went on and as the new constitutional arrangements there [in Northern Ireland] took root. Sadly that has not proved to be the case. On the contrary we have seen a persistent rise in terrorist activity and ambition in Northern Ireland over the last three years. Perhaps we were giving insufficient weight to the pattern of history over the last hundred years which shows that whenever the main body of Irish republicanism has reached a political accommodation and rejoined constitutional politics, a hardline rejectionist group would fragment off and continue with the so-called 'armed struggle'. (Evans 2010)

In stark contrast to the level of much of the dissident campaign, the RIRA's killing of 29 civilians in the Omagh bombing in August 1998 was the worst atrocity of the entire conflict. Following a strong backlash, the RIRA declared a ceasefire, but revived sufficiently to launch a modest bombing campaign in England by 2000. Although their campaign remained mostly low level, by 2010, nearly 200 dissidents had been convicted for their activities, with the RIRA containing the most members (Horgan and Gill 2011) and being the most active group in terms of shootings and bombings, providing half of those successfully prosecuted (Horgan and Morrison 2011; Horgan 2013). Dissident violence revived after 2007, a new wave of dissidence encouraged by the departure of the Provisionals, the completion of their decommissioning of weapons in 2005 and the seismic decision of Sinn Féin to support the Police Service of Northern Ireland in January 2007. Republicans would now be asked by the Sinn Féin leadership to 'inform' on remaining armed republicans, some of whom might be former comrades. For many republicans, the 2007 decision was of greater significance than the entry to a Northern Ireland Assembly in 1998. Now Sinn Féin and militant republicans were clearly at odds; ambiguity had run its course.

An upsurge in republican dissident violence was evident, leading to the killings of two British Army soldiers at Massareene Barracks and a Police Service of Northern Ireland officer in Lurgan, the first security force personnel to be killed by the spoiler groups. Sinn Féin called the British Army killings wrong and counter-productive, but Republican ultras were denounced in much more strident terms by the party's Martin McGuinness, who labelled the perpetrators at 'traitors to Ireland'. In 2011, the dissidents killed a police officer with an under-car bomb and in 2012 shot dead a prison officer. One hundred dissident republicans were in prison in 2012, 60 per cent of whom were incarcerated in the Irish Republic.

Republican spoiler groups remain fixated with the contribution of an armed campaign as a contribution to the removal of Britain's sovereign claim. Although few think they can in isolation somehow force victory and their violence remains paltry compared to the Provisional IRA's campaign, the dissidents believe that their actions can emphasize that Northern Ireland remains contested territory. Their level of electoral backing remains minimal and no dissident candidate has been elected in Northern Ireland. Sympathy, distinct from outright support, may also be in short supply, although the solitary extensive survey test indicated that 14 per cent of those from a nationalist community background (and 30 per cent of nationalist self-identifiers) had some understanding for the reasons for their actions (if not the actions themselves), indicating low but not entirely negligible regard (Evans and Tonge 2012). Moreover, despite the lack of backing for dissidents, a majority of Protestants regard them as a 'major threat' and the republican armed bogeyman remains in the unionist psyche (Tonge 2011). In 2012, only 25 per cent of the population said they would 'encourage a close relative to join the PSNI' (*Belfast Telegraph* 2012b). Although many refused to answer the question, there was greater reluctance amongst Catholics. Meanwhile vigilante 'republicanism' continued to exist in some working-class nationalist areas, propagated by organizations such as Republican Action Against Drugs, rejecting the PSNI's legitimacy.

Continuing Divisions and Sectarian Problems

Northern Ireland offers an example of a highly successful peace process. Naysayers can continue to highlight flaws, most notably the stark level of continuing segmental autonomy and, as Wilson (2009: 235) points out, 'high fences do not make good, but rather mistrustful neighbours'. There is a basic incoherence over how supposedly essentialist identities are to be dissipated amid political structures designed to legitimize and reify communal worth.

The question is left hanging as to when, if ever, Northern Ireland's political system can switch from enforced mandatory coalition between unionists and nationalists to one based upon voluntarism and/or a more common form of government and opposition. The hope of consociationalists is that, as ethnic communities feel more secure, their ethnic solidarity will diminish and dilute and the need to stress oppositional identities will dissipate. Thus far this process has yet to grip. As one example, a decision by Belfast City Council in 2012 to remove the Union flag as a permanent feature atop the city hall, instead flying it only on designated days, was followed by a period of Loyalist protests and rioting.

Wilson (2009) also laments the failure to develop interculturalism rather than the dual nationalism and bi-culturalism enshrined in the GFA. Allegiance to Northern Ireland and state-building are not the priorities of the deal, which instead dwells upon the parity of two national traditions within the same space and inside its political institutions. McGrattan's (2010) critique of the peace process suggests that 'institutional engineering may be less a panacea than a placebo'. He laments the inability of Northern Ireland to escape its past by enshrining communal spheres in its democratic apparatus, allowing ethno-national entrepreneurs to perpetuate their antagonisms and justify their past activities.

Yet interculturalists and other anti-consociationalists tend to ignore three realities: firstly, that Northern Ireland is a divided bi-national identity, in which sincerely held national identities cannot be wished away. Secondly, no peace process globally is reliant upon complete ideological U-turn and entire repudiation of the past. Thirdly, the pessimists ignore the greatly improved security situation in Northern Ireland. On such key indicators as the level of violence (killings significantly down from the figures in the final three decades of the twentieth century) or cross-community membership of the police (now one-third Catholic, more than three times the figure at the time of the Agreement), there has been marked improvement (McGarry and O'Leary 2009). Moreover, pessimists are at odds with the views of the public. By 2010, nearly two-thirds believed that relations between Protestants and Catholic had improved over the previous five years, with only 3 per cent believing that they had deteriorated and only 5 per cent believing that they would worsen over the next five years (Nolan 2012: 136–7).

An apparent growth in Catholic acceptance of (or acquiescence towards) Northern Ireland's place in the UK suggests that the linkages between national identity and constitutional preference are not automatic and that it is becoming easier to harness different national identities within what was once a brutally contested political entity. The supposed triumph of the extremes is nothing of the sort, as the ertswhile hardliners have become the new moderates and even those unwilling to fully accept this acknowledge that apathy rather than violence is more evident in the new Northern Ireland, amid declining levels of voter turnout (Bew et al. 2009).

Part of the problem in tackling Northern Ireland's divisions is attributable to the lack of overwhelming consensus over their cause, as improved inter-communal relations are dependent upon correct diagnosis of the problem. Whilst religious difference was not the root cause of the Northern Ireland problem, it contributed much to the partition of Ireland and infused an ethno-national quarrel with increased communal hostility, amid the alignment of religion with national identity. The extent to which religion infused the conflict remains contested between those who strongly deny its primacy (e.g., McGarry and O'Leary 1995) and a smaller number who emphasize its contribution (e.g., Bruce 1986, 1992). Few of the paramilitaries practised their religion, but they drew upon religious inspirations. The UVF's 'For God and Ulster' slogan emphasized the fusion of religion with territorial defence. The Provisional IRA drew the bulk of its members and support from Catholics and used quasi-religious symbols of suffering at times such as the hunger strikes, but was often critical of the Catholic hierarchy. Stark communalism preceded – and contributed greatly to – the 1970–97 phase of conflict. The difficulty for the Northern Ireland peace process is working out how to shift agreements based upon the recognition of communal difference to a pro-gramme of dismantling that difference. This conundrum is perhaps solved by 'ordinary' people following the examples of their political leaders. Hayes and McAllister's (2013) detailed review of the evidence concluded that com-munity relations had improved significantly in the decade following the GFA, but with much work remaining to achieve integration. Implementation of a programme to ensure a shared future also has to tackle the intellectual ques-tion posed by republicans; why are the differences between the two traditions on the island so small that they can be eradicated amid reintegration, yet so great that a border is necessary to divide the two peoples?

A number of issues remain unresolved in the Northern Ireland peace pro-cess, but its consociation can be judged a remarkable success when the chasm it bridges is taken into account. The militant antecedents of Sinn Féin and the DUP in themselves make power-sharing extraordinary, a rapprochement mirrored at grassroots level in relations between republican and loyalist former prisoners, which are often cordial or at least pragmatic, with common engagement in community transformation projects. The sustainability of political arrangements is remarkable, however, when one considers the con-tinuing depth of electoral polarity and sense of difference. The percentages of Catholics identifying as British and Protestants identifying as Irish are in single figures, 8 and 4 per cent respectively, according to the Northern Ireland Life and Times Survey (2010b). Only 1 per cent of Catholics describe them-selves as Unionist, whilst 0 per cent of Protestants are prepared to identify as nationalist. In the first four Northern Ireland Assembly elections after the Good Friday Agreement, the percentage of Protestants prepared to offer even a lower preference vote to Sinn Féin under the PR-STV (proportional representa-tion through the single transferable vote) system remained below 1 per cent, whilst Catholic transfers to the DUP remained similarly low. Identifications as Irish (which is particularly extensive and intensive) Nationalist and Catholic are core pillars of Sinn Féin voter preference (Evans and Tonge 2013b) and the rival communal identity paradigm of Northern Ireland politics remains paramount. Those looking for evidence of de-pillarization can take succour only in the diminishing percentages of the electorate identifying themselves as either unionist or nationalist – 45 per cent according to the Northern Ireland Life and Times Survey (2010a), a figure higher than the percentage of unionist or nationalist identifiers at 34 and 20 per cent, respectively – and the diminishing percentage of the electorate prepared to endorse the prevailing unionist-nationalist framework by voting in elections. Correlations between religion and bloc party support are as strong as ever in terms of votes cast, but turnout is falling in all types of elections (Tonge and Evans 2010). Abstention is far greater – even the majority choice – of those eschewing religious and ideological labels.

There is some very limited evidence of thawing. There was a modest growth, from 23 per cent in 1998, to 28 per cent in 2010 in the percentage of the electorate adopting the hybrid 'Northern Irish' identity rather than the polar British or Irish affiliations, with the percentage adopting Northern Irishness fairly similar amongst Catholics and Protestants and appearing to be a particularly popular choice amongst young people (Northern Ireland Life and Times Survey 1998, 2010b). Catholics can use the label 'Northern Irish' to emphasize the Irish dimension; Protestants to emphasize the legitimacy of Northern Ireland as an entity. The percentage of Protestants identifying as unionist fell by 8 per cent from 1998 to 2010; the percentage of Catholics identifying as nationalist declined by 10 per cent. Those adopting unionist or nationalist labels now form only a bare majority of the Northern Ireland populace, and only a minority of 18–24-year-olds adopt such labels. Ethnic agnostics may be rising in number, but judging by the acutely communal voting patterns and via examination of abstention patterns, it is the true believers who enter Northern Ireland's polling stations.

These continuing electoral and ideological divisions are often pejoratively labelled sectarian. Having a particular view on which nation should govern the state and reflecting that view in political choice is not sectarian. That said, this is plenty of genuine evidence of sectarianism still present. From 2006 to 2011, the Police Service of Northern Ireland recorded 6,434 sectarian crimes (Police Service of Northern Ireland 2012b). Sectarianism takes many forms, but is most graphically evident in the territorial segregation of Protestants and Catholics throughout working-class Belfast and Derry-Londonderry. Across Northern Ireland, over 90 per cent of public housing is segregated. The number of 'peace walls' in Belfast, physically dividing communities, increased from 20 in the 1970s to 99 by 2012 (Gormley-Heenan and Byrne 2012: 4). Although many of these walls are more porous than in previous years and most of the residents living on either side would like to see the barriers removed eventually, only 13 per cent desire their immediate removal, indicative of the insecurities held by each community, whilst only a minority of residents can envisage a future entirely bereft of peace walls, with Protestants more pessimistic than Catholics (Gormley-Heenan and Byrne 2012: 4–5).

Confrontations over parades, mostly those of the Protestant Orange Order whose parades account for two-thirds of the total number of marches, have been evident. Whilst the vast majority of the region's marches are non-contentious, a small number (146 in 2010–11 of the near 4,000 annual demonstrations) have been subject to Parades Commission restrictions and several of these have regularly led to substantial confrontations (Parades Commission for Northern Ireland 2011: 6). In North Belfast, rioting by nationalist youths became a regular feature of the 'Twelfth', the most important Orange marching day, from the mid-2000s. For the Orange Order, parades are a key expression of loyalty to Faith and Crown, rituals of ethno-national and ethno-religious bonding (Bryan 2000). The Orange Order's membership views such cultural and religious expressions as entirely legitimate, but there is little consensus. Whilst almost half of Protestants believe the Orange Order should be able to march without restriction, only 0.2 per cent of Catholics feel likewise and, although 72 per cent of Catholics believe that the Orange Order should not have the right to march through areas populated mainly by nationalists, only 8 per cent of Protestants support such a prohibition (McAuley et al. 2011: 180). Amid this stark lack of consensus, the quasi-judicial Parades Commission attempts to determine the routes of parades. Orange marches remain one of the few aspects of contemporary Northern Ireland life where hostility from nationalists can be sufficient for dissident republicans to attempt to gain some community traction through their opposition. The Parades Commission has been eschewed by the Orange Order from the outset and its determinations criticized by Unionist political leaders as overly restrictive or inconsistent in respecting the right of Protestants to march. Catholic hostility to what they see negatively as Protestant expressions of triumphalism remains largely undiluted by the peace process and rows over expressions of identity have increased amid assertions of the need for parity of esteem.

Sectarian separation is evident from an early age, the overwhelming majority of Catholics attending Catholic schools from 5 years upwards. At secondary level, there has been a gentle trend upwards in terms of the percentage of children attending integrated schools, increasing to 14 per cent by 2011, the first such school having opened in 1989 (Hayes and McAllister 2013), but most Protestants and Catholics are educated separately. This in itself ought not to be problematic; it is still the case in some cities in England, such as Liverpool where sectarian problems have all but evaporated, but Northern Ireland remains a harder case and those educated separately tend to have few friends or contacts across the divide. When integrated education is advocated by Unionist leaders, whose own followers are more sympathetic to the idea, such proposals can be viewed with suspicion by some Catholics who still see such a project as one of assimilation and dissipation of their own identity. Thus the call in 2010 by the First Minister, Peter Robinson, for an end to the 'benign apartheid' of segregated education and the cessation of state funding for such, met with considerable hostility from sections of the nationalist community, not least from the Roman Catholic church (*Belfast Telegraph* 2010). Other indicators of societal polarity remain stark. The percentage of 'mixed' (Catholic-Protestant) marriages remains in single figures and only 7 per cent of public housing stock houses integrated communities (Nolan 2012).

The Question of Victims

The peace process in Northern Ireland has struggled with issues concerning families of victims and with processes of truth and reconciliation. As such, societal healing has been largely dependent upon the successful functioning of political institutions, amid greatly diminished, but not entirely eradicated, violence. Alongside the 3,600 deaths, there were over 50,000 people injured, approximately 3 per cent of the population (the number injured nearly matches the total number of bombings and shootings) which on population ratios would have meant over 100,000 dead in Britain and 1.8 million injured (Hayes and McAllister 2013). Although a 'low intensity' conflict, Northern Ireland's Troubles had a significant effect within a small country, with more than half of the population claiming they knew someone killed or injured (Hayes and McAllister 2013).

The preponderance of victims on the Unionist side, which views the IRA's 'war' merely as utterly unjustified terrorism, is highlighted by groups such as the Orange Order, many of whose members served in the local security services, with one in five RUC members killed belonging to the Order (McAuley et al. 2011: 105–6). For some families of victims, the presence of Sinn Féin in government, several of the party's Assembly members having served in the IRA, was difficult to accept and Protestants are reluctant to class republicans as victims. Republicans are concerned that state crimes have often not been properly investigated, particularly in respect of collusion between regular state forces and the 'uber-loyalist' Protestant paramilitaries of the UVF and UDA. The £250m Saville Inquiry into the killing of 14 unarmed civilians by the British Army in Derry in 1972 was a major exception, although this has not yet led to any convictions of the perpetrators. The PSNI's Historical Enquiries Team (HET) is charged with policing the past, in that it investigates killings carried out during the Troubles, even though most perpetrators would face a nominal jail sentence under the terms of the GFA. The HET has been criticized for taking a far softer approach towards killings allegedly perpetrated by British soldiers than those in which paramilitaries were involved (Lundy 2012).

Policing the past may bring closure for some victims, but the lack of consensus over how to confront what happened is apparent. The 2009 'Eames-Bradley plan', put forward by the former Anglican Primate of Ireland and the former

Vice Chair of the PSNI, reflected the thinking of the Consultative Group on the Past. It suggested a flat-rate payment of £12,000 to the nearest relative of each victim, a proposal immediately denounced by critics for including payments to relatives of paramilitaries. The Consultative Group headed by Eames and Bradley also recommended the establishment of a Legacy Commission and Reconciliation Forum to help society come to terms with past, but these were not implemented.

Influenced by their friends in the African National Congress, Sinn Féin supports the establishment of a comprehensive truth and reconciliation process. The party's proposals are heavily criticized by Unionists for inferring an equivalence of victims, attempting to rewrite the historical narrative into a justification of the IRA and for raising the prospect of an amnesty, whilst the denials of certain prominent Sinn Féin members regarding their IRA involvement is also cited as evidence against the idea. Bereft of a truth and reconciliation commission and in the absence of amnesties, it is difficult to see how the truth of many of the killings during the conflict will ever be revealed, given that the state is now anxious, post-Saville, to avoid time-consuming and expensive inquiries. The limited ongoing violence adds to the problem, as such a commission might require detailed revelations from the British security forces still at work against armed republicans. A Commission for Victims and Survivors was established in 2008 to represent the interests of the families of victims, including overseeing services such as counselling and advocacy. Sinn Féin has also embarked on a process of 'national reconciliation' in acknowledging the hurt caused by the IRA campaign, but this has gained little traction on the Unionist side and is unlikely to do so as long as that campaign is defended by republicans as having been necessary.

Conclusion

Aside from very limited continuing militant republican activity, a consociational politics of identity has displaced armed conflict in Northern Ireland. Constitutional differences are still apparent between Catholics and Protestants, in that a sizeable, if seemingly diminishing, section of the Catholic population aspires to a united Ireland. Careful conflict management and amelioration, the modern stake for Catholics in the northern state and the pragmatic apparent benefits of UK membership have quelled the rages against discriminatory treatment which fuelled the onset of the conflict at the end of the 1960s. Northern Ireland has become a quieter place, one in which the supporters of all the main parties appeared satisfied (if only moderately) by the performance of the devolved government as it finally embedded after years of post-Good Friday Agreement wrangling. Northern Ireland has also been characterized by growing apathy and ideological disaffiliation, as unionist and nationalist identities become less extensive, although those retaining such affiliations remain strident in their assertion of national, political and cultural identities. A reduction in the percentages of the population associating with the old unionist and nationalist badges has not been concomitant with a significant rise of any party eschewing such labels.

The peace process has been successful in diminishing the level of violence. Although spoilers, in the form of various IRAs, have been present from the outset, their impact has not been great and the 'dissidents' (an unsatisfactory term, given the longevity of armed republicanism) have struggled to sustain an armed campaign, even if their mere existence belies claims that Northern Ireland can entirely be placed in the box marked 'solved'. The obvious question for spoilers is what they believe their more limited armed campaign can achieve that the Provisional IRA failed to achieve. A realist interpretation of the Northern Ireland peace process is that the Provisionals and their political associates in Sinn Féin settled for a peace deal far short of traditional objectives when the failure of its armed campaign became starkly apparent, although such a conclusion does little to explain the precise timing of the peace process given that this scenario was in place in the 1970s. Given the scale of republican compromise, the emergence of spoiler groups, ultras unhappy with a 'sell-out', was more probable than not.

The key feature of the peace process is not, as naysayers claim, the enshrining of sectarianism, although some aspects are hard to dissolve. Rather, it is the consolidation of the Northern Ireland state as it approaches its centenary. The consociational deal of 1998 gave republicans the stake in that state they declined in 1973–4, shoring up Northern Ireland as a political entity. The Irish government's ending of its constitutional claim meant that the difference between armed republicanism and Irish state ideology in respect of the North was now more than merely one of appropriate methodology over how to end British rule. Nationalist hostility to Northern Ireland is less extensive than previously evident in the state's existence, making the task of those still determined to resist even more difficult than was previously the case, even if they remain of sufficient number and determination that their management rather than entire eradication follows. If the northern state is finally accommodating to nationalists, the demand to change the status quo is diminished.

CHAPTER SEVEN

Confederalism and Consociation in Bosnia-Herzegovina

The conflict in the Balkans in the 1990s demolished the comfortable compla-
cency that major ethnic battles could not erupt in post-Second World War
Europe. The post-Tito eruption of nationalist forces within the constituent
federal republics of Yugoslavia and subsequent 'ethnic cleansing' of rival
groups produced a death toll of over 100,000 in Bosnia-Herzegovina alone (a
country of only 4 million) between 1991 and 1995, with several thousand also
killed in Croatia. More than half of Bosnia's 4.3 million citizens were displaced
(Ramet 2005: 186). Bosnia, a multi-ethnic entity, particularly in its urban
areas, became a polity in which identification as Serb, Croat and Muslim
became dominant over shared outlook, a position not reversed by a largely
successful peace process and the absence of conflict since the end of 1995.
Despite being accompanied by criticisms offered by the naysayers attendant
to all peace processes, the 1995 Dayton Accord has been remarkably successful in preventing the re-ignition of a vicious conflict. This base achievement
has tended to be overlooked by those demanding reintegration of Muslims,
Croats and Serbs in a singular territory. Instead, post-conflict Bosnia has utilized concomitant consociational and confederal ideas to maintain a singular
political entity, but one within which the existence of division and territorial
separation are acknowledged as realities. This chapter begins by exploring the
basis of Europe's worst war of recent decades, before assessing why Dayton
has succeeded since 1995, caveats notwithstanding, where other peace plans
failed earlier in the 1990s.

The Ethno-National Basis of Conflict in the Balkans

Tensions between Serbs, Croats, Muslims and Slovenes had long been evident
within the Balkans. Rivalries were not dissipated amid the aggressive assertion
of communism over ethno-national and ethno-religious sentiment during
President Tito's regime from 1953 to 1980. Instead, Tito's establishment of
a Federal Republic of Yugoslavia represented institutionalized ethnicity,
based upon acknowledgement of different components of a highly artificial
confederal construct, but subordinated ethno-nationalism to an overarching communist ideology. However, the 'prisoners of history' notion of a
Balkans permanently beset by seething, uncontrollable ancient hatreds or
omnipresent Serb desires for regional domination, as outlined occasionally

in the literature (see, e.g., Kaplan 2005) is not sustained by prolonged historical examination (Malcolm 1994; Ramet 2005). Much post-Second World War urban intermarriage and peaceful co-existence was evident. Bosnia had seen the relatively harmonious co-habitation of Muslims, Serbs and Croats, although effective governance was often lacking. Indeed, as Pavlowitch (1999: 165) notes, 'the three ethnic groups were entangled in an almost leopard-skin pattern, but there were no institutional mechanisms for accommodating differences among them other than Party authority mitigated by corrupt practices'. Even during the conflict, many Serbs, Croats and Muslims refused to turn on their neighbours, but such liberal sentiment was discouraged, often via violence, by the ethnically-mobilized.

Much of the existing literature blames the 1990s conflict on Serb expansion and the orthodoxy appears justified, albeit with significant caveats. Long-held Serb antagonism towards Kosovan Albanians provided the initial trigger for the onset of Serb ethnic enterprise. Sent by the Serbian President Ivan Stambolic to quell unrest in Kosovo, Slobodan Milosevic, as Deputy President, instead encouraged Kosovan Serbs, who felt a beleaguered minority within a Kosovo long claimed by Serbs as a key part of Serbian territory, despite its Albanian majority. Milosevic famously declared that the Kosovan Serbs would 'never be beaten again', a widely-publicized assertion of Serb nationalism (although the assertion was primarily a response to the beatings of Serbs by local Kosovan police). His increasingly nationalist tone became crucial to his elevation as Serbian President. Whilst protesting loyalty to the Communist Party and denouncing Kosovan nationalists as counter-revolutionaries, Milosevic fused a mixture of populist nationalist aggression, based upon Serbian 'repossession' of territory, with (unfulfilled) pledges of internal reform to mobilize an admittedly somewhat indeterminate concept of a Greater Serbia, the dominant force in Yugoslavia. Milosevic took control of Vojvodina, abolishing its autonomy, and installed a supporter, Momir Bulatovic, in Montenegro. As Serbia's control of Yugoslavia increased, the determination of other parts of the federation to avoid Serbian rule increased and full dissolution became inevitable.

Slovenia and Croatia soon mobilized to resist potential Serbian aggrandisement. Persistently outvoted at the 4,000 strong 1990 Yugoslav Communist Party Congress, the Slovenes quit the Congress. Croatia rejected its Communist leadership in favour of the nationalist leader of the Croatian Democratic Union (HDZ), Franjo Tudjman, who had declared that he thanked God his wife was neither a Serb nor a Jew. Slovenia's move towards independence could be accommodated comfortably, given the absence of hostile minority populations, although the political implications of the Slovenians' move were profound. Croatia had a more complicated ethnic geography, with parts of the south of the country populated by Serbs hostile to the idea of living in a Croat state. Such Serbs revived memories of the previous Croat state, led by the Nazi-supporting Ustasha government, responsible for killing tens of thousands of

Serbs. Crucially, Serb police officers declined to support the new Croat state and, supported by Milosevic and the Serbs on the Yugoslav state council, who mobilized vastly superior forces, an ethnic Serb state of Krajina, under Milan Babic was created within Croatia, its 'headquarters' in Knin. Nonetheless, given Milosevic's eye on territorial prizes in Bosnia, his willingness to do a deal with Tudjman in that respect and antipathy towards Babic, the commitment of the Belgrade government to the Serb enclave was modest. It was effectively protected by the UN for four years before being over-run in 1995.

Croats claimed a strong mandate for independence, with a 93 per cent 'yes' vote recorded in May 1991, on an 83 per cent turnout, although Serbs boycotted the referendum. Predictably, given its own moves towards independence, Slovenia immediately recognized the new Croatian state, with both prematurely recognized by Germany in December 1991, ahead of wider European Community recognition. Amid the crumbling of Yugoslavia, the European Community's (EC) Badinter Commission had suggested referendums to test mandates for independence. This, however, ignored the likelihood of groups in multi-ethnic states determining their own arrangements. Bosnian Serbs conducted their own referendum and effectively seceded from Bosnian authority before the Bosnian government launched a referendum – an event which produced 99 per cent for Bosnian independence, but on a turnout of only 63 per cent, Serbs boycotting the poll.

A Serb counter-narrative to their 'scapegoating' can point to the inability of other actors in the conflict to occupy moral or political high ground. The attempts of Serbs to keep Yugoslavia intact were genuine, albeit guided by self-interest. Slovenia acted prematurely and opportunistically in seceding when further negotiation might still have been possible, and narrow, self-concerned nationalism was not solely attributable to the Serbs (Woodward 1994). Milosevic was still anxious to keep Croats as part of the Communist Party as late as 1990. The Serb Yugoslavs were not *directly* responsible for the creation of new armies and states within the Federal Republic. The 1991 Carrington Plan, devised on behalf of the EC, facilitated the establishment of a multiplicity of sovereign, independent republics within Yugoslavia, bound only by the loosest of free associations, formalizing its dissolution. The West was perhaps too quick to recognize new states. Pre-empted by German acceptance of the embryonic state in December 1991 (a move which did nothing to calm Serb fears), the EC, on the recommendation of the Badinter Commission, recognized Croatia at the start of 1992, after a largely token delay to ascertain whether sufficient minority protection could be guaranteed – entirely unrealistic as the minority had already engaged in a unilateral declaration of independence. The UN followed the EC in Spring 1992.

The right of secession that the Croats demanded in respect of 'Serboslavia' was not reciprocated by a similar deal for the Serbs within southern Croatia. Moreover, within the main theatre of conflict, Bosnia, Serbs were hardly the only nationalist forces present. The Bosnian President Izetbegovic's own Party of Democratic Action (SDA) party took on an increasingly nationalist outlook, whilst the Croatians in the country took their lead from the rise of the HDZ in Croatia proper. Izetbegovic had been imprisoned during the Tito regime for offering a form of Muslim nationalism at odds with the supposed brotherhood and unity ideals of the federal republic. His own forces were joined by former Mujahideen who had fought in Afghanistan and were committed to Islamic Jihad (two of the 9/11 bombers had fought in Bosnia) although they were heavily outnumbered by locals. The assessment of the High Representative of Bosnia from 1999 to 2002 was that 'what is truly worthy of note is that the influence of fundamentalist Islam in the Balkans has been so weak' (Petritsch, 2001: 1). This was largely an ethno-national, not ethno-religious, conflict. The Bosnians' pursuit of self-determination, via Izetbegovic's own independence referendum in response to events in Croatia and Slovenia, made war even more certain, given the absence of a definitive Bosnian nation amid Bosnia's functioning as a multinational republic (Gowan 1999).

Yet the Serb case against rapid secessionism overlooks the obvious fears stoked by the emergence of Serb nationalism. It is also undermined by Milosevic's withdrawal from the Yugoslav state council in 1990 when unable to achieve a sufficient majority to persuade the body in early 1991 to agree to allow the Yugoslav army to move against the Croats. The army moved to 'protect' Serb territories within Croatia and expanded its role to seize other towns in the south and east of Croatia, including cities such as Vukovar. The Serb 'enclave' was rapidly expanded to one-third of Croatia, with 15,000 killed in the process. Many Serbs were later killed or overrun in Operation Storm in 1995, when the West simply ignored reverse acts of 'ethnic cleansing', undertaken on a more brutal scale by Croats on the grounds that they 'simplified matters' in bringing Serbia to the negotiating table. Herman and Peterson (2010) contend (accurately) that the use of the label 'genocide' by the West is highly selective. Even a sharply critical review of their work acknowledges that 'if Serbian "ethnic cleansing" constituted genocide, there is no good reason not to examine the Croatian expulsion of Serbs, during Operation Storm in 1995, within the same frame' (Shaw 2011: 356). However, that Serbs also suffered from mass killings palpably does not alleviate their culpability in precipitating mass ethnic conflict and engaging in occasional, if not systemic, acts of genocide, as at Srebrenica.

The Nature of Conflict in Bosnia

Those acts of genocide in Bosnia (the label of genocide remains contested by Serb political leaders, even among the current relatively moderate nationalists) were the denouement of the Serbian ethnic and territorial aggrandisement viewed by most as the key determinants of the conflict. The Bosnian President, Alija Izetbegovic, made clear from the outset that he was not prepared to allow Bosnia to be part of any Greater Serbia. The Serb one-third of the population was not unduly exercised by nationalist sentiment and co-existed comfortably alongside Muslims in Sarajevo and Croats elsewhere until mobilized by local leaders, notably Radovan Karadzic. The cordial multi-ethnic nature of urban areas began to dissipate, although as late as April 1992, Sarajevo citizens mounted a large multi-ethnic demonstration for peace. The city was then besieged by Serb forces, which shelled Muslim areas.

To counter the encroachment of 'Serboslavia', the 1992 Bosnian independence referendum recorded a near 100 per cent vote in favour, but was boycotted by Serbs. The Serb justification was that it was Bosnia wishing to secede from Yugoslavia; if rights of secession were to be awarded they had the right to withdraw from a 'Muslim-dominated' Bosnia and instead align with Serbs elsewhere, in the remnants of the old Federal Republic. The Serb narrative also downplays their role in ethnic antagonisms, instead highlighting the killing of a Serb by a Muslim in March 1992 as triggering the bloodshed. The siege of Sarajevo by Serb forces overlooking the mainly Muslim city centre began after the March killing. By this point, Milosevic and Tudjman had agreed a division of Bosnia between Serbs and Croats, with mutual major territorial gains for each, at the expense of Muslims who formed 44 per cent of the population. Bosnian Serbs serving in the Yugoslavian Army were transferred to the main theatre of war in Bosnia, constituting a force of 80,000, abetted by 'irregular' Serbian nationalist paramilitary and police forces, who carried out much of the 'ethnic cleansing' under leaders such as Seselj.

Serb territorial expansion was rapid, with over 70 per cent of the country under control at the high-water mark of December 1992. Entire Muslim populations were expelled from cities; 49,000 were removed from Zvornik in north-eastern Bosnia within a single week (those not expelled were killed). In Srebrenica, thousands of dispossessed Muslims had gathered. The UN Commander in Bosnia, General Morillon, pledged that his forces would remain in the area for as long as necessary. Yet the UN declined to declare the area a 'safe haven', guaranteeing UN protection insofar as was possible, instead awarding the area only the lesser status of 'safe area'. The Serbian terms for the 'restraint' of non-invasion were the disarmament of the Muslim forces. In 1995, with the UN powerless to intervene, the Serbs finally moved in, killing thousands of Muslim males.

The Failure of the Vance–Owen Peace Plan

Western governments failed to intervene militarily in Bosnia during the sustained ethnic cleansing of 1992, preferring instead to offer an EC peace plan, promoted by Lord Carrington, based upon the division of the country into ethnic provinces. Russia, still recovering from its own tribulations, offered sympathy (but in material terms little else) to the Serb cause. The West's arms embargo offered no redress to the asymmetry of arms evident at the start of the Bosnian war, in which local Serbs were heavily armed by the Yugoslavian

army. The May 1992 UN London Conference talked a good game on intervention and threatened stringent sanctions, amid growing evidence of war crimes
and Serb-run detention camps, but had no effect. Milosevic and the Bosnian
Serb leader Radovan Karadzic strengthened their positions at the expense of
more moderate political leaders, Milosevic marginalizing the Yugoslavian
Prime Minister Panic. International inertia was exacerbated by the perception that conflict culpability was shared amongst three irrational warring
groups. The Congressional Armed Services Committee in the United States
was informed by the former commander of UN forces in Bosnia, General Lewis
MacKenzie, that 'dealing with Bosnia is a bit like dealing with three serial kill-
ers' (cited in Bennett 1995: 194). James Baker, the US Secretary of State and
then White House Chief of Staff, declared that the US did not have a dog in the
fight. The West continued to indulge Milosevic as a leader with which it could
do business until the Kosovo crisis of the late 1990s (Simms 2002).

When the UN and EU agreed proposals, the US government objected. The
Vance (UN)–Owen (EU) plan offered to divide Bosnia into nine ethnic cantons
and one mixed canton, each to control policing, education and transport.
Although Vance and Owen described their plan as an attempt to 'reconstitute'
Bosnia, the ethnic divisions were more important than the state-wide framework (Silber and Little 1995). Nonetheless, the three Serb cantons were not to
be linked territorially and the plan involved the rolling back of Serb territorial
gains by approximately 30 per cent. As such, the plan did not, as US critics
claimed, legitimize Serb territorial seizures; indeed, as Owen (1995) pointed
out, it did largely the opposite. The UN Security Council approved the use of
sanctions upon the Serbs for non-compliance with the plan. Sensing the end
of territorial gains approaching, recognizing the economic dangers of sanctions and acknowledging the basic fairness of what Vance–Owen proposed,
Milosevic supported the proposals, whilst Izetbegovic and Tudjman, the latter
much more enthusiastically, also believed it was the best deal available in the
circumstances.

Bosnian Serb objections were nonetheless profound. For them, Vance–Owen
meant a rolling back of a year of huge territorial gains. It also meant recognition of a post-referendum Bosnian state with no Serb Republic in return. Under
pressure from Milosevic, Karadzic backed the plan, on condition that it was
ratified by the Bosnian Serb Assembly at Pale. With Karadzic making clear his
objections at that Assembly, backed by the Bosnian Serb Army under Mladic,
the Assembly rejected the plan despite Milosevic's exhortations, ensuring a
continuation of the conflict. Vance–Owen was followed by a tentative, equally
unsuccessful three-way partition idea put forward by Vance's replacement,
Thorvald Stoltenberg, alongside Owen. The plan envisaged a Union of republics, a confederation of Serb, Bosnian and Croatian states, whose union, more
virtual than real, would maintain the fiction of a singular Bosnia-Herzegovina.
Given that the Serbs would be rewarded for ethnic cleansing by being awarded
53 per cent of the territory, it was unsurprising that the Bosnians rejected the

deal, whilst the Croatians, reduced to 17 per cent of the land and who had agreed a better deal in the Milosevic-Tjudman carve-up, were almost as equally unimpressed.

Milosevic's own commitment to Vance–Owen was questionable. He appeared to doubt whether it could be implemented and his urgings to Karadzic were to accept the deal as a tactical necessity. Bennett (1995: 198) asserts that the real impact of the Vance–Owen plan 'was the destruction of the Croat-Muslim alliance and the creation of a three-way conflict'. Croats stood to make gains from the ethnic cantonization of Bosnia, relative to their percentage of the population; Muslims were less enamoured with a plan that they saw as ethnic dismemberment. Bosnian Croats increasingly looked to their embryonic parent state and set up autonomous Croat areas, although the geography and geometry of Croat-Muslim hostilities was variable. Those Croats based in western Herzegovina, one-third of the Bosnian Croats, tended to be more nationalistic in outlook, hostile to Muslims and Serbs and sceptical over the viability of the Bosnian state. Under the leadership of Boban, it was these Croats who established a Croatian mini-state of Herceg-Bosna. In contrast, Croats in central Bosnia were accustomed to living in multi-ethnic areas and held a diminished sense of Croatian nationalism (Silber and Little 1995). A Muslim-Croat ceasefire in March 1994, following an agreement clinched in Washington, paved the way for the concentration of efforts against the Serbs and the establishment of a Muslim-Croat Federation within Bosnia, effectively rendering superfluous the three-way partition ideas of Owen-Stoltenberg as Boban's segregated community was reintegrated into a broader entity. This reintegration did not immediately follow the Washington Agreement. Muslims and Croats retained their separate armies in the aftermath of the deal, not the joint command demanded in its terms, such was the level of hostility. As Glenny (1996: 247) argues, the Washington Agreement was a 'shotgun wedding and amounted to nothing more than a glorified ceasefire', designed to create at least sufficient Muslim-Croat mutual tolerance that attention could be turned to reversing the Serb gains within Bosnia and prepare the ground for the destruction of the Serb enclave within Croatia.

Could the Vance–Owen peace process have worked? Owen argues that had George Bush Senior still been President, the United States would have backed enforcement of the plan and nearly three years of further bloodshed could have been avoided. Yet the Bush administration had also appeared sceptical of the capabilities of the EU and UN to bring about a durable peace agreement and preferred to organize its own diplomatic initiatives. Vance–Owen has been described as a superior plan to the Dayton Accord which eventually followed, Gow (1997) arguing that diplomatic failures to enforce action derived from perceptions of the problem clouded by domestic perceptions of their own issues. Thus the British saw Yugoslavia as potentially as intractable as their own Northern Ireland problem; the French feared succession claims for the impact on their own holding of Corsica; and Germany supported claims to self-determination given the reunification of their own country which had recently occurred (see Ramet 2005: 78).

American reluctance to deploy ground troops was understandable. There was no guarantee of rapid success in what was still seen by many as a Yugoslavian civil war. Moreover, the real antagonists of the situation were still not fully apparent in 1992–3, two years before the genocide of Srebrenica. Serbian aggression was apparent, but the unilateral declarations of independence by the Slovenes and Croats had not impressed all within the US administration, perhaps ironically, given their opposition to communist regimes. Indeed, the US ambassador to Yugoslavia from 1988 to 1992, Warren Zimmerman, whilst hugely critical of Serb aggression, had been hostile to Slovenian secession from the Federal Republic, regarding it as premature (Zimmerman 1999). Amid the lack of clarity amongst Western diplomats, the reluctance to intervene decisively was perhaps understandable. Vance–Owen did have the long-term benefit of dividing Serb opinion, the fracture between the parent Serb state and its illegitimate ethnic 'child' never fully repaired. As the Bosnian Serb General Mladic was later to rue, the split between Belgrade and Pale was the 'greatest tragedy for the Serb nation' (cited in Thomas 1998: 236).

Ripeness for Peace: Force to Create Peace

The Vance–Owen plan might have been interpreted at the time as a ripe moment for peace. Signed by the leaders of all the warring groups in Athens in May 1993, it was not preceded by stalemate, but by continuous Serb territorial advancement which could not immediately be reversed. Serbs were fully aware of the reluctance of the United States to intervene by deploying ground forces amid the succession of initiatives involving Lord Owen. However, the US was anxious to deploy NATO bombing raids, a desire exacerbated by the Sarajevo market shelling of February 1994, perpetrated (and unconvincingly denied) by the Bosnian Serbs. Yet UN peacekeepers on the ground opposed bombing raids as likely to cause civilian casualties and render peacekeeping operations more hazardous, whilst the military effectiveness of bombings was also doubted.

Finally, following the Srebrenica massacre of Muslims by Serbs in July 1995 and the abject failure of the UN to prevent the genocide, the United States moved decisively towards the use of force to create peace. The strategy was three-fold. Firstly, Serb advances would be rolled back to establish a more equitable division of Bosnian territory. Secondly, with the US administration still reluctant to commit ground troops, the Croatian Army was encouraged to begin the process of reversing Serb gains by removing the Serb-held sector of Croatia, which would contribute to 'simplifying matters' according to the US Secretary of State, Warren Christopher. The US was fully aware of the consequences in terms of Serb deaths and refugees, but Operation Storm was launched by the Croats in August 1995. Tudjman's claim that he thought most of the Serbs would stay appeared hollow given the ferocity of the attacks upon Serb-held territory. Thirdly, the US launched a huge bombing campaign, Operation Deliberate Force, against Bosnian Serb positions.

The military pressure finally exerted by the USA thus 'encouraged' the Serbs to move towards peace. The Bosnian Serbs could respond by continuing to attack Sarajevo, but were clearly in retreat elsewhere. Whilst it has been claimed that as late as May 1995 the situation in Bosnia represented a 'fiercely contested stalemate' (Thomas 1998: 237), the balance of forces was shifting. Moreover, Milosevic finally abandoned his Bosnian Serb 'clients' Karadzic and Mladic, who had already been indicted for war crimes (but were still met by the US peace delegation led by Richard Holbrooke). Under pressure, the Serbs ended the siege of Sarajevo, a move reciprocated by the cessation of the US bombing. From this point, a negotiated settlement was possible. The aim of the US bombing campaign was strictly limited, designed to enforce Serbian participation in negotiations rather than roll back all their territorial gains. As the chief US negotiator, Richard Holbrooke told Izetbegovic, 'it is your right to continue the war, but don't expect the United States to provide your airforce' (cited in Glenny 1996: 290).

Although limited, the US intervention and arming of Croats and Muslims brought about a major collapse of Serbian forces in north-west Bosnia in Autumn 1995 and the conflict was arguably close to 'being resolved by straightforward military means' (Malcolm 2002: 270). The US had been cautious over the need for liberal interventionism throughout the conflict. This was largely because they (and other governments, such as the UK's), had been influenced by the 'irrational hatreds' school of thought which conditioned much thinking on the Balkans. It was difficult to identify the liberals who required intervention. Only war crimes and genocide at Srebrenica finally produced a definitive hierarchy of 'illiberals'. From a realist perspective, it was not unreasonable for the US to ask national interest-based 'what's in it for us?' questions in respect of large-scale intervention, to which replies were not readily available if one overlooked humanitarian and moral concerns.

The Contours of the Dayton Accord

Following strenuous efforts led by the US brokerage team under Holbrooke, a 130-page Dayton peace deal was clinched after three weeks of negotiations at the US Air Force base at Dayton in November 1995. The agreement was formally signed in Paris during the following month. Much of the detailed negotiation concerned the final shape of the two territories to be established within one overarching political entity. Haris Silajdzic, the Bosnian Prime Minister who conducted most of the negotiations on behalf of Izetbegovic, was anxious to connect the Muslim enclave of Gorazde, 'trapped' in the prospective Serb Republic, to the Muslim-Croat Federation. This involved the concession of Serb land to allow a connecting corridor road to be constructed by NATO, but the Serbs were adamant that their land share was not to dip below fractionally less than half of Bosnia. The compromises involved the surrender of some recent Croatian territorial gains back to the Serbs as compensation, to the chagrin of the Croatian Foreign Minister, Mate Granic. Agreement was reached only after Tudjman, conscious as Croatian President of the need for pragmatic concessions (and possibly fearful over potential indictment for his own war crimes if compromises were not forthcoming) adopted a more resigned view, demanding only that Bosnian Muslims also concede some land to the Serbs, thus sharing the burden.

The final deal established a Muslim-Croat Federation, the Federation of Bosnia-Herzegovina, covering 51 per cent of the territory and a Republic of Srpksa amounting to 49 per cent, the two entities united to form the overall state of Bosnia-Herzegovina. Bosnian Serbs thus got their own republic, but only on a semi-autonomous basis. It was nonetheless, despite their complaints, a good territorial deal, given Serbs formed less than one-third of the Bosnian population. Muslims and Croats shared territory, but within that entity there was a heavy emphasis upon ethnic cantonization, giving Muslims 27 per cent and Croats 24 per cent (a territorial over-representation for the Croats). It was a deal in which each leader appeared obsessed with territory and the headline 51–49 per cent figure. Although the Dayton Accord contained lots of detail, some of those aspects, such as human rights provisions, 'depended largely on the good faith of the authorities in the two entities to enforce them' (Malcolm 2002: 269).

The Dayton Accord contained 11 annexes, covering military aspects and regional stabilization; territorial boundaries; elections (to be held within 9 months); the constitution; arbitration; the establishment of a human rights commission, comprising a chamber and an ombudsman; refugee returns; monuments; public corporations; civilian implementation; and the deployment of an international police task force. Some of the key items to prevent conflict re-ignition were included in the comprehensive military and regional stabilization provisions, including the deployment of the NATO peacekeeping force; construction of the Gorazde road; withdrawal and disbandment of militias (ambitiously demanded within 30 days); restrictions on military deployments; monitoring of armaments programmes; and liaison between the armed forces of the Federation of Bosnia-Herzegovina and the Republic of Srpska. These annexes also contained provision for the release and transfer of all prisoners. The Agreement was unambiguous (in Annex 7) in offering the right of return for all refugees and displaced persons, the deal also confirming rights of compensation for property lost in the conflict and asserting refugee rights to participate in elections at their original location. An amnesty was offered to all conflict participants other than those suspected of a serious violation of international humanitarian law. A Commission for Displaced Persons and Refugees was established to guarantee these rights and oversee the returns process.

Ethnic shifts in population continued in the immediate aftermath of the Dayton Agreement. Fearful of their future in a Muslim-Croat Federation and anxious over the possibility of retribution for the three year siege of the area, Sarajevo's Serbs fled the city's outskirts en masse in late 1995 and early 1996. Subsequent to this movement, however, the process of returns has been broadly successful. Over two million Bosnian citizens had been displaced during the conflict; within one decade half had returned, and by the mid-2000s, returns (and applications for assistance) had dwindled to a trickle – perhaps indicative that most of those who wished to return had completed the task. Two important caveats to a seeming success story should nonetheless be noted. Firstly, a majority of returns were to areas where the population of the returnee was the dominant one in the locality; those displaced were more willing to return to where they felt safe as the majority population (e.g., Croats returned to majority Croat areas). However, this disproportionality diminished over time and minority returns were more common than majority ones during the 2000s. Secondly, some minority returnees returned only to take possession of property before selling it to buyers from the majority community (Cousens and Harland 2006). Judah (2000: 304) contrasts the successful disengagement of the NATO-led armed protectorate with the partial, at best, return of displaced civilians: 'Soldiers went home. But refugees did not'.

Consociation and Confederation

Confederal and consociational elements were present in the Dayton Agreement. It was a two states in one deal which left 'room for partition and some form of a united state' (Glenny 1996: 290). The federal government of Bosnia-Herzegovina assumed responsibility for foreign and economic policy, a central bank and monetary system, plus control over immigration. The judicial system was also centralized, presided over by a Supreme Court comprising an equal number (two each) of Croat, Muslim and Serb judges, plus three external members. The two states below the federal government maintained their own army, parliament, policing and tax systems, but merged their armies into joint Bosnian-Herzegovinan forces (a requirement of the EU for membership) in 2005.

Consociational features are evident in the power-sharing, proportionality and mutual vetoes built into governmental and legislative arrangements. The central government of Bosnia comprises a directly elected Presidency, a Council of Ministers and a constitutional court, with a bicameral legislature. The three-person rotating Presidency comprises two members (one Bosniac, one Croat) elected from the Federation and one elected by the Republic. A President concerned over the adverse effect of a decision upon their territory may refer the decision to the parliament of their own entity, which could (by a two-thirds majority) vote to block a measure. The Council of Ministers is chosen by a Chair nominated by the Presidency and again comprises a 'one-third each' proportionality of ethnic representation. The Constitutional Court is similarly proportional, with additional representatives selected by the President of the European Court of Human Rights. Proportionality is extended to the governance of the central bank.

In terms of the legislative institutional apparatus, the House of Peoples consists of 10 representatives (five Bosniacs and five Croats) selected by the Federation of Bosnia-Herzegovina's own House of Peoples and five Serbs selected by the Assembly of the Republic of Srpska. The House of Representatives of Bosnia comprises 42 members, two-thirds elected from the Federation and the other third by electors in the Republic. Decision-making requires overall majority support and backing from at least one-third of representatives from each entity. Legislative items deemed potentially detrimental to a particular ethnic group may require a higher threshold of majority support from each. Each legislative institution has a rotating Chair.

Power-sharing and proportionality are not required in the overwhelmingly Serb Republic, which has a unicameral 83-member Assembly. However, the central government's consociational structures are replicated in the Federation's proportionality and power-sharing. The Federation's House of Peoples, elected by first-past-the-post, comprises the same number (30 each) of Bosniacs and Croats (elected on a territorial basis), plus 20 nominations from the ten ethnic cantons. The Federation's House of Representatives (140 members) is elected by proportional representation using party lists. Below the Federation's legislatures lie 10 cantons, each with their own Assembly, with 444 seats in total. Added to nearly 150 municipal councils, over-governance was built into Dayton's structures. The Agreement created three armies, two customs services, five presidents, twelve prime ministers, 100 ministers, 760 parliamentarians, 13 police forces and 1,200 judges and prosecutors (Geslin 2006: 175; Chivvis 2010: 49).

Criticisms of rigid consociationalism and lower-level cantonization are familiar, principally that these arrangements enshrine ethnic division and institutionalize ethnicity; offer no clear means of the dissolution of identities in favour of a common Bosnian identity or loyalty; fail to account for individual identities, or for alternative identities to those licensed by the state; and lead to stagnation, not progressive decision-making. None of these criticisms is easily rebutted, although integrationist arguments risk overlooking the abject conditions and position-in-extremis from which the Bosnian polity has been constructed. Utopianism was in short supply in 1995 and some organic growth of Bosnia and Herzegovina has developed amid the prospect of EU membership.

Indeed, the Dayton Accord acknowledged and legitimized, but did not deepen, ethno-nationalism. Rather, Dayton held out the optimistic prospect of a single Bosnian army, judiciary, intelligence and tax systems at an unspecified point (the reintegration of the Muslim and Croat military forces would prove difficult enough) and the aspirations towards single state unity were greater than the separatist urges, but Dayton's ambitions in these respects outweighed grassroots realities in the immediate post-war years. Modest integration has been evident since 2000, even though Bosnia's parliament narrowly rejected greater transformation. Communal autonomy and self-governance were dominant Dayton themes below the single state insistence. Croats, Serbs, Muslims and 'Others' were recognized as the constituent peoples of the country. Dayton was an accord which tried to steer gently integrationist, liberal and multi-ethnic courses against a prevailing wind which had been unremittingly partitionist and segregationist for the first half of the 1990s. The maintenance of a united Bosnia-Herzegovina (albeit somewhat nominal) was arguably riskier than ethnic partition, which would have potentially resulted in further population transfers to ethnic states. Partitioning Bosnia into three distinct entities might have offered a long-term solution to the intra-nationalist rivalries within the Bosnian state. However, it risked the embedding of inter-state nationalist enmity from the new states which would be formed, not least because new 'mini-Croatia' or 'mini-Serbia' would see themselves as part of a greater entity surrounding a rump Bosnian Muslim state.

Izetbegovic was obliged to accept the confederation he had explicitly rejected in 1992. Bosnia-Herzegovina was maintained – just – as a singular state, at the head of which Muslims, Serbs and Croats shared power, initially on the basis of minimum cooperation. Yet Dayton also effectively created two states within one; the Bosnian (Muslim)-Croat Federation and the Republic of Srpska (a small area around Brcko remained contested and awarded to neither entity). The ethnic cantons within the Muslim-Croat Federation, further divided into municipalities, assumed considerable importance. The Serbs were rewarded for their expansionist adventure by a semi-autonomous republic, but one which still formed part of Bosnia-Herzegovina rather than an entity with closer formal links to its 'parent' Serbia. As defeats go, the Serbs' was certainly not calamitous in territorial terms, notwithstanding the ruinous impact upon the economy. Given the ethnically homogeneous, 97 per cent Serb, nature of the Republic of Srpska (Geslin 2006: 179), it is unsurprising that its people and leaders are more quizzical of their position within Bosnia. The conflict erupted when less ethnically homogeneous entities (although Slovenia was similar) were permitted self-determination. The Republic of Srpska is almost the ethnically 'pure' state fantasized by some Serb leaders, although not necessarily Milosevic (contrary to popular wisdom), who had spoken on occasion of the need for a more pluralist Serbia which accepted minorities. Nonetheless, the very small other ethnic groups are over-represented in the Republic of Srpska's assembly. The big losses for the Serbs were the presence of the Bosnian state 'umbrella' and the absence of Sarajevo from their territorial acquisitions, the city designated as the capital of Bosnia-Herzegovina and largely a Serb-free city post-Dayton. Serbs were largely excluded from the Muslim-Croat Federation, representing only 1 per cent of the police and 5 per cent of the judiciary (Cousens and Harland 2006: 107). The ethnic nature of the two states within a state led to intervention from Bosnia's Constitutional Court in 2000, designed to enforce the equal status of the constituent peoples of Bosnia at all levels within both of the entities comprising the state.

The West's obsession with keeping Bosnia-Herzegovina as a single entity lay in sharp contrast to its ready acceptance of the rapid dismantling of communist Yugoslavia. Via recommendations from the Badinter Commission based on the flimsiest assurances of minority protection, emergent states were recognized. Yet the Dayton Accord contains a multiplicity of logics, not always complementary, which recognize the 'facts on the ground', that, as even an opponent of the partition of the country argues, Bosnia is 'a country whose citizens are deeply divided on the most intractable of faultlines – national identity, state allegiance and the legitimate focus of sovereignty' (Bose 2002b: 199). Given this, preservation of the state might be seen as miraculous, drawing upon the considerable political dexterity shown via Dayton – an agreement which simultaneously combined consociationalism, confederalism and devolution with the potential for secession.

Bosnia-Herzegovina's political arrangements have been accompanied by numerous rows, exemplified by the failure to form a government for 14 months in 2010–11. Almost three-fifths of citizens within Bosnia would regard its break-up as unacceptable, but this does not mask ethnic differences, with only 36 per cent of Serbs saying this, whereas most Muslims and Croats appear content (Irwin 2012: 51). Amongst all three groups, however, 'normal' issues, such as the economy and education, appear greater priorities than conflict-related matters. Although not a burning issue for most, Serbs desire the Serb Republic and links with Serbia, not Bosnia. This outlook was consolidated in an agreement in 2006 between the Republic of Srpska and Serbia. Perhaps surprisingly, but cognizant of wider loyalties, Article III of the Dayton Agreement declared that the Federation or the Republic 'shall have the right to establish special parallel relationships with neighbouring states', albeit 'consistent with the sovereignty and territorial integrity of Bosnia and Herzegovina'. The clause permitted the Republic of Srpksa a bilateral arrangement which could challenge the latter stipulation. For political elites within the Republic, the destabilizing has come from beyond their entity, created, according to a special adviser to the Republic's Prime Minister, Gordon Milosevic, by the manner in which 'some politicians in Bosnia-Herzegovina, including some within the international community, seem to want a "unitary" system of government, not the federal system created by Dayton' (Milosevic 2008).

Continuing Ethno-National Militancy?

Perhaps the most successful aspect of Dayton was its ability to marginalize potential spoilers. With the 'ethno-state parents' of Milosevic, Tudjman and Izetbegovic approving of the top-down deal, it was hard for ethnic entrepreneurs to assert that their national group had been betrayed by compromise. Some Bosnian Serbs nonetheless accused Milosevic of treachery. Fearful of their future in the Muslim-Croat Federation, some burnt their homes on quitting the embryonic entity, to prevent acquisition by Muslims, who dominated the new Sarajevo canton. The President of the Serbian Radical Party, Vojislav Seselj, railed against the abandonment of pan-Serb unity (although Milosevic had been attempting this since the Vance–Owen plan of 1993) arguing, with some prescience, that it would herald retreats in Montenegro and Kosovo (Thomas 1998). Anti-Dayton Serb forces, whilst numerous, were too divided to mount effective opposition. Due to these divisions and Milosevic's increasing control of the media, Serb acquiescence to Dayton was the norm.

There were tensions on the Bosnian Muslim side between the newly-formed Party for Bosnia and Herzegovina, led by the former Prime Minister Silajdzic and committed to a multi-ethnic party, and more reactionary forces which remained in the SDA. Presidential and parliamentary elections were conducted amid allegations of malpractice, with nearly nine out of ten voters backing the overtly nationalist representatives of each side, namely the Muslim SDA, the Serbian Democratic Party (SDS) and the Croat HDZ (Bideleux and Jeffries 2007). Expressions of nationalism were products of a desire to maintain the best deal possible in the new dispensation. There was neither the desire nor capacity amongst former combatants to re-ignite the conflict. The main difficulties lay in the power struggle between moderate and militant nationalists in the Republic of Srpska. Recognizing the new realities of Western involvement in the running of Bosnia, the SDS leader, Biljana Plavsic, moved against those most closely associated with Bosnian Serb aggression, including Karadzic and Mladic, but was forced to quit her party in so doing. Only amid the installation of a government led by the relative moderate Milorad Dodik, accompanied by the sackings of renegades by the Office of the High Representative, did the most militant forms of Bosnian Serb nationalism begin to dissipate. There were clashes between Serbs and the small remaining Muslim population in the Republic into the 2000s and Bosnian Serb–Serbia relations remained close, bilateral agreements signed in 2001 and 2006.

A brief flirtation by HDZ militants to force Croatian secession from Bosnia in 2000–1 ended amid the removal of the political leaders of the nationalist uprising by the High Representative, but significantly, the HDZ had been confronted by 'the indifference or even hostility of many ordinary Croats' (Bideleux and Jeffries 2007: 380). Yet the apathetic response of most Croats could not complacently be equated with support for the Federation. As Sumantra Bose (2002b: 258) – no fan of Croatian nationalism – put it: 'All the assurances and built-in constitutional safeguards of equality, parity, consensus etc have failed to obviate a dominant perception amongst BiH [Federation] Croats that they are the subordinate partner in an accidental marriage which is blighted by mutual suspicion'. Croats and Serbs fear becoming lesser players, as minority groups within a majority Bosnian Muslim state, hence their antipathy towards the bolstering of Bosnia-Herzegovina.

Serbia clung onto the 'Serboslavia' entity dream beyond Dayton, however unrealistic the prospect. Elements of the country remained loyal to Milosevic, and his acolytes continued to dominate senior policing appointments, presiding over a network of internal criminality. Milosevic and his supporters attempted to overturn election reverses in 1996 and presided over an increasingly corrupt and criminal state. The size of vote against Milosevic's party and the extent of mass protests against Milosevic's election-rigging indicated how the President was far removed from a hegemonic position in the Serbian state, and his 'socialist-nationalist' party's fragile hold on expressions of Serbian national sentiment diminished.

Milosevic's final outworking of Serbian nationalism was located in the arena of his first: Kosovo. Having long argued that the region was an integral part of Serbia and abolished distinctive Kosovan political institutions (even though Serbs constituted a mere one-tenth of the population), Milosevic attempted to face down the Kosovan Liberation Army (KLA), which was committed to Kosovan independence. The KLA, which targeted Serb police and soldiers, were regarded as terrorists by the Serbs, to be met with a strong 'counter-terror' programme, which consisted of various atrocities. By the late 1990s, the West was no longer prepared to indulge Milosevic, who was obliged to accept Kosovo as a self-governing entity (albeit under nominal Serb sovereignty) under international protection and was forced to withdraw all Serb forces, or face an invasion by NATO and Russian forces. Kosovo declared itself an independent Republic in 2008, based upon plans for self-government devised by Ahtisaari, although international recognition is incomplete.

Milosevic was charged with war crimes by the International Criminal Tribunal for the former Yugoslavia (ICTY) in 1999, the first former Head of State to be charged with such offences, as NATO bombed Serbia. Milosevic lost the Presidential election in 2000 (the opposition, led by Kostunica, funded by the US) despite his attempts to rewrite the result and defy a general strike. Milosevic increasingly lost control of the police and military. The Serbian authorities arrested Milosevic on separate corruption charges, but President Kostunica (unlike his Prime Minister Djindjic) appeared cautious over dealing with his predecessor's wartime activities, expressing concerns over the likely conduct of the ICTY. With Kostunica's concerns soon being overridden, Milosevic's death from natural causes in the ICTY prison in The Hague left numerous questions unanswered. Little evidence of his direct involvement in the authorization of massacres had been unearthed and his public pronouncements sometimes demonstrated a favouring of a multiethnic Serbia. Yet Milosevic's actions fuelled Serbian nationalism and were at least indirectly responsible for the conflict which followed. An increasingly cooperative approach to the arrest and extradition of suspected war criminals was developing, leading to the incarceration of Karadzic and Mladic, whilst liberalization of the stagnant economy was undertaken in preparation for EU accession. Amid a new moderation, there were only muted Serbian reactions to the arrests of figures prominent in the conflict. Insofar as old Serbian nationalism remained, it was confined to a reluctance to accept the full gravity of what had occurred between 1991 and 1995. Massacres such as those at Srebrenica were acknowledged as wrong, but there was reluctance to use the label 'genocide' to describe what occurred. Amid the zealous criticism of Serbia's modest record in bringing perpetrators to justice, the previous indulgence by the West of Karadzic and Milosevic tended to be conveniently forgotten. Milosevic had been seen as a person to be negotiated with by figures across the political spectrum, from communists who saw him as the only person capable of preserving Yugoslavia (effectively 'Serboslavia') to western liberals who believed that he was less nationalistic than other ethnic entrepreneurs, such as Tudjman or even Izetbegovic.

Maintaining Peace by External Intervention: Sackings, Reconstruction and War Crimes Trials

Formerly warring parties could not be trusted to manage peace on their own and, at the height of external peacekeeping, there was one peacekeeper present for every 67 Bosnians (Cousens and Harland 2006: 121). A 60,000 NATO force eventually became a much smaller EU force, but an external watch remained. Although Dayton had laudable liberal ambitions in terms of its multi-ethnic reintegrationist ambitions, its implementation was decidedly illiberal. A High Representative was appointed by the Peace Implementation Council (PIC), established to oversee the implementation of Dayton. Successive High Representatives exercised highly interventionist powers of interference, increased by the PIC at Bonn in 1997 and thus dubbed the 'Bonn Powers'. The PIC forced through 246 decisions in 1997 alone, to ensure compliance with the Dayton Accord. This cast aside the democratic process, leading to sackings of elected officials for supposed non-compliance with Dayton, or, on a less charitable alternative interpretation, simply being too ethno-nationalist in policy outlook. Whilst the first High Representative, Carl Bildt, was equipped with lesser powers than those bequeathed to successors and thus tended to move cautiously (see Bildt 1998), the second, Carlos Westendorp, was less circumspect amid his 'arming' by the Bonn arrangements, in removing the President of the Republic of Srpska, Nikola Poplasen, following the President's refusal to reappoint the (relative) moderate Milorad Dodik as Prime Minister (Judah 2000).

The Croatian HDZ leader, Ante Jelavic, was removed from the tripartite Presidency and barred from holding any elected post by the third High Representative, Wolfgang Petritsch, for supposedly wishing to secede from Bosnia, after the HDZ moved towards strengthening Croat cantons at the expense of the Muslim-Croat Federation. Petritsch sacked 23 other officials in a single day. Jelavic's successor, Dragan Covic, was removed by Petritsch's successor, Lord Ashdown, who also sacked 60 Bosnian Serb officials in a single day in 2004, for failures to apprehend suspected war criminals and other non-compliance issues. For critics, this was a grotesque and unwarranted interference in the democratic process and negated ideals of self-determination (Chandler 2000). In scorning Petritsch's claim that nationalist officials had failed the voters who elected them, Bose (2002b: 276) contends:

> The sacked officials may indeed have failed to meet the expectations and demands of international community bureaucrats. But it is stretching credulity to claim that they had 'failed the voters who had elected them'. The voters who elected these persons to their offices generally did not do so in the hope and expectation that they would toil to promote inter-ethnic harmony and coexistence.

Political leaders and their parties were elected as ethnic tribunes, an accompanying feature of early consociational years which ought not necessarily to be seen as detrimental to a peace process. If political leaders operated in too nationalistic a fashion, in contravention of the consociational and confederal terms of the Dayton Agreement, they were removed regardless of the wishes of the electorate. The PIC and Office of the High Representative acted as judge and jury, a self-appointed constitutional court. Democracy, Bosnian-style, was hardly constructed from below. The actions of the High Representative showed contempt for the expressed wishes of the electorate. Whilst a greater good was argued to be at stake, external interference showed a marked lack of faith in local electorates and inhibited the reconstruction of civil society. State-building via the establishment of a set of democratic institutions was accompanied by highly anti-democratic decision-making which belied assertions of the integrity and credibility of Bosnia as a nation.

External intervention extended across swathes of reconstructed Bosnia, including its Constitutional Court, central bank, with international representatives present on election, human rights, media, property, public corporations and national monuments commissions. International finance also played a crucial role in the reconstruction, with $5 billion spent in the first six years post-Dayton, although, as Cousens and Harland (2006: 77) note, this was far less than the sum spent on peacekeeping and stabilization forces, amounting to over $30 billion in the first decade of their deployment. The original 60,000 strong NATO implementation force (IFOR) became a stabilization force (SFOR) and was reduced to a mere 7,000 EU special force (EUFOR) by 2004. EU pressure to strengthen the central government led to a modest rewriting of the Dayton Agreement in 2006, at the expense of the Federation and Republic. EU membership was a goal even of nationalist-leaning Bosnian Serbs, whilst also remaining an aspiration of the Serbian government. This aspiration increased the pressure on the Serbian and Republic of Srpska governments to deal more effectively with suspected war criminals.

Although the Dayton Agreement declined to attribute blame to any particular party, the attitude of the West soon changed and a succession of leading figures in the conflict were brought to trial at the ICTY, which had been established by the UN Security Council in advance of Dayton, in 1993. The Dayton Agreement excluded those indicted for war crimes from holding any public office. More than 50 Bosnian Serbs accused of the running of Muslim 'detention' (or 'concentration') camps and of committing atrocities against Muslims and Croats had already been indicted prior to Dayton, another reason why Bosnia Serbs were less sanguine concerning aspects of the deal – notwithstanding the establishment of the Republic of Srpska – than their Serbian 'masters'. However, even their 'parent', who had long abandoned the Bosnian Serbs, was to be indicted. Meanwhile, Bosnian Serb leaders such as Karadzic and Mladic could no longer live openly, but took years to be arrested, apprehended in 2008 and 2011, respectively.

Serb nationalists argued that the ICTY's proceedings concentrated mainly on Serb crimes, when Croats were at least equally guilty of ethnic cleansing as evidenced in, for example, the removal of the Serb enclave of Krajina within Croatia (celebrated as a public holiday in Croatia), and Muslims, including 'imported' Mujahideen, had been equally brutal. Even the Commander of the Bosnian forces for part of the period argues that Izetbegovic was not the western-loving Muslim liberal commonly portrayed, but instead was a Muslim nationalist content with the dismemberment of Bosnia if it meant the establishment of a more Muslim state (Halilovic 1998). This is not, however, an orthodox view of Izetbegovic and the more accepted view is that Bosniac Muslims were caught in a Serb-Croat carve-up of hitherto multi-ethnic Bosnia (Ramet 2005). Two-thirds of those charged by the ICTY have been Serb, although this was broadly in line with the ratio of killings during the conflict. Serb antagonism to the ICTY has been inflamed by the way in which Croatian military leaders, such as Ante Gotovina, a general implicated in the Krajina massacre, have had initial convictions overturned, in that particular case leading to a freeing after less than two years of a 24-year prison sentence. Croatian nationalists rejected the legitimacy of the original sentence and Serbs claimed that Croatian protests had influenced the overturning of the conviction.

Conclusion

Despite acquiring numerous naysayers, the peace process in Bosnia has been successful in preventing a return to conflict and stabilizing a polity which appeared impossible to reconstruct in 1995. The peace process has demonstrated the values of consociation and confederation – unusually used in conjunction in this case – as political tools designed to achieve conflict management. Ethnic cleansing outcomes have not been reversed and Bosnia-Herzegovina is not a fully functioning unitary entity – and may never achieve that status. Ethnic mini-states remain more important than Bosnia as a fully integrated polity. Yet, crucially, no ethnic group is oppressed – or objectionably second class, whatever the claims of some – within the overarching state.

The Dayton Accord's record in preventing a return to violence, facilitating fair elections and permitting refugee returns bears close inspection. Extensive external interference, lacking amid divisions between Western allies during the conflict itself, has been effective in preventing a resumption of ethno-national conflict. If the absence of war is a base aim, there is little ongoing threat of any resumption of hostilities and the crude nationalisms which ignited the conflict have been marginalized. This, of course, owes much to their sating beyond Bosnia itself, with the securing of the reconfiguration of the Balkans amid the maturing of the embryonic states of the early 1990s.

An obvious question begged is whether the success of the peace process has yielded appropriate political arrangements. Consociational structures institutionalized ethnically-based political representation and yet were based on the gamble that ethnic leaders will not be entrepeneurs intent on destabilizing those arrangements. When that gamble failed, the West was forced to seek recourse to the Bonn Powers, a decidedly undemocratic and authoritarian exercise of authority via western colonial governance. Political legitimacy has at times been conferred rather than accrued.

Ethnic political structures are unlikely to diminish identities, but peaceful co-existence, perhaps leading to eventual modest reintegration, incremental consolidation of the central government and the disappearance of ethnic cantons within the Federation are perhaps the most realistic aspirations concerning the post-Dayton endgame. The fixation with maintaining a confederal unity of Bosnia-Herzegovina seems curious given, firstly, the mass secessions from the former Yugoslavia and, secondly, the reality that the Republic Srpska is a largely homogeneous ethnic entity. The denial of full country status stems principally from a desire not to reward the most aggressive ethnic entrepreneurs with the victory of a new Serb state to accompany Serbia proper, but it is difficult to conceptualize the Serb Republic in another way. Moreover, the Bosnian Serb leadership remains far more committed to the Serb Republic than it may ever be towards Bosnia. What appears to drive the political process which has accompanied the peace is fear that formal separation of Bosnia into two component parts will lead to further partition, amid the dissolution of the Muslim-Croat Federation into two distinct entities – ones which may not neatly be territorially divided and which could potentially convert currently mild intra-communal rivalry into inter-state violence over territory. Overall, Dayton has worked as a peace process, but as a political project designed to engender primarily loyalty to a Bosnian state, it remains in the starting stalls.

CHAPTER EIGHT

ETA's Slow Defeat: The Basque 'Peace Process'

It is a moot point whether there has been a peace process worthy of the title in the Basque region. Political violence arising from the claims of Basque independence has been evident since the 1970s, but its near-eradication perhaps owes more to the military and political exhaustion of militant Basque nationalism than any sophisticated peace or political process. Insofar as there has been a discernible 'process', it has mainly comprised efforts to finally eradicate the lingering and increasingly irrelevant threat posed by ETA (*Euskadi ta Askatasuna* – Basque Homeland and Freedom) in its pursuit of secession from the Spanish state and the establishment of an independent Basque state. In tackling the problem of secessionist demands, the Spanish government has appeared less interested in conflict resolution via negotiation than achieving the outright defeat of ETA and its political allies in the outlawed Batasuna party (formerly Herri Batasuna, but referred to in this chapter consistently as Batasuna), an uncompromising approach which appears to carry much favour amongst the Spanish electorate.

After providing an outline of the growth of Basque militancy, this chapter traces the attempts by Basques seeking an independent region to advance their goals by violence and then via Basque pan-nationalism, a unity of political purpose across different Basque nationalist organizations. The chapter explores the limits to this strategy amid the determination of the Spanish government to resist dialogue with what it regards as unreconstructed Basque terrorists within ETA. For the government, ETA is a failed, anachronistic terrorist group which ought to be defeated rather than indulged. It assesses the key unresolved political issues of secession and self-determination associated with the perpetuation of an episodic campaign of ETA violence, one increasingly, perhaps perpetually, infused with ceasefires.

Negotiating the Historical Arguments on Basque Ethno-Nationalism

Limits of space and focus prohibit any detailed examination of the case for a historical Basque homeland, an area subject only to regional particularism from a Spanish government determined to preserve the territorial integrity of the state. In providing a political outlet for ethno-national Basque sentiment, the Partido Nacionalista Vasco (PNV) relied upon an essentialist combination of language and race and the belief in a 'pure' Basque people as cornerstones of the assertion of the separateness of the Basque region. The Basque region's distinct political history was evidenced by the *fueros* (local charters) taxes and exemptions from Spanish military service which the area had once enjoyed. The PNV used its historical interpretations to create the symbols of nationhood, such as a flag and anthem (Mees 2001). Economic disadvantage did not feature; traditionally Basque regions fared well and, as a consequence, attracted large numbers of 'immigrant' workers to cities such as Bilbao, diminishing the distinctiveness of the Basque people. The rapid industrialization of the region and associated economic and social upheaval fuelled a conservative, religious Basque nationalism which also developed via distinctive Basque trade unions. Only later, in the 1970s, did the Basque provinces suffer economically, with high youth unemployment fuelling resentments, but ETA was not formed as a product of economic deprivation or relative or actual structural disadvantage. The mobilization of Basque nationalism owed much more to 'irrational' primordial contentions concerning the differences of the Basque people (less overtly racial these days), distinctive culture and language, which were then extended into political action, accompanied from the 1960s by violence. Although nationalist militancy tends to be strongest amongst the Basque working class, these ethnic markers are not susceptible to economic treatment, explaining the durability of the problem.

Any political recognition of distinctiveness was impossible to achieve amid the suppression exercised by the Franco regime, which prohibited the deployment of Basque symbols or the use of the Basque language. Francoist suppression has been seen as a key cause of Basque nationalism taking a violent direction; indeed there has been an academic consensus that 'Franco was ETA's father' (Mees 2001: 818). If that was the case, however, the offspring has long since been independent of parent, as most ETA killings occurred following Franco's departure and long after those ETA members who had killed during the Franco years had been offered a pardon. ETA was never merely an anti-fascist resistance movement. Spain's transition to democracy and the introduction of the constitution in 1978, with the Statute of Autonomous Communities (the Gernika Statute), failed to impress some Basques, even though it created a Basque parliament and a regional government, police force and education system. The 1978 Constitution was designed to devolve power whilst ensuring the integrity of the Spanish state and prevent pan-nationalist unity amongst other groups potentially seeking statehood, notably the Catalans. The Constitution insisted that federation between autonomous communities would not be permitted. Perhaps paradoxically, it recognized nationalities within Spain, but subordinated these to the Spanish nation.

The Basque claim to an independent homeland has always been further complicated by Euskal Herria's straddling of two jurisdictions, requiring a Spanish–French bi-national political response, and by the contest over what constitutes the 'Basque Country'. There remains dispute between Basques and Spaniards over whether Navarre should be added to Alava, Vizcaya and Guipuzcoa as part of the Basque country on the Spanish side, joining the provinces of Behe-Naforroa, Lapundi and Zuberoa, the 8 per cent of the Basque territory and 14 per cent of the population, under French jurisdiction. The Navarrese, who would constitute 18 per cent of a redefined Basque entity (and 50 per cent of the territory) do not accept the authority of the Basque parliament and the main Basque nationalist party, the PNV is much weaker here (as were the political associates of ETA when permitted to stand), with significant Basque nationalism evident only in the north of the region. The Spanish government's position, as outlined in Navarre's Statute of Autonomy, has been that Navarre's status can ultimately be a matter for the local electorate to determine. A bi-national approach has been evident only in the willingness of the French government to join its Spanish counterpart in crackdowns on ETA activity, effectively removing the Iparretarrak (ETA of the North). The actions of Iparretarrak also irritated sections of ETA, which had used the French Basque region as a relatively safe haven in the 1970s and ETA did not ariculate in its discourse the need to use violence against France.

There is a clear asymmetry in the extent of support for Basque nationalism across the two jurisdictions. Ninety per cent of the 3 million Basques live on the Spanish side of the border and, although the PNV and EA both have sections in France (and Batasuna had a related organization), they are pale shadows of their organizations in Spain. On the French side, Basque nationalism is politically weak, with its political representatives averaging less than 20 per cent of the vote over the last three decades, amid the comfortable co-existence of Basque and French identities, with exclusive Basque identity very much a minority taste. In contrast, an exclusive sense of regional identity is found to a greater degree in the Spanish Basque region than amongst any other autonomous area (Moreno et al. 1997). The percentage of Basque region citizens locating themselves in the 'exclusively Spanish' or 'mainly Spanish' categories remains low compared to 'exclusively Basque' identifiers. Exclusive Basque identification is far from pervasive, however, remaining in the 20–30 per cent category since the mid-1980s (it was higher in the immediate aftermath of the introduction of the 1978 Constitution), but Spanish identification is always lower (Martinez-Herrera and Miley 2010: 20–1). The percentage of Basque region dwellers describing Spain as 'my country' is below one in five (Martinez-Herrera and Miley 2010) What is now apparent is a comfortable co-existence of Basque and Spanish identities amongst over 60 per cent of Basque citizens; a further solid core, slightly below one-third of Basques, identifying exclusively as Basque and rejecting any Spanish identity and a small percentage, invariably in single figures, of exclusively Spanish identifiers (Muro 2008: 161). If exclusivity of identity were the sole criterion, there appears to be little rationale for the award of Basque independence. Given the non-malleable nature of exclusive Basques, however, and their rejection of all things Spanish, the intensity of argument at times threatens to deafen the extensiveness counter-argument.

Military and Political Struggle: the Ambitions of ETA

ETA's emergence during the 1960s came amid the ruthless suppression of even the moderate forms of Basque nationalism that had been exercised by the PNV since its foundation in 1895. ETA's formation from a PNV breakaway group reflected the frustration with the lack of progress on Basque self-determination. The PNV could barely function during the 1940s and 1950s and the frustration at its impotence led to the formation of a youth breakaway group, Ekin, and the eventual formation of ETA. From the outset, ETA represented an uneasy fusion of often contrary impulses of right-wing nationalism, racism, anti-colonialism, socialism, Marxism, religion and anti-clericalism. Basque nationalism originated from a deeply conservative and religious culture and the revolutionary socialism espoused particularly during the 1980s seemed an unconvincing bolt-on. As Sullivan (1988: 270) comments of ETA's and Batasuna's leaders, few 'displayed much interest in concrete proposals to change the Basque country's social and economic structure. Socialism was seen in vague terms as a fairer society and the stress was on idealism and self-sacrifice rather than on a distinct political programme.' The demands of the 'national struggle' always outweighed socialism.

ETA's killings began in the 1960s, the first intentional such action in 1968, and its violence was sustained at a significant level in the 1970s. The assassination of the Spanish Prime Minister Blanco in 1973 was accompanied by hundreds of other killings, peaking in 1980, with the death toll of ETA victims having risen to over 800 by the 2000s. Whilst many expected ETA to disappear amid the amnesties offered as part of the post-Franco transition, ETA merely intensified its efforts to force Spanish withdrawal from the 'occupied' Basque country. Although the largest single category of ETA victim has been police officers, nearly half of the organization's killings have been of either civilians or politicians, with actions such as the Barcelona supermarket killings of 21 in 1987 ebbing lingering sympathy afforded the organization when tackling Franco's repression. Most ETA killings have taken place after the Spanish transition to democracy and two-thirds have taken place within the Basque country. On occasion, ETA has taken its 'war' to Madrid, where the organization has claimed more than 100 victims. Of the 59 per cent of ETA killings which have been of non-civilians, the police service has provided the biggest source, followed by the army (Sanchez Cuenca 2007: 294). By the onset of the twenty-first century, ETA struggled to recruit even from its core membership areas of Guipuzcoa and Vizcaya, where it has been most significant in rural parts (Mansvelt Beck 1999). Within the Basque heartlands, the concepts of *ekintza*, armed actions as part of national struggle, and *abertzale*, backing for that struggle, became routine (Conversi 2000). Participation in that 'struggle' ranged from armed ETA activity to the ostracism of the police and civil guards which formed part of the contest for legitimacy.

ETA has split on several occasions, the most significant fracture being that between ETA Politico-Militar (PM) and ETA Militar (ETA-M) during the 1970s. ETA-PM eventually eschewed armed struggle after merging with Euskadiiko Ezkerra, whilst ETA Militar became effectively the ETA, supportive of armed struggle and backed by Herri Batasuna, formed in 1978 (see Campbell and Connolly 2012). ETA-M argued that only militarism could achieve results, using the slogan 'Actions Unite, Words Divide'. Yet with ETA palpably incapable of achieving its political goals in isolation and probably not in conjunction with fellow-nationalists, its continued existence is under the greatest questioning since the organization was formed. It appears to have reached a juncture not untypical of a small terrorist group where the organization 'exists to maintain itself more than to accomplish its ostensible purposes' (Crenshaw 1999: 34). Survival, in the vague hope of better days ahead, appeared to be its raison d'être by the 2000s.

This notwithstanding, the ability of ETA to endure in some form over several decades surprised most observers, given that its rapid demise was predicted from the Spanish transition to democracy in 1978 onwards (Sullivan 1988). Those taking a longer view concluded that ETA's violence was part of a seemingly unbreakable action-repression-action cycle, but the diminution (albeit not entire eradication) of ETA's capacities has nearly ended the sequencing. Additionally, there is the problem of how to achieve the 'civilianization' of its membership. Those immersed in ETA's armed struggle have known little else. Even a sympathetic account of ETA in the 1980s, which attempted to rationalize the group's armed actions, acknowledged that at times they were perpetuated by individuals who 'continue to fight because they do not know what else they can do' and because they 'define themselves in terms of armed struggle' (Clark 1984: 279). Whilst Clark's analysis did not downplay the political aspects of ETA, this attempt at psychological explanation risks assuming that members of terrorist groups are entombed as prisoners of history or mindset, trapped by prior investment in struggle. It risks overlooking the capacity of thousands of members of armed groups in other conflicts to move from paramilitary activity and demobilize with a low rate of recidivism.

The Extent of Support for Basque Self-Determination

Support for Basque self-determination, as distinct from ETA's prosecution of armed struggle for its achievement, has been consistently high. Most Spaniards were enthused by the 1978 Constitution marking the transition to democracy. The Statute of Autonomy ratified in 1979 put into effect the principles of the constitution, establishing clear principles (and limitations) of devolution for the Basque region. Although there was a three-to-one majority in favour of ratification amongst Basque voters, the victory seemed slightly less than satisfactory. More than 40 per cent of Basques, nearly twice the national average, abstained from the referendum and the percentage 'no' vote was triple that of Spain in its entirety.

The muted endorsement was unlikely to sate the continued violent campaign for Basque independence. ETA was cognizant of the need to respond to the new political context and its diminished allure as 'freedom fighters' against fascism, as Spain democratized. ETA's response was to establish a political wing, Batasuna, to justify continuing 'armed struggle'. Abstaining from 'illegitimate' Spanish and Basque parliaments, Batasuna quickly became a significant force in elections to the Basque parliament. Its first contestation of Basque parliament elections in 1980, at the height of ETA violence, yielded 18 per cent of the vote. However, Batasuna did not recognize the legitimacy of that parliament, viewing the institution as a puppet Spanish-created legislature. Only a full Basque parliament with sovereignty over the Basque Country, including the Navarrese, was acceptable.

Spain's transition to democracy divided Basques between those with a satisfied sense of Basque nationhood, receptive to the creation of Basque political institutions and the liberation of Basque culture (Perez-Agote 2006) and those for whom the Basque Country was still subject to occupation regardless of the changed colonial regime. Basque militants in the latter camp pointed to the sweeping powers of the Spanish police and Guardia Civil, the harsh treatment of prisoners and that the number of prisoners incarcerated for political crimes rose back to Francoist levels within two years of Spain's transition to democracy (Clark 1984: 274).

The ETA (and later Batasuna, via its support for armed struggle) project was designed to combine strident assertions of Basque ethnic identity, of which the PNV was capable, with a harder, 'cutting edge' of violence designed to emphasize that this was not merely a cultural war for recognition of identity; it was primarily a territorial struggle for sovereignty. In these beliefs, ETA was not bereft of sympathy. At the onset of Spanish democracy in 1978, more Basques believed ETA to be patriots than regarded them as terrorists and even two decades later, after sustained but fruitless ETA violence, the percentage of Basques describing ETA members as 'criminals' was low, at 32 per cent (Muro 2008: 161). Yet ETA could not take a great deal of comfort in the apparent continuing ambivalence towards the organization. By 2006, the proportion of Basques who 'totally rejected' ETA had risen from 23 per cent in 1981 to 61 per cent, whilst the percentage offering 'total support' for ETA amounted to only 2 per cent, one quarter of the figure of the early 1980s (Muro 2008: 160). Using survey and electoral data, Sanchez-Cuenca (2007: 302; 2010: 80) calculates mean support for ETA during its campaign at 0.18, where 1 equals full support and 0 equals no support. Whilst ETA could always rely upon an inner core of support and an outer ring of ambivalence or sneaking regard, the perpetuation of its activities had also created extensive antipathy towards the organization, even in the region where many had once seen the group as freedom fighters. ETA was not carrying public opinion in its fight; it was slowly alienating it to an admittedly not negligible rump of supporters. Yet civil society was incapable in isolation of producing peace. Organizations dedicated to promoting peace emerged in the Basque Country, notably Gesto por la Paz (Gesture for peace) and Elkarri (Among all of us), which encouraged people to speak out against terror, but the ETA/Batasuna core was unmoved.

The lack of support for ETA's tactics needs to be disaggregated from the broader political issues perpetuated by the organization. Basque nationalism constitutes a sweeping movement of many hues, straddling a plethora of groups, covering the Right (notably the PNV) and the Left (the trade unions), and is not reducible to formal political activity. Concepts of nation and identity are similarly complex. Although, as noted above, only a minority of Basques see their identity as exclusively Basque, a slight majority of those living in the Basque Country view the area as a nation, a figure rising to two-thirds amongst those 'natives' always resident in the area and whose parents were born in the Basque region (La Calle and Miley 2008: 715). Such figures indicate the extensive sense of nationhood, although they are no higher than those found for Catalonia, where nationalism has adopted non-violent patterns. Amongst this 'native' core, support for the right to Basque self-determination is highest, at around three-fifths, but amongst the overall Basque population it is (narrowly) a minority belief (La Calle and Miley 2008: 719). There is an obvious paradox in that the combined share of the vote of all Basque nationalist parties which support the right to self-determination exceeded 50 per cent at each regional parliament election from the 1990s until the 2009 election, when the Basque socialists of the PSOE won a surprise victory. This suggests there have been alternative reasons for supporting the PNV and other Basque nationalists, rather than the anti-self-determination People's Party (Partido Popular, the PP) and the Socialist Workers Party (Partido Socialista Obrero Espanol, the PSOE) in regional contests. Basque nationalist parties have been seen as tribune parties, better able to represent Basque interests within a regional setting than the 'Madrid parties', and contests could adopt a nationalist versus non-nationalist flavour, particularly in the era of the Lizarra and Ibarretxe Plans. Amongst the Spanish population in its entirety, only just over one-quarter back the idea of a referendum on self-determination within the Basque Country, although only half oppose, with a significant number, perhaps weary of the issue, undecided (CIS 2011).

Support for Basque self-determination extends into a social movement via the trade unions, with the two Basque unions, the large Euskal Langileen Alkartasuna (Basque Workers Solidarity, the ELA) and the smaller and more left-wing Langile Abertzaleen Batzordeak, Nationalist Workers Committee, the LAB), covering nearly 70 per cent of workers in the region. The Basque nationalist Left also has two daily newspapers, GARA and Berria, the latter emerging after the newspaper Egunkaria was terminated by the Spanish state. Combined with sympathetic radio stations, the Basque cause still has sufficient promotional vehicles for it to be a daily part of discourse, and attempts to clamp down on such outlets have elicited sympathy for militant Basque nationalism. Militant Basque nationalism has also mobilized youth support via Jarrai-Haika-Segi, although its street violence (*kale borroka*) has been seen as indicative of the weakness of the 'parent' organization. With the Organic Law on Political Parties outlawing Batasuna from 2002, a prohibition approved by 87 per cent of the Spanish Parliament and endorsed by the Supreme Court, Batasuna has been removed as a political entity and its assets liquidated. Militant Basque nationalism now has four distinct forms of outlet: the use of 'flag-of-convenience' parties effectively representing Batasuna interests; the broader Abertzale Left, a coalition of Leftist groups which has urged compromises from ETA; youth activity, including protests and riots; and ETA armed actions, the lattermost mode of operation now seemingly consigned to the past.

Peace but little Political Process: the Defeat of ETA and its Associates?

The response of the Spanish government to Basque violence in the 1980s was to force peace through strength. Defeating ETA was the priority and arguably the 'peace process' of the late 1990s and 2000s contained the same ambition, but utilizing legal methods. The PSOE government of the early 1980s used the Grupos Antiterroristas de Liberacion (GAL), mercenary paramilitaries hired by the state, to 'terrorize the terrorists'. This state counter-terror was preceded by ad hoc formations of Spanish loyalist groups determined to combat ETA, the most notable killing, performed by the pro-state ultras, being that in 1978 of the ETA-M leader involved in the assassination of the Spanish Prime Minister five years earlier.

Use of the GAL moved illegal state responses beyond the ad hoc and occasional towards state-sponsored terrorism. It was sanctioned by the Interior Ministry and led to the deaths of 67 people, many in France and sometimes unconnected to ETA, between 1983 and 1987. In addition to assassinations, GAL was involved in the breaking of ETA's financial operations. GAL's operations were sanctioned at high levels within the central and regional states, with the Interior Minister, Jose Barrionuevo and the governor of Guipuzcoa among those eventually convicted of authorizing kidnapping and murder, respectively. Run mainly by the Spanish secret service, the GAL's activities were facilitated by growing cooperation between the Spanish and French authorities in anti-terror alliances, although the GAL's activities remained secret for several years afterwards and were strenuously denied by the Prime Minister of the period, Felipe Gonzalez.

Despite the GAL's actions, ETA's rate of killing, at around 40 per year for the remainder of the 1980s, remained fairly constant, and it was subsequently claimed that the organization 'emerged from the GAL period stronger as a terrorist force and probably much stronger politically than before' (Woodworth 2001: 412). This is strongly disputed by Bew et al. (2009) who argue that the GAL altered the balance of the conflict by disrupting ETA and making it much more difficult subsequently for the organization to use havens in South-West France. The truth lies somewhere in between. The GAL put ETA on the defensive and the organization never fully recovered, but it subsequently amply demonstrated its resilience. Ultimately, it has been ETA's inability to shape political agendas that has been its problem and even a higher rate of killings might not have achieved those political ambitions.

With the Spanish parliament having ordered a full investigation into the GAL and the government increasingly embarrassed by disclosures, subsequent coercive activities needed to be legal and open. The second coercive phase actioned by the Spanish government involved the outlawing of ETA associates, with the 23-strong Batasuna leadership arrested in 1997 for the 'glorification' of militarism and sentenced to seven-year prison terms. There has been considerable support for the repressive measures used by the Spanish government. The Association of Victims of Terrorism has continued to oppose any 'concessions' to Basque prisoners, with far greater impact than Basque prisoner representatives in Etxera, which continues to pressure for the repatriation and early release of ETA's members from Spanish prisons. Only occasionally has the Spanish government's attempts to isolate ETA and Batasuna had negative impact. The absurd attempt to blame Al-Qaeda's Madrid train bombings, which killed 191, upon ETA, when it was clear this was not the style of the organization, contributed to the PP's 2004 election defeat.

Public antipathy to ETA was heightened following its disastrous kidnapping and killing of the PP Basque local councillor, Miguel Angel Blanco in 1997. ETA's demand – the repatriation of all Basque 'political prisoners' to the Basque Country within 48 hours – was unrealizable and the wave of revulsion against ETA extended to the Basque Country, where 100,000 had demonstrated against the action in Bilbao, even before news of Blanco's death broke (Woodworth 2001). The public mobilized under the slogan !Basta Ya! (It's Enough Now) and briefly it appeared that ETA might be forced to abandon its violence immediately through the weight of public hostility. Increasingly, ETA's campaign seemed anachronistic and pointless. Yet, whilst the demonstrations were huge, they did not effect an immediate shift in ETA policy. Six more 'soft target' councillors were killed during the following five years and within weeks of the Blanco killing, Batasuna mobilized thousands of supporters in pro-ETA street demonstrations and street violence. Apparent political progress via Basque pan-nationalism (see below) was accompanied by continuing political violence, interrupted by an 'indefinite' ceasefire in 1998 which lasted only until the following year. Batasuna's support rose in the regional election within one year of Blanco's murder.

The first in a plethora of ETA ceasefires in the modern phase of the peace process came in 1998. This was followed by various others, regularly fractured.

In late 2006, for example, a nine-month ceasefire ended with a bomb attack on Madrid's Barajas airport which killed two people. A further ceasefire was called in June 2007, but two years later ETA killed two police officers and in March 2010 the organization killed a French police officer. In September 2010, ETA announced that 'all offensive armed actions' were over and in January 2011, the organization declared a 'permanent and general ceasefire which will be verifiable by the international community'. Each declaration was followed by a demand from the Spanish government for the full dissolution of ETA.

Attempts to defeat ETA have been accompanied by efforts to remove its political associates. Although Herri Batasuna was legal for two decades, the Spanish government has persistently banned the party (a prohibition not replicated in France) since the late 1990s, an outlawing which has adopted a seemingly permanent form since the Spanish constitutional court upheld the ban in 2003. Already, the party had adopted flags of convenience, from 1998 standing for election as Euskal Herritarrok. Batasuna was in decline at the time of its ban. By 2001, its regional parliament vote share was 11 per cent, yielding only seven seats compared to the PNV's 44 per cent vote share and 33 seats. Nonetheless, the ban removed 900 councillors and 63 mayors. Already the Basque nationalist newspaper *Egin* and the radio station *Egin Irratia* had been closed by the state, as part of a broader judicial purge (the 18/98 edict) against any organization deemed as conniving in terrorism. Parties, municipal organizations, youth groups and media organizations were all subject to prohibition.

Batasuna averaged a 17 per cent vote share during the 1980s and 1990s, just more than half of the 32 per cent share obtained by the PNV. The Spanish government's banning of Batasuna (its entire ruling executive was arrested in 1997) was upheld by the European Court of Human Rights and the state was successful in portraying to the public the indistinguishable nature of ETA and Batasuna. There was some overlap of membership and considerable financial links. Batasuna rallies tended to end with pronouncement of support for ETA. By no means all Batasuna voters unconditionally supported ETA, but Justice's (2005: 314) analysis embracing numerous variables suggested that 'acceptability of violent political participation is a highly significant factor leading to votes in favour of Herri Batasuna'. At its electoral height, Batasuna had become the largest party on 62 councils in the Basque region, with Guipozcoa providing particularly fertile territory. Here can be found the highest percentages of Basque speakers and identifiers, each correlated to levels of nationalist political militancy. Unsurprisingly, the party was of no significance in Spanish parliamentary elections, holding only two seats in the 1990s and none, under its prohibition, since that time.

The removal of Batasuna was partially circumvented by the appearance of parties willing to articulate Batasuna positions, although the Supreme Court has regularly disqualified ex-Batasuna candidates appearing on other party lists. The replacement of Batasuna in various guises has also embarrassed the Spanish government as it has merely changed the name, but not the actuality, of significant militant Basque nationalist organizations and electoral performances. The Communist Party of the Basque Homelands (EHAK) initially carried some of Batasuna's ideas and temporarily built upon Batasuna's regional parliament seat share, with Batasuna urging its potential supporters to back EHAK in 2005. In the 2007 local elections, EAE-ANV's (Basque Nationalist Action) emergence as a Batasuna successor led to bans on nearly half of its candidates. 'Legal' EAE-ANV obtained 73,000 votes and 'banned' ANV secured 114,000 votes. A total of 437 councillors were allowed to take their seats (from a potential total exceeding 700). ANV held a majority of local government seats on one-third of the councils in three Basque provinces and the overwhelming majority of Basque councils held ANV representations. In the 2009 Basque regional parliament elections, two parties seen as closely aligned to ETA, Askatasuna and Democracia 3 Millones were barred from participation. The Sortu coalition (itself banned) and then Bildu offered many of Batasuna's separatist arguments, whilst eschewing support for violence. In 2011, the leader of Batasuna, Arnaldo Otegi, received a draconian ten-year prison sentence for attempting to reform Batasuna, even though during the trial he had described ETA as an unnecessary hindrance to the political organization. In 2013, Batasuna announced it was dissolving its structures. Its effective successor, Bildu, had extended Batasuna's traditional hardcore support to an impressive 25 per cent of the vote in the 2012 parliamentary elections and trailed the PNV by only six seats.

External Influences: the Input of the Irish Model and pan-Basque Nationalism

An alternative interpretation of the Basque peace process moves beyond a 'defeat-of-ETA' thesis, instead locating events within a greater voluntarism amongst Basque nationalist militants in shifting towards non-violence. On this reading, militant Basque nationalism has been capable of putting considerable pressure upon the Spanish authorities. Thus Whittaker (2007: 137) claims that 'without the constant pressure exerted by ETA violence, political elites in Madrid may not have felt as impelled to grant concessions to demands for Basque autonomy and for a fundamental restructuring of the central state'. Without attributing such developments to ETA's role, Conversi (1993) claims that an unprecedented amount of devolution has taken place within Spain. Yet the most fundamental restructuring took place in 1978 as part of the democratic transition and subsequent increases in autonomy have also been apparent in non-violent regions, notably Catalonia. The Basque region, with its claims to nationhood, has not always been treated as an exceptional case.

The lines adopted by Batasuna (under its various guises) have been to simultaneously condemn Spanish government repression whilst also presenting the gradual movement away from militarism as a positive choice by ETA, by which Basque independence can be realized under a negotiated solution. Under this portrayal, the Spanish government, beset with economic difficulties, is portrayed as weaker on the political front than in its military aspects, although in both it is considerably stronger than the forces of Basque nationalism. Support for an armed campaign had become a millstone for Batasuna, detracting from an otherwise credible political message concerning how rights of self-determination had been afforded to other nations across Europe in the 1990s and 2000s. As such, Batasuna, in its new guises, moved away from support for 'armed struggle'. Amid the plethora of ceasefires, ETA did not repudiate the idea of armed actions or apologize for the conduct of its armed campaign, but the desire of relative moderates in what remained of its political arm was to move away from violence, which had long ceased to hold any utility. Whilst the organization could still mount significant operations in the 1990s and 2000s, such as the killings of Guardia Civil and of the Head of the Anti-Terror Surveillance Force in Bilbao, political advancement was not an accompaniment.

In calling ceasefires which it insisted were of its choosing and not the products of external pressure, ETA could highlight its longevity as an organization which endured for over half a century despite strong repression and with a hardcore persistently estimated as comprising fewer than 500 members (Sanchez-Cuenca 2010: 76). As such, the move away from militarism has been portrayed as a benevolent, voluntary act designed to further the peace process. A less voluntaristic reading would be that ETA's armed campaign was spent, ideologically and in terms of its utility. An unwinnable campaign persisted and the perpetuation of the struggle had, by the 2000s and perhaps earlier, become more important than the political advancement accruing to that campaign. For the more politically-oriented Basque militants, this situation palpably required alteration.

The movement away from violence has partially followed the model of the Irish peace process and Batasuna and its flags-of-convenience have been fond of the comparisons with Sinn Féin and the (Provisional) IRA, two organizations which, of course, also failed to realize their ultimate political goals, but salvaged much from that failure. Whilst the language was careful, Batasuna came close to disavowing ETA violence and indicated its desire for a non-armed Basque independence movement, in language akin to that used by Sinn Féin in the late 1990s and early 2000s regarding the role of 'armed struggle', before the removal of the Provisional IRA. Batasuna's successors were more upfront in renouncing violence.

In shifting away from armed conflict, the Irish pan-nationalist model, involving the supposed coming together of the forces of constitutional and 'extra-constitutional' nationalists and beginning with Sinn Féin-SDLP dialogue during the late 1980s, was influential in the Basque case. The Basque equivalent was the political alignment of Batasuna and the PNV during the 1990s. In terms of the respective ideologies of the two parties, there was not a huge distance to travel. Both asserted Basque nationhood as a historical right and questioned the legitimacy of the Spanish government to devolve rights to an existing nation under the constitution. Ross (1996: 495) claims that the two parties enjoyed a symbiotic relationship, in which the PNV was supposedly ambivalent about ETA's 'war' and Batasuna's demonstration of a significant level of backing for ETA's violence 'did nothing to weaken the PNV's position in negotiations with the Madrid authorities'. Against this assertion, however, it is unclear what gains, in terms of enhanced Basque autonomy, can be directly attributable to ETA, Batasuna or the PNV since 1978–9.

Moreover, there were substantial differences in modus operandi over the appropriate means of the fulfilment of historical Basque 'rights' between Batasuna and the PNV. The latter was sufficiently unyielding in its rejection of ETA's violence that, in 1988, it signed the pact of Ajuria Enea, an 'Agreement for the Pacification and Normalization of the Basque Country', an unambiguous condemnation of violence supported by all parties except Batasuna. Concurrently, the PNV briefly toned down its emphasis upon Basque independence and criticized other organizations, not merely Batasuna but also Basque Solidarity (EA) (which had been formed partly via a split from the PNV earlier in the 1980s) for their obsession with that cause at the expense of material interests (Ross 1996).

ETA launched its 'Democratic Alternative' in 1995, although this amounted to little more than a statement of traditional militant demands for recognition of Basque sovereignty and the right to self-determination for the Basque Country, the mode of such determination to be agreed amongst Basques. It was accompanied by renewed ETA violence, including attempts to assassinate the leader of the PP, José Aznar and the Spanish King, Juan Carlos. Nonetheless, ETA, already operating in reduced circumstances due to diminished funding from its 'revolutionary taxation' of local businesses, had been weakened by the arrest of its leaders in Bidart in 1992. More significant than ETA's violence were the moves towards pan-nationalism, which began with the PNV's announcement of the replacement of the anti-terror pacts of Ajuria Enea with the PP and PSOE at a 1995 peace conference, which ended the 'political leper' status of Batasuna. The peace conference brought together for the first time the forces of Basque nationalism, as the PNV, EA and Batasuna agreed to press for a programme of self-government (see Gillespie 1999). The PNV was pushing at an open door in aiding Batasuna, which had lost support during the first half of the 1990s.

The usurping of the 'anti-terror' alliance facilitated the 1998 Lizarra-Garazi declaration (often known as the Pact of Estella or the Irish Forum), reached after months of secret dialogue between the PNV and ETA. Basque nationalists were encouraged by developments in Northern Ireland, which had seen IRA ceasefires followed by the inclusion of Sinn Féin in serious dialogue with the

British government, leading to the political accommodation of power-sharing and acknowledgement of the legitimacy of the cause (and possibility) of a united Ireland. The first section of the Lizarra-Garazi declaration analysed the Northern Ireland peace process, claiming that the Good Friday Agreement had highlighted the unwinnability of the war for either side, whilst the second part identified the key issues to be resolved (territorial unity and self-determination) and called for inclusive talks without preconditions and in the absence of violence. The Irish connection was bolstered by the apparent influence of Sinn Féin upon Batasuna, via regular meetings, and the input of Fr Alec Reid, the Belfast Catholic priest and interlocutor in the Northern Ireland peace process, in the drafting of the Lizarra-Garazi declaration. It appeared to have a profound influence upon ETA and Batasuna, Mees (2001: 810) arguing at the time that the 'unilateral and indefinite ceasefire declared by the radical nationalist ETA paramilitaries is hardly imaginable without the strong influence of the peace process in Northern Ireland', sentiments broadly endorsed by Letamendia and Loughlin (2006).

Yet the Lizarra-Garazi declaration was considerably different from the key declarations of the Northern Irish peace process, which at least offered outlines of self-determination and the possible means for their achievement. There was far less clarity over the means of attainment in the Basque case, which, given the ambiguities pertaining to the Northern Ireland process, was quite something. Lizarra-Garazi amounted to little more than a Basque nationalist statement of aspirations for self-determination and pledges to work towards a non-violent resolution of the problem. ETA and Batasuna wanted the PNV to move towards developing political institutions which covered all the Basque area, including Navarre – an Assembly of Basque Municipalities – whilst the PNV, which had prospered until now in the regional parliament and had little desire for a rival institution, wanted above all else a prolonged period of peace (Muro 2008). In shifting towards ETA and Batasuna, the PNV leadership was obliged to deal with internal dissent from figures such as Joseba Arregi, who contested ETA's representativeness among ordinary Basques.

The Lizarra-Garazi declaration extended Basque solidarity across a broad movement of 24 political parties, trade unions and other organizations, to press the Spanish government to acknowledge the right of Basque self-determination and to facilitate its exercise. As the declaration was followed immediately by an ETA ceasefire and with a swelling of Batasuna's vote, it was understandable that there was considerable optimism surrounding the Basque peace process. The avowed willingness of Batasuna to enter dialogue without pre-conditions was articulated by the party's leader, Arnaldo Otegi, who claimed that 'Ireland was a mirror for us and so was the republican movement. Negotiation was always regarded here as something suspect. But Sinn Féin and the republican movement showed us that negotiation did not have to lead to political treachery' (*Irish Times* 1998). The Ardanza (PNV President)-Otegi dialogue was elevated to something akin to the Hume

(SDLP)-Adams (Sinn Féin) talks in Northern Ireland. The latter, however, provided input to subsequent declarations by the British and Irish governments, with additional contributions from loyalists. Basque discussions remained internal to nationalists.

Lizarra-Garazi, an ETA ceasefire and a rise in Batasuna's vote was a promising start for the pan-nationalist agenda. The Spanish government was aware of the changed context and for the first time direct talks were held between the two sides in Zurich (see below). Overall, however, the Basque nationalist percentage vote declined in 1998 to a bare majority of the overall share, the lowest since the establishment of the regional parliament (Bew et al. 2009: 224). More ominously, the ETA ceasefire was fragile, despite local election gains for Basque nationalists in 1999. Amid the absence of serious political progress following the Lizarra-Garazi declaration, the organization was to begin a period of oscillation between ceasefires and violence. The PNV appeared content with its traditional approach of eliciting concessions from the Spanish government, whereas ETA and Batasuna wanted much more radical transformation towards acceptance of the principle of self-determination. ETA's inability to maintain sustained cessations of violence diminished the organization's credibility, emphasizing its weakness. Its return to violence was not, unlike the IRA's fracture, accompanied by 'spectaculars' and indicated the probability of internal friction, confirmed when a group of ETA prisoners called upon the organization's leadership for a change of approach. Arrests of its suspected members continued apace. ETA's temporary returns to violence in 1999 and again in 2006 achieved nothing, whereas the IRA's huge bombings in Britain highlighted to the British government that any negotiations without Sinn Féin would be worthless. ETA did, nonetheless, produce a substantial level of violence in 2000, killing 20 people, including judges, police officers and politicians. The 2006 return to violence followed a formal nine-month ceasefire and was marked by the killing of two immigrant airport workers and the 2010 ceasefire was followed in 2011 by a curious restatement of a cessation supposedly already in place.

In an attempt to re-unite the forces of Basque nationalism and encourage ETA towards a permanent renunciation of violence, the PNV President of the Basque Country, Juan Jose Ibarretxe launched a plan for self-determination in 2003. Launched during a lull (but not a cessation) in ETA violence in 2002–3 and on a high tide of PNV votes at the 2001 regional election, the Ibarretxe Plan belatedly attempted to provide detail for the principles of self-determination agreed across a variety of Basque organizations in 1998. It argued for a referendum in the Basque Country on whether the 'nation' should become an area of free association, an entity just short of full statehood, rather than merely an autonomous region. Under this loosening of ties with the Spanish state, the Basque Country would enjoy its own representation within the EU and adopt a separate judicial system. The Basque Country would hold the option of eventual full secession from the Spanish state.

Such was the radical nature of the Ibarretxe Plan that it enjoyed only a bare majority even in the Basque parliament. Unsurprisingly, the proposals found little favour amongst the PP and PSOE, both parties perceiving the plan as a roadmap to Basque secession. Already embittered over the supposed Batasunization of Basque society indulged by the PNV, the PP and PSOE severed their associations with the largest Basque nationalist organization and agreed, in 2000, a Pact for Freedom versus Terrorism, in effect a replacement for the old Ajuria Enea, which demanded that Basque nationalists repudiate the Lizarra-Garazi declaration. Angered by the Basque parliament's endorsement of the Ibarretxe Plan, the Spanish parliament overwhelmingly (313 to 29 votes) rejected the Basque nationalist approach and a suspension of the Basque Statute of Autonomy was briefly threatened. In response, the PNV attempted to turn the 2005 Basque regional elections into a surrogate referendum on the Ibarretxe Plan, but the loss of 140,000 votes ensured that the proposals, as the outworking of nearly a decade of Basque pan-nationalism, were doomed, even though Basque nationalists (of very different hues) captured nearly three-fifths of the vote. Whilst Irish pan-nationalism could mobilize Irish American help and create at least some interest in the US administration in encouraging British political movement, no such luxury was available to Basques attempting to move an unyielding Spanish government which perceived the problem predominantly in security terms. The only recent external inputs to the Basque conflict have been modest, such as EU INTERREG projects linking Basque territory across the French–Spanish border. Moreover, there is no external broker permitted, given the Spanish perception that the problem is an internal affair solely under its jurisdiction.

ETA's declaration of a permanent ceasefire in March 2006 – 'permanent' in this case meaning nine months, adopted a more conciliatory tone than previous bellicose utterances from the organization. The inclusion of the word 'permanent' in the ceasefire announcement was an attempt to satisfy the Spanish government, which insisted on the term but remained suspicious of ETA's peace *bona fides* even after delivery of the word. What was perhaps remarkable of the growing number of ETA ceasefires, aside from their diminished credibility, was their lack of pre-conditions, such as that of prisoner releases, an aspect that had been non-negotiable (other than in terms of timescale) for the Provisional IRA. The demand for the recognition of Basque rights as a people contained in ETA's ceasefire statement could be interpreted as merely a restatement of a traditional assertion of the need for self-determination. It contained a hint that ETA might be moving towards a more culturally-based, more indeterminate rights-based stance and moving away from rigid territorial demands (already couched in the language of self-determination rather than independence) but cultural autonomy has never been the ultimate raison d'être of the ETA project. In 2004, Batasuna appeared to hint, via a speech by Otegi, in what Bew et al. (2009: 232–3) label the 'Anoeta declaration', that independence was no longer a pre-condition. Rather, peace and prisoner releases were the priorities, with a new constitutional framework to be discussed without pre-conditions. Under the optimistic cultural and political autonomy interpretation, there was an outside possibility that a more explicit recognition of Basque nationhood by the Spanish government (a device effectively granted to Catalonia) might assuage all but the most hardline of ETA militants and offer scope for progress, if accompanied by tangible measures such as prisoner releases. Yet Batasuna and ETA were still insistent on the idea of an ultimate exercise in self-determination – a referendum – which went beyond what the Spanish government was to concede.

Why did the peace process of 1998–2006 fail to gain traction? Mees (2003: 163–70) highlights the intransigence of veto-holders. The Spanish government failed to take the Zurich talks with ETA sufficiently seriously, leaking details, imprisoning an ETA interlocutor and failing to offer any confidence-building measures, contrasting this with the more positive role of the British government in its dealings with the IRA. ETA's lack of interest in compromises short of its full demands stymied efforts to begin detailed negotiations. Moderate nationalists (although it is contentious whether they were ever veto-holders) were fooled by ETA's ceasefires and overestimated the capacity of Batasuna relative moderates to steer the dominant military arm of Basque militancy towards peace. Thus a key problem was that of 'weak politicos', who, according to another study, can only operate effectively in taming militarists when regime receptivity is evident (Irvin 1999). Substantial divisions were evident within Basque nationalism, between the constitutional PNV, ETA and Batasuna militants (themselves divided over the utility of violence) and a so-called 'third space' of leftist groups opposed to any return to 'armed struggle' whilst rejecting the legitimacy of the PP and PSOE.

Although comparisons can be drawn between Basque and Irish pan-nationalism, each attempting to pressurize on the issue of self-determination, there are clear limits to the parallels that can be drawn between the two peace processes. For the Spanish government, structural amelioration of discontent was not a possible remedy, given that Basque citizens were not second class, whereas Irish nationalists had suffered economic disadvantage, which could be rectified via investment abetted by fair employment legislation. The IRA's weaponry and capability, as demonstrated by its bombings in the 1990s, were stronger, as was its support base, giving it more of a veto on a settlement. Above all, however, political dexterity was possible via the creation of new political institutions and power-sharing, whereas the political options for the Spanish government, other than the concession of rights of secession which were beyond its limit of acceptable possibilities, were more limited. Thus for the Spanish government, coercion was preferable to concession.

In his critique of the parallels drawn between the Basque and Northern Irish cases, Alonso (2004: 696) makes the point that Basque nationalism's interpretation of the Northern Irish process was 'based on the two following wrong assumptions': of the effectiveness of pan-nationalism as compensation for electoral and military inadequacies and that the process involved a British and Irish recognition of the right to self-determination, when the reality was different. Yet this is where the parallels between the peace processes can indeed be drawn – Basque nationalists and Irish republicans were both embarking naively (or, more conspiratorially, to dupe some of their own supporters) on a pan-nationalist exercise to make some political progress, even though very little was evident in terms of traditional goals. The other element of pan-nationalism (and Alonso is very critical of Fr Alec Reid's role in facilitating this in both processes) was to give political breadth and cover to armed organizations struggling to maintain their campaign, notwithstanding occasional upsurges. Pan-nationalism did reshape politics as it forced moderate constitutional nationalist party members to choose between their natural nationalist leanings and defence of communal 'rights', drawing them potentially closer to the armed groups most vigorously asserting that communalism and the 'opposite' state forces. It did not, however, achieve its political desires. Although elements within Batasuna saw the Northern Irish peace process as a strategic model to be followed to escape more years of pointless violence, hardliners within ETA were more cognizant of the compromises (and defeats) involved in the process and viewed the value of the Irish model mainly in terms of legitimizing negotiations between a government and an armed group (Alonso 2004).

Negotiations with ETA

Informal and exploratory dialogue (although it asks much of the word 'dialogue') between the Spanish government and ETA has existed, mainly in the form of state-authorized interlocutors sounding out ETA positions, since the mid-1970s. Indeed Clark (1990: 225) highlights ten government or ETA attempts to negotiate or engage in preliminary dialogue between 1975 and 1985 alone. Lines of communication remained open (just), but a series of political and violence-related obstacles inhibited attempts to develop dialogue, whilst there has never been a sustained period of confidence-building measures to move dialogue to full negotiation. Most of the initial attempts at constructing some form of discourse were based upon ETA's articulation of what would produce a ceasefire. Its 'KAS alternative' – a minimum proposal for the establishment of Euskal Herria advocated by the Koordinadora Abertzale Sozialista (KAS), or Patriotic Socialist Coordination, a loose collection of political parties, trade unions, armed groups and other leftist organizations – demanded an amnesty for Basque prisoners; the legalization of all political parties; the removal of the Spanish police force and Guardia Civil; recognition of Basque sovereignty and the primacy of the Basque language; plus a vaguer demand for the emancipation of the working class. Other discussions were based around the amnesties awarded to ETA-PM members as they eventually, by 1982, abandoned violence as a tactic.

Substantial discussions between the intelligence services and ETA took place in Geneva during the mid-1970s and again in 1984 (Bew et al. 2009). The Spanish government, represented by sections of its security forces, and ETA, held further dialogue during the intermittent Algiers process of 1986–9, amid a lull in violence. The PSOE-led government hoped to lead ETA-M down the route taken by ETA-PM with similar prospects of amnesties. With ETA-M uninterested and demanding direct negotiations with government representatives and full consideration of its KAS alternative, the Spanish government responded by declining to locate Basque prisoners in their home region, scattering them across Spain. Attempts to create sustained dialogue have been difficult for a variety of factors. In recent times these have principally concerned the belief within the Spanish government of the possibility of outright victory and the final dissolution of ETA. Moreover, whilst it may be true that Basque and even Spanish public opinion (although the latter is very conditional on the level of violence) has tended to favour a negotiated settlement (Clark 1995; Muro 2008), the PP and PSOE will not win or lose general elections on a successful resolution of the Basque conflict. Arguably, in only one election, the 2004 post-Madrid bombings contest, was the Basque issue decisive and then only in the odd circumstances of erroneous blame, although the revelations concerning the GAL did appear to damage the PSOE during the 1990s.

Other issues affecting the antagonists have included the linkage of willingness to negotiate ceasefires, rejected until recently by ETA because security operations against the organization continued; tensions between the Basque and Spanish governments over who is best placed to conduct dialogue; the fragmentary nature of ETA, often divided between pro- and anti-ceasefire elements and invariably prone to splits and internal tensions; the determination of both sides to control the talks agenda and the lack of credible intermediaries – and the unwillingness of others to put themselves in that position, given that some interlocutors have been killed and all have technically been acting beyond Spanish law (Clark 1990).

Exploratory dialogue was resumed in Zurich between ETA and Spanish government representatives in 1998–9, amid the optimism (on the Basque side) developed via the onset of regional pan-nationalism. Yet the approach of the PP under Aznar was not to deal with ETA as a group which could or should be incorporated into a sustained political process. The PP's outlook was hostile even to the PNV, which it believed rode on the back of ETA violence and whose relationship to terrorism was too ambivalent. (This did not, however, prevent the PP sometimes relying on support from the PNV in the Spanish parliament, in return for more concessions in terms of Basque autonomy). Under Aznar the party criticized not merely the PNV, which he described as a 'fundamental and grave part of the Basque problem' (interview in *La Vanguardia*, 11 June 2000) but any party which encouraged, however slightly, movement towards greater autonomy from the state (Blakeley 2006). Aznar's beliefs were conditioned by two ideas: strong opposition to terrorism and his party's political approach which remained implacably 'Gaullist and hostile to other national-isms within the Spanish state' (Shaw 2009: 50).

Aznar's approach as Prime Minister from 1996 to 2004 was to eschew rap-prochement with ETA and Batasuna and his departure from office did not bring retrospective reassessment of his security-oriented views:

> I have experienced terrorism at first hand. Many of my friends and political colleagues have been killed by terrorists whose only merit was to have a hood, a gun or a bomb. Nonetheless, even in the most difficult times, I have always believed that weakness and appeasement are the wrong choices. Terrorism is not a natural phenomenon: it doesn't happen spontaneously: it's not something ethereal. It can and must be fought using all the tools provided by the law and democracy – and most importantly it can be defeated if there is the will to defeat it. (Aznar 2012)

There was a brief flurry of optimism in the mid-2000s when, following the electoral ousting of Aznar, the PSOE Spanish Prime Minister Zapatero indicated a new willingness for talks, notwithstanding parliamentary pro-scriptions on talking to terrorists. This appeared a departure from the usual PSOE-PP bipartisanship on formal discussions with ETA (the PP was still hostile to the idea). The government and ETA sounded out each other's positions on possible talks (Bourne 2010), whilst the inclusion of the word 'permanent' in ETA's ceasefire announcement in 2006 attracted much excitement, but proved illusory. Yet the resumption of violence did not entirely end a tenta-tive three-way PSOE-PNV-ETA dialogue, which only finally expired during the following year after meandering fruitlessly. In 2008, there was briefly revived dialogue between government intermediaries and ETA, over the arrests of ETA members on extortion charges. Prospects for full talks appeared to recede at the start of the second decade of the twenty-first century, as there appeared few incentives for the government to intervene rather than merely allow ETA to wither. Fewer than 4 per cent of Spaniards believed that ETA's terrorism was in the top three problems confronting the country and only 0.1 per cent saw the issue as the main problem (CIS 2011). ETA did not claim any victims from 2003 until the end of 2006 and inflicted a modest 11 deaths between the end of its ceasefire that year and the resumption of the cessation, on a more enduring basis, in 2010. Significantly, most Spaniards believed that police action against ETA had contributed substantially to the decision of ETA in 2010 to call its ceasefire, with the second largest category of explanation, also highlighted by a majority of Spaniards, being the judicial actions against the framework of ETA, outweighing alternatives such as the significance of PP-PSOE anti-terror pacts; pressure on ETA from the Basque nationalist left (37 per cent of respondents cited these), peace demonstrations (35 per cent), or the Northern Ireland peace process (20 per cent) (CIS 2011). Security-based options appeared popular and useful.

In 2011 the Spanish Defence Minister, Carme Chacon, declared that there was nothing to negotiate with ETA, indicating that the government's main aim had been fulfilled; the gradual stifling of the organization and repudiation of its political demands. However, the prospect of discussions with the Patriotic Left, in the form of the Bildu coalition, which included some of the remnants of Batasuna, appeared possible if the removal of ETA was complete. Yet end-of-conflict measures would be difficult to enact, with only the repatriation of Basque prisoners receiving endorsement from the electorate. Blanket amnesties or individual pardons for ETA prisoners are opposed by a large majority (over 80 per cent) of Spaniards and individual pardons would be unpopular beyond the Basque region.

Conclusion

The Basque peace process has reflected an asymmetry of forces between the Spanish state and ETA, which encouraged Basque nationalists hitherto committed to armed struggle to rethink their methodology. Whilst the influence of other peace processes, notably the Irish model, has been significant, this has also acted to provide cover for potential movement away from fundamental principles. Militant Basque nationalism has made little progress in achieving movement towards acknowledgement by the Spanish state of a Basque right to self-determination or acceptance of the right of the Basque region to form an independent country. Co-sovereignty remains a non-option, whilst full federalism is not used by the Spanish state for fear it would lead to the eventual break-up of the state. Given the considerable existing extent of self-government (devolution tantamount to quasi-federalism), there is little room for further macro-level political manoeuvre. The shift towards softer, neo-nationalist alternatives, grounded more in rights-based politics, rather than the hard politics of who governs, as occurred in Northern Ireland, has not fully developed in the Basque Country. One possible route might be for the Spanish government to concede in principle the idea of self-determination whilst either preventing its full exercise (it will not permit a referendum on Basque withdrawal from the state as it is too risky) or drawing up sufficient caveats for the prospect of Spanish sovereignty to remain likely (similar to the North–South two-state qualifications to self-determination in the Downing Street Declaration in the Irish case).

There may be scope for compromise on non-constitutional issues, such as the 'repatriation' of prisoners, release of those prisoners and even amnesties, although there appears little political incentive for the Spanish government to engage in such blanket measures, and the most conciliatory noises have merely suggested case-by-case reviews. Non-constitutional issues are also dangerous; what would be required of ETA weapons, for example, if the end of conflict is agreed, as decommissioning might look like surrender? Rather than move towards a negotiated settlement, the approach of successive PP and PSOE governments in recent times has been to maintain military pressure on ETA and politically to erase Batasuna, or any other identifiable associates of ETA, from the Spanish polity. If this constitutes a peace process, it is of the remarkably asymmetric variety. The Basque situation never constituted a mutually hurting stalemate, nor even a stalemate. Ripeness for negotiation, let alone conflict resolution, has not been present for years, although there was perhaps an opportunity in the 1998–2003 period. Whilst the Spanish government has struggled to entirely eradicate ETA, it has been largely successful in containing its threat, to the point where the group has struggled merely to survive, let alone mount a serious campaign against the 'occupation' of the Basque Country. There has been scant political encouragement for a more pragmatic wing of ETA-Batasuna to come to the fore, although it should be acknowledged that a more conciliatory Spanish government could not *guarantee* its emergence. The approach of the government has been based upon coercion, not concession. For ETA, there remains the fear that its final dissolution would remove entirely the issue of Basque independence amid acquiescence of what it conceives as Spanish nationalism.

As is common in peace processes, the stark language of victory and defeat is avoided, yet ETA is on the brink of military and political subsidence. The joint military-political pressure upon ETA-Batasuna, whilst effective, has nonetheless slowed the full transformation to politics within militant Basque nationalism, as the claim that a political alternative is available is not easily available to the remnants of Batasuna – unlike the claims readily made by Sinn Féin in Northern Ireland. ETA and Batasuna have slowly been obliged to accept that the considerable strength of Basque nationalism was important in yielding political, economic and administrative autonomy in the Spanish constitution, but insufficient to break the centralist tendencies of a Spanish state determined to preserve its territorial integrity. Basque militancy remains, but it is difficult to see how the Spanish government can accommodate the demand for self-determination, in case this would lead to secession from the state. Whilst there is conflicting evidence as to the precise level of support for independence, a referendum would merely highlight the extent of division on the issue and is unlikely to produce a 'settled will' verdict. The constitutional options pertaining to the Spanish government are limited and have contributed to its desire to 'remove' Basque militancy rather than indulge even its political outworking, as can be seen from the abrupt response to the Ibarretxe Plan. The outcome of the Basque peace process, insofar as it ever existed, is a further dwindling of ETA capacity or a final withdrawal by ETA, with attendant risks of a small level of continuing spoiler activity from renegades for whom the Basque independence struggle and militarism are inseparable.

CHAPTER NINE

When a Peace Process Fails: Sri Lanka

Many peace processes end in failure. This final chapter analyses one such case, the defeat of the Liberation Tigers of Tamil Eelam (LTTE, or Tamil Tigers) in their pursuit of secession from the Sri Lankan state and the establishment of an independent homeland for the 3 million Tamils in the north and east of Sri Lanka, 18 per cent of the island's overall population. The Tamils' political aspiration, based upon primordial conceptions of identity and the assertion of historical right of nationhood, was extinguished as the Tamil Tigers were routed by Sri Lankan forces in 2009. This defeat of the LTTE ended a military campaign which spanned three decades and involved the deaths of over 80,000 people, of whom nearly 30,000 were killed in the final three years of conflict. Sri Lanka remained a unitary state in which the promises of inclusive government from the Sinhalese majority towards the Tamils, the largest ethnic minority, would now be tested. The persistence of civil war from the 1980s until its conclusion in 2009 was juxtaposed with a succession of peace processes which at times appeared likely to succeed. The chapter examines why optimism for a successful resolution of the conflict dissipated amid the destruction of the Tamil Tigers as a military force, accompanied by mass killings of Tamils unconnected to the conflict.

The Emergence of Tamil Ethno-Militancy

The development of armed Tamil militancy reflected a perception that Tamil ethnic interests were under-represented within a state in which the Sinhalese form three-quarters of the population. Tamils were themselves divided between 'original' Sri Lankan Tamils (13 per cent of the population) and ex-Indian (Up Country) Tamils (5 per cent). Tamil feelings of under-representation were heightened following independence in 1948 and the birth of Sri Lanka (replacing the old Ceylon title) and implementation of a new constitution in 1972, with the majority (Buddhist) Sinhalese seemingly encouraged to settle in (Hindu) Tamil homelands. Although the Sri Lankan conflict was not a religious war, the assertion of Buddhism was part of a Sinhalese identity which wished to move beyond the old colonial domination of Ceylon, and ethno-religious advancement of the Buddhist nation tended to be to the exclusion of consideration for other national and religious groups on the island.

A growing Sinhalization of the state, part of this process of assertion of independence, was evident from the 1950s with Up Country Tamils denied the franchise and the Sinhalese proportion of the parliamentary seats increasing from two-thirds at the end of the 1940s to four-fifths by the conclusion of the 1970s (Nissan 1996: 10–11). Ethnic riots occurred in 1958 and the sense of separation between Sinhalese and Tamil grew. Whilst it was claimed in the 1970s by a sympathetic analyst that the 'Sinhalese temperament . . . is an accommodating one' (Jeyaratnam Wilson 1974: 125), the Sinhalese-dominant administration proved incapable of adjudicating competently between the centrifugal forces of Sinhalese nationalism and Tamil separatist tendencies, demonstrating a lack of political dexterity and an inability to create an integrationist project.

Yet, ethnic conflict was not inevitable and most assumptions pre-conflict were that Sri Lanka would develop as a fully functioning democracy. As Silva (2002: iv) puts it in her attack upon 'tired ethnography', the growth of convenient fictions propagated by ethnic entrepreneurs and the emphasis on differences belied historical reality:

> Sinhala and Tamil nationalist historical narratives share a common plot that presumes that the two groups are and were mutually exclusive. These nationalist histories mirror each other in enshrining notions of ethnically pure territory and identity, despite the history of mixed settlement, intermarriage and bilingual and bicultural communities in most parts of the island. This proliferation of ethno-nationalist history has disabled the very notion of hybrid identities, mixed marriages, or multiple stories of a multicultural island.

Whatever the fiction and myth underpinning contemporary enmity, the fear of domination by the other community began to pervade Sri Lankan political life. The Sri Lankan government had talked a good game on concessions to Tamil autonomy from the 1950s onwards, but had failed to deliver, fuelling Tamil resentment. The lack of action was due to ethnic outbidding in the parliamentary arena, the main opposition party invariably also being Sinhalese and tending to be critical of any moves towards devolution as a threat to the territorial integrity of the Sri Lankan state (Meyer 1984). Furthermore, there was growing suspicion of Tamil intentions amongst the Sinhalese, with a developing perception that they wished to make common cause with the large Tamil population in Southern India, rather than foster allegiance to the Sri Lankan state. With two-thirds majorities required in parliament for legislative measures, the Sinhalese, with three-quarters of the population and thus the vast bulk of MPs, could dictate the political agenda. Some concessions to Tamils were made, such as the uplifting of Tamil to the status of joint official language with Sinhalese in 1987, but the perception of second-class political status persisted. Indeed, Up Country Tamils were for decades not considered natural Sri Lankan citizens. Moreover, Tamils were underrepresented in public sector employment, as the state favoured the loyal Sinhalese. Yet economic explanations of the growth of Tamil militancy are inadequate. The young militants who were to sign up for armed struggle were often educated and drawn from the lower middle class.

The political response of the Tamils by the 1970s was to desire their own state and the Tamil United Liberation Front (TULF) was formed in 1976, to articulate this demand. The TULF was somewhat Janus-faced as an entity, harnessing Tamil militancy whilst, as the parliamentary official opposition, reassuring the government of its constitutional credentials. Yet constitutionalism was waning on both sides. The government introduced a draconian Prevention of Terrorism Act in 1979, quickly enshrined into permanent law, which effectively introduced internment without trial and legitimized brutal methods of interrogation (Alison 2009).

The Tamil Tigers and the Conduct of the Civil War

Tamil secessionism began to adopt a military form during the 1970s. Founded in 1976 as an amalgamation of disparate leftist separatist groups, the Tamil Tigers (the tiger label was 'awarded' by the wary Sinhalese) developed into a considerable military force, capable of sustained and high-profile actions. Whilst the Tamils they purported to represent were mainly Hindu, the LTTE was mainly secular and neo-Marxist in outlook. Yet Marxist-Leninist ideas were more influential in terms of organization than ideology, the LTTE's leftist credentials always appearing subordinate to its ethno-nationalism.

The LTTE leadership was drawn mainly from the Karaiya fishing caste of Tamils, rather than the wealthier Vellala caste, but caste differences were suppressed by national struggle. Vellala Tamils were less influential in the Tigers and many fled abroad in the 1980s, but they then formed part of a diaspora prepared to back the campaign for a Tamil homeland. Indeed, the Tigers drew upon significant support from a well-organized Tamil diaspora, with offices in Paris, London and Toronto. Sections of this diaspora operationalized ethnicity as an ideological principle, with full acceptance of Tamil identity only possible via separatism (Winslow and Woost 2004).

Initially, much LTTE activity was aimed at Tamils associated with the government, viewed as traitors, but the range of targets was soon extended and a campaign against the largely Sinhalese state forces began, quickly extended to politicians. The LTTE's victims included the former Indian President Rajiv Gandhi (an act which greatly diminished international support beyond the Tamil diaspora) in 1991 and the Sri Lankan President Ranasinghe Premadasa two years later. The growth of the Tigers as a large-scale force was assisted by severe ethnic clashes in 1983, effectively an ethnic pogrom which followed the killing by the LTTE of 14 Sri Lankan soldiers in Jaffna. The aftermath saw 150,000 Tamils flee Sri Lanka, fuelling Tamil arguments that their safety could only be assured by a separate political entity created out of the existing state. The Sri Lankan government attempted to blame the ethnic fighting upon the Tamils, yet the 1983 clashes consisted almost entirely of attacks by members of the Sinhalese population against Tamils (Manor 1984).

Initially the recipients of arms and training from India, the Tigers later extended arms procurement to the Middle East and other parts of Asia. The LTTE engaged in an explicitly ethnic campaign which denied the possibility of co-existence with the Sinhalese within the same state, resulting in ethnic cleansing. Non-supporters of the Tamils' struggle were also expelled, including over 70,000 Muslims, whilst several hundred Muslims were killed by the LTTE in Tamil areas. Some locations, such as Jaffna and Mannar, saw virtually the entire Muslim population forcibly removed.

Support from Tamils for the LTTE within Sri Lanka was achieved by a combination of coercion and torture, genuine empathy and acknowledgement of the commitment of volunteers, symbolized by the cyanide capsules worn by the organization's members, to be used in the event of capture by the Sinhalese forces. The superior military capability of the Tigers, alongside commitment, ensured that it became the dominant force amongst Tamil secessionists, eclipsing groups such as the Tamil Eelam Liberation Organization (TELO) which was wiped out by the LTTE, whilst other groups such as the Eelam People's Revolutionary Liberation Front were forcibly disbanded. Robberies, extortion and people smuggling funded the growth of the LTTE, providing the finance to develop its arms import operation. Having initially been hostile to the presence of women in the organization, the LTTE's growth embraced both sexes across all aspects of activity.

The military strategy of the Tamils was highly aggressive, based mainly upon attacks on Sri Lankan defence forces, but also utilized to achieve internal communal dominance. Much attention focused upon the deployment of suicide attacks carried out by the Black Tiger section of the LTTE, not least because such tactics were used in the Prime Ministerial and Presidential killings. Totalling nearly 400, such attacks formed a key part of the militia's modus operandi, used on more occasions than by any other armed group. Developing remarkable strength to combat Sri Lankan forces numbering nearly 300,000, the LTTE adopted the size and form of a country's regular defence forces, operating with impunity from the Tamil proto-state established in the north. The Tigers' various divisions included artillery, naval and, in the 2000s, air forces (aircraft were purchased from South Africa) in addition to intelligence and internal security units and an overseas branch. The LTTE's air capability required the Sri Lankan government to drill the civilian population in Colombo, Sri Lanka's capital, in air raid precautions and install anti-aircraft weaponry.

In declaring itself a regular defence force, the Tamil Tigers proclaimed adherence to the Geneva Convention, yet engaged in numerous breaches, including the mass killings of captured Sri Lankan forces. Although the LTTE claimed to wish to avoid civilian casualties, no particular political reason necessitated this and attacks were far from confined to military targets. In

1994, for example, the LTTE bombed a United National Party rally, killing several of the party's prominent members. In addition to the suicide assassinations of a Prime Minister and a President, the LTTE killed 37 MPs, 10 party leaders and 7 Cabinet members.

Although the LTTE established a political party, the People's Front of Liberation Tigers, this was always subordinate to the military arm and folded during the 1990s. The LTTE's political arm was then revived for the ceasefire accords of 2002. This political arm controlled Tamil areas, presiding over autonomous policing, judicial, media and sporting institutions. It extended internationally, with LTTE support networks and numerous offices offering lucrative backing, until the increased fracturing of support following the 2002 ceasefire and then the resumption of violence hastened a trend of proscription as a terrorist group (Tamil fundraisers had already been arrested in, for example, Switzerland during the 1990s). Amid extensive clampdowns and sequestration of funds by national authorities, the LTTE was also condemned for its use of child soldiers, their deployment diminishing in the 2000s amid international protest.

External Intervention: the Breakdown of the 'Indian-Led' Peace Process, 1987–90

Much of the blame for the ultimate breakdown of the succession of peace processes lay in the lack of strategic acumen of the Tamil Tigers. Having captured three-quarters of the Northern and Eastern Provinces of Sri Lanka by the end of the twentieth century and established their own network of control, the Tamils failed to recognize a potentially ripe moment for cessation, eschewing detailed negotiations with the Sinhalese government from this position of strength. The outcome was a turning of the military tide. The Tamil Tigers had long eschewed compromise and the nuances of political agreements, having usurped one-time politically sympathetic groups, notably the TULF, in their bid for outright conflict victory and communal dominance.

From the late 1980s onwards, the uncompromising approach of the Tigers was reflected in its rejectionist attitudes to possible deals based upon regional autonomy and the strengthening of Tamil local authorities. The LTTE showed little interest in compromise, even when the government overcame strong parliamentary opposition to enact devolutionary measures. Proposals for decentralization via under-funded district councils were regarded as adequate rather than as stepping-stones towards eventual autonomy and independence. Tamils highlighted the trend towards secession in other global conflict zones, yet the Sri Lankan government was always unlikely to move briskly towards a solution facilitating secessionism. Even if the political desire had been evident, the territorial division was insufficiently neat to facilitate comfortable separation. Whilst very few Sinhalese lived in the Tamil-dominated northern region of Sri Lanka, the eastern region, also seen by the LTTE as part of the

Tamil state, was much more mixed, constituting one-third of the population, almost as large a proportion as the Tamils. Partition thus risked the ignition of a much deeper ethnic cleansing.

External intervention from India following the 1983 riots led, firstly, to an all-party conference and Indian-hosted discussions between the Sri Lankan government and all shades of Tamil opinion, including that of the Tigers in 1985. By 1987, the numbers in the Tamil Tigers had grown to 13,000, dealing with them was costing a rising proportion of GDP and tourism was in sharp decline. The rise of the Tamils was such that it was claimed that a hurting stalemate existed, although this was a premature analysis of a conflict with a considerable course to run (Wiggins 1995: 49). The stalemate perception arose from the inability of Sri Lankan forces to obliterate the LTTE, as they had pledged to do in 1987 amid a major offensive. It was in this context that the Sri Lankan government was prepared to accept Indian government 'interference', as a broker capable of taming the Tamils, in the Indo–Sri Lanka Peace Accord in 1987.

As a bilateral deal between the Indian and Sri Lankan governments, the Accord gambled that India's 'special relationship' with the Tamils might somehow resolve the political issues at the heart of the conflict. The Indian government had given substantial covert assistance to Tamil militants from 1983 to 1987 in order to help extend its own influence within Sri Lanka, but assumed wrongly that it could now put the violence genie back in the bottle, despite the absence of a clear political programme from the Sri Lankan government designed to address grievances. The Indian assistance for the LTTE, whilst initially also conditioned by human rights concerns, was reckless. Insofar as the Indo–Sri Lanka Accord was accompanied by any political pronouncements, these pledged commitment to a multi-ethnic, unitary Sri Lanka; the status quo in other words. Whilst there was a pledge to merge the northern and eastern regions of the country into a contiguous devolved entity, a proposal in line with Tamil thinking, the amount of power to be devolved was minimal. Moreover, territorial contiguity was to be subject to referendum, in which the people of the north and east could decide their future. With the Tamils only a minority in the east, such a proposal was always likely to be undone.

The Indian Peacekeeping Force (IPKF) deployed following the Accord was welcomed initially by many Tamils. Yet far from accepting a deal which potentially awarded greater autonomy to Tamil areas and made the north and east contiguous devolved Tamil areas, the LTTE, which had been marginalized in the talks leading to the agreement, unilaterally attacked the peacekeepers (and local Muslims deemed as collaborators) charged with disarming militias. The LTTE feigned compliance with an overly ambitious demilitarization programme, which required the decommissioning of all weapons within three days of the peace accord, a process which looked like one of immediate surrender, given that arsenals were to be transferred to Sri Lankan authorities. In return, the Sri Lankan government offered an amnesty and prisoner releases to Tamil fighters. For an organization which embraced suicide attacks, amnesties and prisoner releases were perhaps of less interest than to some other armed groups. The LTTE surrendered only 15 per cent of its arsenal, before quickly rearming in readiness for a new offensive (Bose 2002a: 647).

The scale of the Tamil Tigers' onslaught forced the withdrawal of the peacekeeping mission by 1990, even after the size of the force had increased 20-fold from the original 3,000-strong mission. As the LTTE assumed control of swathes of northern and eastern territory and the IPKF mission was clearly failing, vengeance became common. Up to 8,000 Tamils were killed by the Indians, earning it the sobriquet 'Innocent People Killing Force' (Bose 2002a: 653), although the LTTE–IPKF conflict during this period was overshadowed by the 25,000 deaths in the battles waged by the Janatha Vimukthi Peramuna (JVP) against Sri Lankan and IPKF forces. The failed experiment in external regulation of the conflict ended in 1990, when the Indian Foreign Minister, Kumar Gujral, unilaterally declared that Indian troops would be withdrawn and would never return to Sri Lanka (Joshi 1996). From hereon, the conflict would be conducted internally, although the Tamils would mobilize diaspora cheerleaders for another two decades.

Originally a Marxist Sinhalese organization, the JVP wished to overthrow the Sri Lankan government as part of its 'socialist-populist' agenda which perceived all ethnic struggle as artificial and needing to be overcome by class consciousness, given that the Sinhalese and Tamils were equally oppressed (Gunasinghe 1989: 250–1). Unable to achieve this, the JVP reacted strongly to LTTE activities and developed predominantly into a Sinhalese nationalist organization prepared to confront Tamil militants – effectively a loyalist counter-terror group which killed several thousand people during the late 1980s before moving in a political direction.

The Collapse of Peace Processes in the 1990s and 2000s

For much of the decade following the Indo–Sri Lanka Accord, the LTTE was excluded from attempts by the government to reach a consensus on political change, the Sri Lankan authorities preferring emergency legislation and military approaches as the framework to contain Tamil militancy. A pan-Tamil constitutional front on reform was evident within the 1991–3 parliamentary select committee on devolution for the Tamil areas, but devolution was insufficient for the LTTE, which assassinated the architect of the committee, President Premasada, before the conclusion of its deliberations.

After the retreat of Indian troops in 1990, the Tamil Tigers turned their attention back to targeting domestic forces, attacking all branches of the Sri Lankan armed forces, even sinking two ships in 1995 and downing a Sri Lankan plane, then engaging in ethnic cleansing, despite having called a ceasefire at the beginning of the year. Amid considerable ebb and flow, control of parts of the north of Sri Lanka, including the Jaffna Peninsula, changed hands several times during the 1990s. Occasional truces were also evident, such as the one which allowed Tamil Catholics to participate in a visit to Colombo by the Pope in 1995, both sides anxious to reinforce non-sectarian claims, although occasional sectarian actions, such as the LTTE's attack on the sacred Buddhist relic, the Temple of the Tooth, were evident. In 1995–6, a sustained government offensive temporarily recaptured Jaffna and ousted the LTTE from its urban base in Kilinochchi, with thousands of LTTE members killed in the onslaught. It was a prelude to what would follow in 2009.

By 2002, there appeared to be a more propitious scenario for peace. The United National Front (UNF), led by Ranil Wickremasinghe had won a comfortable election victory during the previous year and had declared itself committed to sealing a peace agreement with the LTTE, even though some of its members had been targeted by the Tamil militants. This was the high-water mark of the liberal peace envisoned by the UNF leadership, based upon international peace brokerage and financial aid, free market economic reforms and flexible governance (Bastian 2011).

Having called month-by-month truces since the end of 2000, the LTTE announced an indefinite ceasefire and allowed external monitoring of its cessation by the Nordic countries in the Sri Lanka Monitoring Mission. For the first time since 1995, the LTTE hinted at compromise on its fundamentalist demands for secession and independence, declaring support for a more limited form of self-government. The 2002 Oslo declaration (Norway took the lead among the Nordic states in brokering a peace deal) committed both sides to work towards a federal solution. Given the Tigers' total domination of armed force at this stage within the Tamil community, having obliterated internal opposition, it appeared to have the capacity to deliver a deal. The LTTE appeared to be recognized as the legitimate and solitary representative of the Tamil people in the negotiations. Heavy casualties had been suffered by both sides, enticing them towards a peace deal. International involvement in brokering peace extended to talks in Phuket and Berlin, in addition to the Nordic involvement. In total, it appeared that the Sri Lankan conflict had reached a ripe moment for peace. Only retrospectively was it declared to have been 'unripe', indicating the unsatisfactory nature of the concept.

Yet dissent within the LTTE and within the Sri Lankan government over the ceasefire was soon evident, whilst the Sri Lankan President was always hostile towards the process and accused the Nordic peace brokers of indulging the LTTE. Soon after the ceasefire, the LTTE's chief negotiator cautioned against a 'peace trap', in which years of talks sap the determination of insurgents to change the status quo (Goodhand and Korf 2011: 1). As a first step, the LTTE demanded government recognition of its administrative authority over the north and east of Sri Lanka, to translate the ceasefire acknowledgement that the LTTE controlled these areas into a more durable political reality – a regional state in waiting. Yet no meaningful administrative authority was ever conceded, the government hoping against all previous evidence, that a large internationally-financed fiscal peace dividend would act as a substitute for political radicalism and movement on sovereignty (Uyangoda 2011). Given that the LTTE regarded itself as an army which had fought the Sri Lankan government to a standstill, political inertia was not an option. The LTTE's position demanded, as a minimum, regional autonomy, self-government and internal self-determination, but in the absence of movement towards any of this, the conflict was likely to be re-ignited (Smith 2011).

Negotiations with the LTTE were likely to be popular only for so long as there was clear political and military progress and unbroken peace. In the absence of both, Sinhalese nationalism and Buddhist religious sentiment, neither of which had ever truly signed up to the peace process, would arise from its latent state. The Federation of Buddhist Organizations turned as early as 2002, before the process had even begun to embed, insisting that the LTTE was a terrorist organization to be eradicated and that no government should negotiate with the organization; that there was no such thing as 'Tamil territory' and that areas captured by the LTTE should be used for resettlement by the Sinhalese and other groups and that Sri Lanka was unequivocally and righteously a unitary state (Holt 2011: 139–40).

The UNF was defeated in the 2004 election and President Wickremasinghe ousted by the electorate a year later. The federal solutions supposedly on the negotiating table were laid out within a unitary Sri Lanka and the extent of commitment of the Sinhalese to federalism was far from clear, a factor overlooked in the euphoria generated by the potential permanence of the LTTE's cessation of violence. Within the government, there was disquiet over the veracity of the Tamil ceasefire, scarcely surprising considering that the Sri Lankan Monitoring Mission reported daily breaches of the agreement within three years, compared to a total of over 100 on the government side during the same period. Within the LTTE, there was a serious north versus east split, leading to the formation of a new grouping, the TamilEela Makkal Viduthalai Pulikal, or Karuna Group, based around the leader of the rebellion against Prabhakaran's northern LTTE forces. This offshoot condemned the LTTE in northern Sri Lanka for ignoring Tamils in the east and accused the northern leadership of child conscription, a charge confirmed by the Sri Lankan Monitoring Mission, which found hundreds of cases annually between 2002 and 2005, in clear breach of the ceasefire agreement, in addition to extortion and the maintenance of luxurious lifestyles. Taking several thousand Tigers with them, Karuna and his Eastern Tigers moved against the Tamil Tigers, working with the Sri Lankan armed forces, whilst also becoming an electoral force. It was the LTTE's most serious internal reversal, a division from which it never fully recovered and was a factor encouraging the Sri Lankan forces to push for final victory.

Breaches of the ceasefire by the Tamil Tigers became even more common, whilst elements within the government believed a decisive military push to oust the LTTE was now achievable. This view was reinforced after the 2004 general election, when the United Freedom's People Alliance became the largest parliamentary grouping, helped by its most prominent figure, Chandrika Kumaratunga, then leader of the Sri Lanka Freedom Party, insisting that tougher action was required against the LTTE, at the expense of the UNF's preference for a negotiated solution. Having nearly been killed by the LTTE and seen the breakdown of its ceasefire in the mid-1990s, Kumaratunga was sceptical of conciliatory approaches, believing that these were interpreted as a sign of governmental weakness and a betrayal of the nation. Kumaratunga had offered concessions to Tamils in 1995, offering to restructure Sri Lanka as a Union of Regions amid indications from the LTTE, which proved false, that they might consider federal structures. Her proposals were received favourably by Tamil moderates, but fell well short of full autonomy and found an unreceptive audience from Tamil militants.

Kumaratunga's more hardline approach after the failure of her 1990s initiatives even involved tactical alliance with the JVP, the organization which killed her husband in 1998, such was her antipathy towards the LTTE (Holt 2011). This approach was supported by President Rajapaksa, elected in 2005 with the backing of Sinhalese nationalist parties, including the JVP and who viewed the LTTE as an unreconstructed terrorist organization whose demands could not be sated short of the secession he opposed. Rajapaksa continued to make common cause with Sinhalese nationalist or leftist opponents of dialogue with the LTTE to defeat the reviving armed rebellion by political and military means.

Civil society was divided over the value of a peace dialogue with the LTTE. Whilst the National Anti-War Front, the National Peace Council and other groups organized peace rallies for much of the 2000s, a combination of forces ranging from Sinhalese nationalist parties to Buddhist monks opposed any return to peace negotiations (Orjuela 2008). Moreover, the hostility of the LTTE to peace groups and assertion that the Tigers alone represented the will of the Tamil people, however untrue, was difficult to challenge. Peace work tended to be swept aside by ethnic impulses, whilst many of the efforts of civil society peacemakers were piecemeal and reliant upon ad hoc funding from abroad, doing little to create Sinhalese empathy for Tamils, beyond sections of the moderate urban middle class and failing to spread Tamil cognizance of Sinhalese political difficulties. A stereotypical perception emerged of members of the peace movement as 'predominantly Sinhalese, male, Colombo-based, Christian and English speaking' (Orjuela 2008: 245), somewhat divorced from the theatre of conflict.

Although the 2002 ceasefire agreement was not formally ended until 2008, by that stage a military push against the LTTE, the fourth and decisive phase of fighting, was well advanced. The last chance for an avoidance of resumption of hostilities passed with the failure of peace talks in Geneva in 2006. The Head of the LTTE's political office, Anton Balasingham, cautioned the military arm against the idea of a difficult total war, but his influence was diminishing amid long periods spent abroad and poor health. Balasingham's stature had waned after he had tried and failed to legitimize the LTTE with the US administration. The United States treated the organization as an unreconstructed terrorist group, not necessarily representative of the Tamil population, omitting the LTTE from peace conferences in Tokyo and Washington in 2003 where financial allocations for peace projects were drafted (Balasingham 2004). This snub led to the first withdrawal from the ceasefire agreement by the LTTE, although full-scale hostilities were still to resume.

In 2007, LTTE casualties began to increase sharply, 2,319 deaths in 2006 rising to 4,318 in 2008 as emboldened Sri Lankan forces, backed by covert weapons imports from China and Pakistan (both later endorsed Sri Lanka's victory at the United Nations) began to press towards victory and insisted that talking was over until the Tigers agreed to disarm (Rifaat Hussain 2010: 408–9). In January 2009, the Jaffna peninsula had been captured by the Sri Lankan Army and the capital of the Tamil proto-state, Kilinochchi, had fallen. The Sri Lankan Navy launched a highly effective blockade to prevent the delivery of weapons cargo to the LTTE, intercepting nearly a dozen major shipments from 2005 to 2008. Although the LTTE offered a ceasefire in March, this, unlike its previous cessations, was an offer borne of desperation not strength. Similarly desperate were the small number of suicide air sorties aimed at Colombo. In May 2009, confined to a few hundred acres of land, and largely bereft of weapons and supplies, the LTTE's remaining 12,000 members either surrendered or, like their leader, Velupillai Prabhakan, were killed by Sri Lankan forces.

The final months of conflict were marked by war crimes on both sides. Whilst the LTTE, in its ever shrinking territorial confinement, used fleeing fellow Tamils as human shields and executed those attempting to leave, the Sri Lankan army made little effort to spare corralled civilians in instances where it suited their military purposes to target an area, regularly breaching their own declared 'no fire zones' and shelling civilian refugees and even hospitals. The army also executed an unknown number of captured prisoners and raped some other detainees. Although 40,000 civilians were permitted to escape after the army's capture of Mullaitivu District, Sri Lankan forces were far less restrained elsewhere.

The Eradication of the Problem? Post-Conflict Sri Lanka

In congratulating the Sri Lankan government on its victory over the LTTE, the UN Human Rights Council endorsed the removal of anti-state terrorism as a justifiable campaign, a triumph of a war on terror and a liberation of the Sri Lankan people, without being unduly concerned over the methodologies deployed (Hoglund and Orjuela 2011). The Lessons Learnt and Reconciliation Commission was established by the Sri Lankan government to assess the latter stages of the conflict, blaming the LTTE for human rights violations and largely exonerating state forces, whose actions, including the killing of civilians, were viewed primarily as inadvertent responses to LTTE actions. A genuine truth and reconciliation commission it was not, and its conclusions elicited widespread international criticism. In 2011, a UN investigative panel declared that it had discovered 'a very different version of the final stages of war' than the 'zero civilian casualties' façade of the Sri Lankan government, instead contending instances of 'war crimes and crimes against humanity' (United Nations 2011: ii). The charge sheets offered by the UN against the government included intentional attacks upon civilians and upon humanitarian enterprises, murder, extermination, persecution and disappearances, whilst the LTTE was accused of murder, child labour and the placement of civilians near locations of military objectives (United Nations 2011: 71).

Between 2009 and 2011, the Sri Lankan government released most of the LTTE members captured during the conflict, along with over 250,000 civilians trapped amid the advance of Sri Lankan forces. The treatment of some LTTE detainees during this period was criticized as brutal, although there was a knowledge deficit. International organizations were denied inspection rights and the UN was obliged to leave on 'safety grounds' in 2008, although Tamils had pleaded with the force to stay, fearing the consequences of Sri Lankan army incursions. Some leading LTTE members escaped to India at the conclusion of the conflict and the possibility remained of their return and re-ignition of hostilities. However, it was difficult to envisage a revived LTTE possessing anything approaching its old military capability. A more pressing issue was the return of the hundreds of thousands of people dispossessed during the conflict. Although Muslims appeared willing to return to Tamil areas, the Sinhalese appeared less keen. Tamils had suffered the greatest displacement, however, even before their banishment in the final stages of the conflict. By 1994, Tamils had already formed 78 per cent of the 524,000 internally displaced persons (Nissan 1996: 27).

Economic growth had continued amid the conflict, with the exception of a brief reverse during the final months of battle during 2009. As such, there was no requirement for large-scale post-conflict reconstruction. In the first post-conflict year, 2010, GDP grew by 8 per cent and tourism rose by nearly 50 per cent compared to the previous year. Military spending increased as the government consolidated its new grip on the north and east of the country by constructing military bases. External investment fell well short of government targets, however, reflecting uncertainty that the political position had truly stabilized.

Military victory for the Sri Lankan government did not lead to the reintegration of the two main ethnic groups. Ethnic segregation was more acutely territorial than ever previously and educational separation was the norm, the rival education systems contributing to the reinforcement of negative stereotyping of the rival community. Amongst Tamils, there was little indication that the constitutional status quo of a unitary state would ever find acceptance. At the end of the conflict, 83 per cent declared this option unacceptable, whereas the most popular constitutional option was the two-state separatist solution (Irwin 2012: 92–3). In stark contrast, 95 per cent of Sinhalese rejected the two-state idea and majorities were also against confederal or federal solutions (Irwin 2012: 92–3). This left only enhanced devolution as a constitutional option, offering cross-community consensus as a way forward, although it would be unlikely to dissipate hardline Tamil sentiment amongst a minority demanding much more. Having defeated the armed wing of Tamil secession-ism, there were no particular incentives for the Sri Lankan government to be magnanimous.

The Sri Lankan President established an all-party parliamentary committee to assess what changes, if any, should be introduced to the constitution. These contained some protections for Tamils, given that constitutional amend-ments could only be made via support from each region of the country, whilst there was also a restatement of language and religious rights and equality, but the proposals were more about continuity than change. Moreover, President Rajapaksa's post-victory rhetoric scarcely promised nuanced recognition of the position of different identities within the state:

> We have removed the word minorities from our vocabulary . . . No longer are the Tamils, Muslims, Burghers, Malays and any others minorities. There are only two peoples in this country. One is the people that love this country. The other comprises the small groups that have no love for the land of their birth. (Cited in Hoglund and Orjuela 2011: 24)

For Tamils in the north, the failure to find a satisfactory constitutional solution remains the biggest single problem facing the country and sizeable sections remain scornful of interim change, even though Tamils overall in Sri Lanka appear almost as concerned by unemployment and inflation. It is in this northern Tamil heartland that the Sri Lankan government will struggle to assert authority, even following the demise of the Tigers. The LTTE established a full-scale alternative civil administration in the north, not easily replaced by forces still seen as illegitimate by swathes of the population.

Conclusion

Writing in the 1990s, one analyst of the Sri Lankan conflict, representing popular orthodoxy, asserted that 'military means will not resolve the conflict: a process of negotiations leading to a political solution remains necessary' (Nissan 1996: 40). Yet the conflict ended through military victory, there were no serious negotiations in the endgame, no development of trust between the antagonists and no political solution. The outworking of the Sri Lankan peace process was a return to hard-nosed realist thinking. If governments think they can beat secessionist insurgents on the battlefield, they may attempt this, without offering political concessions. For the Sri Lankan forces, tackling the LTTE was more akin to dealing with a regular army than a covert terrorist group, a factor which, notwithstanding the strength and commitment of the

Tigers, made outright victory possible, one in which the rules of war were ignored – and the lack of subsequent action against the perpetrators of war crimes highlights further inadequacies of peace processes. From the outset of the conflict, Sinhala-Buddhist affirmations of a hegemonic identity enforced within a post-colonial unitary state dominated government thinking. Met with equal intransigence by the LTTE, which was also weakened by splits amongst Tamils, the outworking of the clash of wills was a military, not a political, denouement. Yet with political imagination and some population movement in the eastern region of Sri Lanka, a secession solution was arguably no more difficult to enact than in some central and eastern European entities.

The Sri Lankan peace process ultimately collapsed after several phases of conflict, due to a combination of lack of will on both sides for a political compromise and government belief in the prospects of outright military victory. The LTTE believed military successes, evident for years against the Indian Army and the Sri Lankan forces, was sufficient to gain its demands. The Tigers failed to develop the political sophistry to match their undoubted military prowess. Having initially considered developing a liberal peace through economic aid and reform, the Sri Lankan government used strategies of coercion, containment and confrontation, having never been convinced of the need for political change or the *bona fides* of the Tigers in terms of fidelity to a sustained process of negotiation.

This Sinhalese victory has seen a dilution of Tamil demands, amid removal of the potential bargaining power (had it been exploited) accruing to the LTTE's armed strength. The Tamil National Alliance (TNA) now articulates demands for federal structures offering full constitutional guarantees of autonomy for the Tamils and wants government recognition of the right of self-determination for the 'Tamil nation'. Yet with the TNA holding only 14 seats in a 225-seat parliament and with the Tamils bereft of military power, there is scant pressure upon the Sri Lankan government to recast a unitary state to recognize a Tamil nation in this way. Such a change would also require consent via referendum, which may not be forthcoming. Yet majoritarianism without cognizance of the need for the equal legitimacy of the Tamil identity within state structures risks a revival of conflict, albeit not on the scale seen for three decades prior to 2009. Swathes of Sri Lankan territory are now mono-ethnic and the historical myth-making, primordial sense of identity, assertions of ethno-national identity and exaggerations of difference which fuelled the conflict have yet to be addressed in any post-conflict process.

Other than via a semi-workable territorial division and the utility of communal autonomy, Sri Lanka ticks few boxes for a consociational deal (see Ismail 2005). There is not a tradition of parity between the Sinhalese and Tamil traditions, at least since independence in 1948. Dominant parties in the Sinhalese tradition are ethnic ultras more than accommodationists. The Tamil political disposition is secessionist rather than state loyalty-driven. The two traditions are very different in population size, and proportionality in government would be so overwhelmingly Sinhalese that few from that community might accept mutual legislative vetoes. There is also the issue of how the Muslim community, divided over solutions based upon regional autonomy given their regional dispersion, could be incorporated into power-sharing structures. Yet if consociationalism is unworkable, secessionism unacceptable and devolution untried, there remains a risk that peace through total victory may be temporary. An insufficient number of Tamils buy the argument that what happened in 2009 was a victory for all the Sri Lankan people, not merely the Sinhalese.

Conclusion

The ubiquity of deployment of the term 'peace process' has led to questioning of the value of the concept, whilst the utility of such processes in resolving conflicts remains subject to much controversy. Realist scepticism over whether peace processes amount to little more than sticking plaster has yet to be assuaged. A world without discord is elusive and peace processes may merely manage or contain conflicts, rather than resolve underlying divisions, with the obvious risk of the re-ignition of violence. Yet the success of some peace processes, including in some of the supposedly intractable cases or vicious conflicts discussed in this book, belies the claims of naysayers concerning the inevitability of perpetual conflict. The success of peace brokerage indicates that conflict management processes benefit from policy learning in terms of negotiating techniques. Greater sophistry in the post-conflict management of hitherto warring groups is increasingly evident. The statistic that, in 31 per cent of conflicts which ended between 1950 and 2005, violence recurred within five years (Mack and Nielsen 2008) indicates that peace is often fragile, but it also shows the resumption of hostilities is a minority choice, demonstrating that peace processes have a reasonable chance of success. Recurring violence, whilst unexceptional, is not the norm and, as policy learning in peace processes develops further, it is reasonable to hope that conflict revivals become increasingly abnormal.

That disasters still occur in peace processes has been illustrated in this book; a failure to anticipate conflict or offer viable peace plans has been evident in all of the case study conflicts. The Oslo Agreement, Sunningdale and Vance–Owen plans, to cite three, were all credible proposals which failed to satisfy ethno-national entrepreneurs disinterested in peace at the time they were launched. Political sophistry cannot compensate for a stark lack of political will, as evidenced in the Israel–Palestine case, or the perception that a total victory may be possible and worthwhile, as demonstrated in Sri Lanka. Violence may also diminish of its own accord without a major process of negotiation or peace deal having occurred, the exhaustion of ETA in the Basque region being an example. In such cases, the hegemony of the dominant state remains undimmed, albeit usually accompanied by limited political concessions.

The will of participants to move permanently from conflict is the most difficult aspect of processes to quantify at the outset of any process, regardless of the objective circumstances associated with the maintenance of violence.

Indeed this book has been critical of existing theories where they do not appear to explain unresolved conflict situations, or rely upon tautological argument. Theories of mutually hurting stalemate and ripeness, in particular, have limited explanatory or predictive capacity, underestimating the ability of conflicts to endure despite an obvious asymmetry of forces and underplaying the capacity of parties in conflict to regularly adjust their tactics. Such theories rest upon cognitive assessments of the position of other parties which may be impossible to ascertain amid the fog of conflict. The onset of peace processes requires rational calculations by combatants that similar or better results can be achieved by non-violence. However, theories of ripeness and mutually hurting stalemate have limited utility in explaining how this point is reached. Such ideas are tautological at worst and descriptive at best, and they tend to be military-focused in assuming a deadlock in conflicts. Where a peace process does not succeed, the moment is retrospectively deemed to be unripe.

The extent of inclusive and viable political opportunity structures, at local and national levels, allowing movement from violence and cognizance of their potential utility, provides a better indicator of how conflicts can be transformed. Exclusion from structures of power, alongside attendant economic inequalities, fuels conflicts and addressing those issues is likely to yield change far more than reliance upon one-dimensional 'enemies fighting to a standstill' stalemate ideas. Far broader and deeper conceptions of the rationality of peace are needed beyond the notion of a military draw or war-weariness. Moreover, perceptions of stalemates and conceptualizations of ripeness are rarely universal. There has never been a peace process unaccompanied by denunciations by spoilers and renegades determined to continue the pursuit of violence in the furtherance of political goals. If, however, the main antagonists are afforded space within political opportunity structures, ultras and militants may be sufficiently marginalized as to offer little destabilizing threat, withering amid the new consensus.

Political learning may make a substantial contribution to the diminution of conflict in the twenty-first century. The nature of conflict has changed from inter- to intra-state, as the demise of the Cold War and inter-bloc conflict led to a proliferation of ethnic antagonisms previously restrained by the dominant class paradigm (Guelke 2010). Fortunately, the growth of ethno-national struggles was accompanied by adaptability amongst peacemakers, which in many cases has prevented ethnic pluralism and arguments for self-determination producing recurring violence. Potential conflict has in some cases instead been accommodated by rights-based agendas and cultural and political recognition. The political apparatus devised to address this more common form of conflict has improved in scope and sophistication. These improvements have been accompanied by other learning, in processes of negotiation, mutual exchange, problem-solving, international peacekeeping and restorative justice.

Whilst 'peace processing' is not simply an exportable commodity with universal application, international growth of conflict management techniques and deftness of political solutions has been apparent. This enhanced political dexterity has been accompanied by a growth in the mission and capacity of the UN, in particular, to implement and build peace. This capacity has been bolstered by the increased willingness of countries to intervene to help restore UN missions where insurgents continue to threaten. Amid the current omnipotence of liberal interventionism, the containment of the Revolutionary United Front and staging of democratic elections in Sierra Leone in the 2000s provides one such example (Dorman 2010). Whilst the UN remains overly reactive and often cannot forestall outbreaks of violence, its missions have become more accomplished in preventing the spread of conflict. The same can be said of regional organizations involved in peace-brokering, such as the EU, Arab League and African Union. Beyond the military, post-conflict political interventions may be decidedly illiberal, as was the case in Bosnia with the dubious sackings of hundreds of elected ethnic representatives, but seemingly justified as proactive measures designed to stabilize peace.

Some caution needs to be exercised in assuming the ubiquity of processes of conflict management and the universality of peace processes. Religious-ethno conflict – that where religious affiliation and aggression has some form of territorial dimension – has expanded significantly so far this century and remains impervious to standard political treatments. Peace processes require at least a modicum of desire for inclusion in a political process by combatants at some stage; not all religious militants have trod that path. These 'glocal' conflicts fuse the global (international religious aggrandisement) with the local (national ethno-religious grievance). By concentrating on the amelioration of the grievances afflicting local religious networks, offering parity and assimilation, it may be possible for peacemakers to defuse antagonisms regardless of the proclaimed fidelity of religious groups to transnational struggle (Murden 2009).

This volume offers some sympathy to the idea of consociational solutions in divided societies. Despite only modest success globally, the short-term alternatives to consociation and pillarization are usually far worse – failures of assimilation, accompanied by ethnic cleansing or genocide – and the number of successful examples is likely to grow beyond the modest number of cases such as Northern Ireland and the confederal-consociation of Bosnia-Herzegovina. In acknowledging division, consociational political arrangements offer a *continuous* management of conflict rather than relying upon a 'one-off' big deal to settle issues. This is not to accept blindly the excessive claims of consociationalists that enforced power-sharing is apposite in the most divided societies, or in cases where ethno-religious militancy is such as to make secure power-sharing merely a utopian ideal. The recent attempts to build power-sharing in Iraq and Afghanistan, bereft of strategic rationale and insufficiently cognizant of the nature of divisions, have shown the follies of such an approach in extreme instance. Consociation has only rarely worked to end any conflict defined as high-level, averaging over 1,000 deaths per year, but relative successes (and no clear alternatives) can be seen in theatres of acute division such as Lebanon and Kenya. Consociationalists are far more realistic than integrationists in what needs to be done immediately in managing ethno-national conflict. The criticism of consociationalism is that its exponents tend to adopt the maxim of the economist John Maynard Keynes, in a very different context, that in the long term we are all dead anyway. As such, consociationalists do not offer a long-term prognosis for the dilution of ethnic sentiment, beyond hoping that elite-level cooperation in political institutions between ethnic group leaders will dissipate ethnic tensions at the grassroots. It may – but when and how?

Consociationalists may be correct that the most appropriate means of conflict management may be through proportionality in representative institutions and respect for communal autonomy. Enforced integration in an immediate post-conflict setting is likely to prove disastrous, with a strong probability of conflict restarting. A belief in an organic approach to reintegration is justified in the years following conflict, but when unaccompanied by a longer-term plan for societal reintegration, does not offer the promise of movement towards reconciliation, instead leading to the restatement of difference. Consociation's own essentialist formulas also need revision. Communal autonomy may be a claimed pillar of consociational deals, but in the cases where it has worked it has already been evident as a 'fact on the ground' and consociation has done little to bolster pre-existing autonomy.

This book ends on a cautiously optimistic argument. It contends that while divisions may be permanent, violence is solvable. Peace processes rarely fully resolve division, which given the existence of different identities, ideas and territorial claims, is unsurprising. What peace processes can (and increasingly do) achieve as a minimum is to place violent conflicts in remission for sufficient lengths of time as to render the problem benign, not malignant. Political learning may make a substantial contribution to the diminution of conflict in the twenty-first century. The nature of conflict has changed from inter- to intra-state and the political apparatus devised to address this more common form of conflict has improved. Where the engagement of combatants is all-embracing, peace processes have grown in scope and sophistry. The commonsense assertion that the sources and justifications of violence need to be analysed before embarking on a peace process has taken root. Brokerage has improved via knowledge of what can and cannot work, based on the adage that the more one studies and practises, the better one gets at a task. Processes of decommissioning, disarmament and demobilization have become increasingly common, overseen by non-partisans. The range of dexterous political prescriptions has advanced in terms of application and has built upon acquired knowledge. Equally welcome has been the increased willingness to offer a more holistic conception of a peace process, extending beyond ceasefires and the 'big deal' towards issues of reconstruction and redevelopment. These have been accompanied by often difficult and sensitive programmes of restorative or retributive justice, designed to heal gaping psychological wounds which have followed the physical damage wreaked by combat.

Societal and political reintegration of those who fought wars has been accompanied by efforts to aid all casualties of war, civilian and non-civilian, via economic advancement, which needs to improve evenly displaced communities. Comprehensive programmes of resettlement, reparation and, via truth and reconciliation processes, acknowledgement of the damage and hurt caused by the conflict, have also been attached increasingly to peace processes. There remains huge inconsistency in approaches towards reconciliation, with some perpetrators of genocide facing the retributive justice of war crimes trials, whilst others evade censure merely by story-telling. Ultimately, the success of programmes of restorative justice depends upon the extent to which they are seen as legitimate by the bulk of the population. A majority of black South Africa backed the country's Truth and Reconciliation Commission (although many Whites and Afrikaners did not) and favoured its approach over vengeance or retribution. International opinion was supportive, believing that anti-state violence had been perpetrated in a just cause. Yet other cases are not so clear cut. Where recent history remains strongly contested, several versions of the 'truth' may emerge, whilst truth processes may allow some of the worst perpetrators of violence to escape censure, El Salvador's truth commission offering one example.

Where retributive justice is the chosen path, international courts need to highlight how and why the scale of ethnic aggrandisement was utterly unjustified and need to be even-handed, the latter a difficult requirement amid the inevitable 'blame-games' and non-objective histories of conflicts which emerge. A major challenge for peace processes is to ensure that they do not offer insulation for ethnic aggressors from the demands of international justice. Ends-based features of peace processes have to be tempered by the need to deter future leaders who might be tempted to engage in ethnic aggrandisement. Ultimately, conflict prevention is always superior to cure. Where conflict cannot be prevented, the ending of violence needs to be accompanied by a form of justice which further diminishes the prospect of the conflict ever returning.

Bibliography

Abukhalil, A. (2007) 'The New Sectarian Wars of Lebanon', in N. Hovsepian (ed.) *The War on Lebanon: A Reader*, Moreton-in-Marsh: Arris, 358–67.

Abul-Husn, L. (1998) *The Lebanese Conflict: Looking Inward*, London: Lynne Rienner.

Alexander, A. and Rose, J. (2008) *The Nakba: Why Israel's Birth was Palestine's Catastrophe and What's the Solution*, London: Bookmarks.

Alison, M. (2009) *Women and Political Violence: Female Combatants in Ethno-National Conflict*, London: Routledge.

Allport, G. (1954) *The Nature of Prejudice*, Cambridge, MA: Addison-Wesley.

Alonso, R. (2003) *The IRA and Armed Struggle*, London: Routledge.

Alonso, R. (2004) 'Pathways Out of Terrorism in Northern Ireland and the Basque Country: The Misrepresentation of the Irish Model', *Terrorism and Political Violence*, 16.4, 695–713.

Amer, R. (2007) 'The Resolution of the Cambodian Conflict: Assessing the Explanatory Value of Zartman's Ripeness Theory', *Journal of Peace Research*, 44.6, 729–42.

Arian, A. (2005) *Politics in Israel*, Washington, DC: CQ Press.

Arthur, P. (2002) 'The Transformation of Republicanism', in J. Coakley (ed.) *Changing Shades of Orange and Green*, Dublin: UCD, 84–94.

Ashour, O. (2009) *The De-Radicalization of Jihadists: Transforming Armed Islamist Movements*, London: Routledge.

Axelrod, R. (1984) *The Evolution of Cooperation*, New York: Basic Books.

Aznar, J. (2012) 'How Dare the World Shun Israel on Terrorism', *The Times*, 24 July.

Baechler, G. and Spillman, K. (eds) (1996) *Environmental Degradation as a Cause of War*, Zurich: Verlag Ruegger.

Balasingham, A. (2004) *War and Peace in Sri Lanka: Armed Struggle and Peace Efforts of Liberation*, Mitcham: Fairmax.

Barakat, H. (1988) 'A Secular Vision of Lebanon: Transformation from a Mosaic to an Integrated Society', in H. Barakat (ed.) *Toward a Viable Lebanon*, London: Croom Helm, 361–77.

Bastian, S. (2011) 'Politics of Market Reforms and the UNF-Led Negotiations', in J. Goodhand, B. Korf and J. Spencer (eds) *Conflict and Peacebuilding in Sri Lanka*, London: Routledge,132–49.

Beilin, Y. (2004) *The Path to Geneva: the Quest for a Permanent Agreement 1996–2004*, New York: RDV.

Belfast Telegraph (2010) 'Peter Robinson calls for end to school segregation', 16 October, available at http://www.belfasttelegraph.co.uk/news/education/

peter-robinson-calls-for-end-to-school-segregation-14978235.html, accessed 26 November 2012.

Belfast Telegraph (2012a) 'Most Catholics would not vote for united Ireland . . . now or in 20 years', 11 June.

Belfast Telegraph (2012b), 'A new headache for the Chief Constable . . . just 25% would urge a loved one to join the police', 11 June.

Ben-Ari, R. and Amir, Y. (1986) 'Contact between Arab and Jewish Youth in Israel. Reality and Potential', in M. Hewstone and R. Brown (eds) *Contact and Conflict in Intergroup Encounters*, Oxford: Blackwell, 45–58.

Bennett, C. (1995) *Yugoslavia's Bloody Collapse*, London: Hurst.

Berdal, M. (1996) *Disarmament and Demobilization after Civil Wars*, Oxford: Oxford University Press.

Berman, E. and Labonte, M. (2006) 'Sierra Leone', in W. Durch (ed.) *Twenty First Century Peace Operations*, Washington, DC: United States Institute for Peace.

Berrebi, C. and Klor, E. (2008) 'Are Voters Sensitive to Terrorism? Direct Evidence from the Israeli Electorate', *American Political Science Review*, 102.3, 279–301.

Bertram, E. (1995) 'Reinventing Governments: The Promise and Perils of United Nations Peace Building', *Journal of Conflict Resolution*, 39.3, 387–418.

Bew, J., Frampton, M. and Gurruchaga, I. (2009) *Talking to Terrorists. Making Peace in Northern Ireland and the Basque Country*, London: Hurst.

Beydoun, A. (2004) 'Confessionalism: Outline of an Announced Reform', in N. Salam (ed.) *Options for Lebanon*, London: I.B. Tauris, 75–96.

Bideleux, R. and Jeffries, I. (2007) *The Balkans: A Post-Communist History*, London: Routledge.

Bildt, C. (1998) *Peace Journey: The Struggle for Peace in Bosnia*, London: Weidenfeld and Nicolson.

Blakeley, G. (2006) '"It's Politics, Stupid": The Spanish General Election of 2004', *Parliamentary Affairs*, 59.2, 330–48.

Blanford, N. (2009) *Killing Mr Lebanon: The Assassination of Rafik Hariri and its Impact on the Middle East*, London: I.B. Tauris.

Bobrow, D. and Boyer, M. (1997) 'Maintaining System Stability: Contributions to Peacekeeping Operations', *Journal of Conflict Resolution*, 41.6, 723–48.

Bogaards, M. (1998) 'The Favourable Factors for Consociational Democracy: A Review', *European Journal of Political Research*, 33, 475–96.

Bose, S. (2002a) 'Flawed Mediation, Chaotic Implementation: The 1987 Indo-Sri Lanka Peace Agreement', in S. Stedman, D. Rothchild and E. Cousens (eds) (2002) *Ending Civil Wars: The Implementation of Peace Agreements*, Boulder, CO: Lynne Rienner, 631–62.

Bose, S. (2002b) *Bosnia after Dayton: Nationalist Partition and International Intervention*, London: Hurst.

Boulding, K. (1978a) 'Future Directions in Conflict and Peace Studies', *Journal of Conflict Resolution*, 22.2, 342–54.

Boulding, K. (1978b) *Stable Peace*, Austin, TX: University of Texas Press.

Bourne, A. (2010) 'Political Parties and Terrorism: Why Ban Batasuna?' Paper presented to the Elections, Public Opinion and Parties annual conference, University of Exeter, September.

Brancati, D. and Snyder, J. (2011) 'Rushing to the Polls: The Causes of Premature Post-Conflict Elections', *Journal of Conflict Resolution*, 55.3, 469–92.

Bregman, A. (2002) *Israel's Wars: A History Since 1947*, London: Routledge.

Bregman, A. (2003) *A History of Israel*, Basingstoke: Palgrave Macmillan.

Bruce, S. (1986) *For God and Ulster! The Religion and Politics of Paisleyism*, Oxford: Oxford University Press.

Bruce, S. (1992) *The Red Hand: Protestant Paramilitaries in Northern Ireland*, Oxford: Oxford University Press.

Bryan, D. (2000) *Orange Parades: The Politics of Ritual, Tradition and Control*, London: Pluto.

Brynen, R. (2008) 'Palestine: Building Neither Peace Nor State', in C. Call with V. Wyeth (eds) *Building States to Build Peace*, Boulder, CO: Lynne Rienner, 217–48.

Burke, J. (2011) *The 9/11 Wars*, London: Allen Lane.

Call, C. (2008) 'Ending Wars. Building States', in C. Call with V. Wyeth (eds) *Building States to Build Peace*, Boulder, CO: Lynne Rienner, 1–24.

Campbell, C. and Connolly, I. (2012) 'The Sharp End: Armed Opposition Movements, Transitional Truth Processes and the *Rechtsstaat*', *International Journal of Transitional Justice*, 6.1, 11–39.

Cetinyan, R. (2002) 'Ethnic Bargaining in the Shadow of Third Party Intervention', *International Organisation*, 56.3, 645–77.

Chandler, D. (2000) *Bosnia: Faking Democracy after Dayton?* London: Pluto.

Chernick, M. (2003) 'Colombia: International Involvement in Protracted Peacemaking', in S. Lekha and K. Wermester (eds) *From Promise to Practice: Strengthening UN Capacities for the Prevention of Violent Conflict*, Boulder, CO: Lynne Rienner.

Chivvis, C. (2010) 'Back to the Brink in Bosnia?', *Survival*, 52.1, 1–14.

Chomsky, N. (2003) *Middle East Illusions*, Lanham, MD: Rowman and Littlefield.

CIS (Centro de Investigaciones Sociologicas) (2011) 'Conflict and Social Problems Survey', http://www.cis.es/cis/export/sites/default/-Archivos/Marginales/2900_2919/2917/e291700.html, accessed 25 July 2012.

Clark, R. (1984) *The Basque Insurgents: ETA, 1952–1980*, Madison, WI: University of Wisconsin Press.

Clark, R. (1990) *Negotiating with ETA: Obstacles to Peace in the Basque Country 1975–88*, Reno, NV: University of Nevada Press.

Clark, R. (1995) 'Negotiations for Basque Self-Determination in Spain', in W. Zartman (ed.) *Elusive Peace: Negotiating an End to Civil Wars*, Washington, DC: The Brookings Institution, 59–76.

Clausewitz, C. (1873) *On War*, London: Trubner.

Coakley, J. (2009) 'Implementing Consociation in Northern Ireland', in R. Taylor (ed.) *Consociational Theory: McGarry and O'Leary and the Northern Ireland Conflict*, London: Routledge, 122–45.

Cochrane, F. (2008) *Endings Wars*, Cambridge: Polity.

Cohn-Sherbok, D. and El-Alami, D. (2008) *The Palestine–Israel Conflict*, Oxford: Oneworld.

Collier, P. and Hoeffler, A. (1998) 'On Economic Causes of Civil War', *Oxford Economic Papers*, 50, 563–73.

Collings, D. (1994) 'Reflections on a Question', in D. Collings (ed.)

Peace for Lebanon: From War to Reconstruction, London: Lynne Rienner, 287–310.

Conversi, D. (1993) 'Domino Effect or Internal Developments? The Influences of International Events and Political Ideologies on Catalan and Basque Nationalism', *West European Politics*, 16.3, 245–70.

Conversi, D. (2000) *The Basques, the Catalans and Spain: Alternative Routes to Nationalist Mobilisation*, London: Hurst.

Corm, G. (1988) 'Myths and Realities of the Lebanese Conflict', in N. Shehadi and D. Mills (eds) *Lebanon: a History of Conflict and Consensus*, London: I.B. Tauris, 258–74.

Cornwell, R. (2010) 'Obama Won't Restrain Israel – He Can't', *Independent*, 18 March.

Cortright, D. (1993) *Peace Works: The Citizen's Role in Ending the Cold War*, Boulder, CO: Westview.

Cousens, D. and Harland, D. (2006) 'Post-Dayton Bosnia and Herzegovina', in W. Durch (ed.) *Twenty-First Century Peace Operations*, Washington, DC: United States Institute for Peace, 49–140.

Cox, G. (1986) *The Ways of Peace: A Philosophy of Peace as Action*, Mahwah, NJ: Paulist Press.

Cox, M. (2008) 'Bosnia and Herzegovina: The Limits of Liberal Imperialism', in C. Call and V. Wyeth (eds) *Building States to Build Peace*, Boulder, CO: Lynne Rienner, 249–70.

Crenshaw, M. (1981) 'The Causes of Terrorism', *Comparative Politics*, 13.4, 379–99.

Crenshaw, M. (1999) *How Terrorism Ends*, Washington, DC: United States Institute of Peace Working Group Report.

Dajani, O. (2005) 'Surviving Opportunities: Palestinian Negotiating Patterns in Peace Talks with Israel', in T. Wittes (ed.) *How Israelis and Palestinians Negotiate*, Washington, DC: United States Institute for Peace.

Darby, J. (2001) *The Effects of Violence on Peace Processes*, Washington, DC: United States Institute of Peace.

Darby, J. (2003) 'Borrowing and Lending in Peace Processes', in J. Darby and R. Mac Ginty (eds) *Contemporary Peacemaking: Conflict, Violence and Peace Processes*, Basingstoke: Palgrave Macmillan.

Darby, J. and Mac Ginty, R. (eds) (2003) *Contemporary Peacemaking: Conflict, Violence and Peace Processes*, Basingstoke: Palgrave Macmillan.

de Chastelain, J. (2004) 'The Northern Ireland Peace Process and the Impact of Decommissioning', in M. Bric and J. Coakley (eds) *From Political Violence to Negotiated Settlement: The Winding Path to Peace in Twentieth Century Ireland*, Dublin: UCD, 154–78.

de Silva, D. (2012) *Pat Finucane Review*, available at http://www.patfinucanereview.org/report/index.html, accessed 16 December 2012.

Dedring, J. (1987) 'Towards Appropriate Peace Research', *Peace and Change*, 7.3, 1–21.

Deeb, L. (2007) 'Hizballah and its Civilian Constituencies in Lebanon', in N. Hovsepian (ed.) *The War on Lebanon: A Reader*, Moreton-in-Marsh: Arris, 58–74.

Dekmejian, R. (1978) 'Consociational Democracy in Crisis: the Case of Lebanon', *Comparative Politics*, 10.2, 251–66.

Deschouwer, K. (2005) 'The Unintended Consequences of Consociational Federalism', in I. O'Flynn and D. Russell (eds) *Power Sharing: New Challenges for Divided Societies*, London: Pluto, 92–106.

Diez, T. and Tocci, N. (2009) *Cyprus: a Conflict at the Crossroads*, Manchester: Manchester University Press.

Dimitrijevic, N. (2006) 'Justice beyond Blame: Moral Justification of (the Idea of) a Truth Commission', *Journal of Conflict Resolution*, 50.3, 368–82.

Dingley, J. (2010) *Terrorism and the Politics of Social Change: A Durkheimian Analysis*, Aldershot: Ashgate.

Dixon, P. (1997) 'Paths to Peace in Northern Ireland: Civil Society and Consociational Approaches', *Democratization*, 4.2, 1–27.

Dixon, P. (2005) 'Why the Good Friday Agreement in Northern Ireland is not Consociational', *Political Quarterly*, 76.3, 357–67.

Dixon, P. (2008) *Northern Ireland: The Politics of War and Peace*, Basingstoke: Palgrave Macmillan.

Dixon, P. (2011) 'Is Consociational Theory the Answer to Global Conflict? From the Netherlands to Northern Ireland and Iraq', *Political Studies Review*, 9.3, 309–22.

Dixon, P. and O'Kane, E. (2011) *Northern Ireland since 1969*, Harlow: Pearson.

Dorman, A. (2010) *Blair's Successful War: British Military Intervention in Sierra Leone*, Aldershot: Ashgate.

Downs, A. (1957) *An Economic Theory of Democracy*, New York: Harper.

Dowty, A. (2008) *Israel/Palestine*, Cambridge: Polity.

Doyle, M. and Sambanis, N. (2000) 'International Peacebuilding: a Theoretical and Quantitative Analysis', *American Political Science Review*, 94.4, 779–801.

du Toit, P. (2003) 'Rules and Procedures for Negotiated Peacemaking', in J. Darby and R. Mac Ginty (eds) *Contemporary Peacemaking: Conflict, Violence and Peace Processes*, Basingstoke: Macmillan, 65–76.

Dunning, T. (2011) 'Fighting and Voting: Violent Conflict and Electoral Politics', *Journal of Conflict Resolution*, 55.3, 327–39.

Durch, W. (2006) 'Are We Learning Yet? The Long Road to Applying Best Practices', in W. Durch (ed.) *Twenty-First Century Peace Operations*, Washington, DC: United States Institute for Peace, 573–602.

Durch, W. and Berkman, T. (2006) 'Restoring and Maintaining Peace: What We Know So Far', in W. Durch (ed.) *Twenty-First Century Peace Operations*, Washington, DC: United States Institute for Peace, 1–48.

Duyvesteyn, I. (2012) 'How New is the New Terrorism?' in J. Horgan and K. Braddock (eds) *Terrorism Studies: A Reader*, London: Routledge, 27–40.

el-Hoss, S. (1994) 'Prospective Change in Lebanon', in D. Collings (ed.) *Peace for Lebanon: From War to Reconstruction*, London: Lynne Rienner, 249–58.

English, R. (2004) *Armed Struggle: the History of the IRA*, London: Pan.

English, R. (2009) *Terrorism: How to Respond*, Oxford: Oxford University Press.

Esman, M.J. (2004) *An Introduction to Ethnic Conflict*, Cambridge: Polity.

Evans, J. (2010) 'Speech to the Worshipful Company of Security Professionals', London, 16 September, available at http://www.telegraph.co.uk/news/uknews/terrorism-in-the-uk/8008252/Jonathan-Evans-terrorism-speech.html, accessed 18 December 2012.

Evans, J. and Tonge, J. (2012) 'Menace without Mandate? Is There any Sympathy for Dissident Irish Republicanism in Northern Ireland?', *Terrorism and Political Violence*, 24, 1–18.

Evans, J. and Tonge, J. (2013a) 'From Abstentionism to Enthusiasm: Sinn Féin,

Nationalist Electors and Support for Devolved Power-Sharing in Northern Ireland', *Irish Political Studies*, 28.1, 39–57.

Evans, J. and Tonge, J. (2013b) 'Catholic, Irish and Nationalist: Evaluating the Importance of Ethno-National and Ethno-Religious Variables in Determining Nationalist Political Allegiance in Northern Ireland', *Nations and Nationalism*, 19.2, 357–75.

Everts, P. (1973) 'Developments and Trends in Peace and Conflict Research: 1965–1971', in *Proceedings of the IPRA 4th General Conference*, Oslo: IPRA.

Falk, R. and Bali, A. (2007) 'International Law at the Vanishing Point', in N. Hovsepian (ed.) *The War on Lebanon: A Reader*, Moreton-in-Marsh: Arris, 208–24.

Farha, M. (2009) 'Demographic Dilemmas', in B. Rubin (ed.) *Lebanon: Liberation, Conflict and Crisis*, Basingstoke: Palgrave Macmillan.

Finkelstein, N. (2003) *Image and Reality of the Israel–Palestine Conflict*, London: Verso.

Finlay, A. (2011) *Governing Ethnic Conflict: Consociation, Identity and the Price of Peace*, London: Routledge.

Frampton, M. (2009) *The Long March: The Political Strategy of Sinn Féin 1981–2007*, Basingstoke: Palgrave.

Frangieh, S. (2004) 'Redressing Syrian–Lebanese Relations', in N. Salam (ed.) *Options for Lebanon*, London: I.B. Tauris, 97–116.

Fraser, T. (2008) *The Arab–Israeli Conflict*, Basingstoke: Palgrave Macmillan.

Frisch, H. (2005) 'Has the Israeli–Palestinian Conflict become Islamic? Fatah, Islam and the Al-Aqsa Martyrs' Brigades', *Terrorism and Political Violence*, 17, 391–406.

Frisch, H. (2006) 'Motivation or Capabilities? Israeli Counterterrorism against Palestinian Suicide Bombings and Violence', *Journal of Strategic Studies*, 29.5, 643–69.

Galtung, J. (1969) 'Violence, Peace and Peace Research', *Journal of Peace Research*, 18.3, 167–91.

Galtung, J. (1971) 'The Middle East and the Theory of Conflict', *Journal of Peace Research*, 8.3, 173–206.

Galtung, J. (1975) 'International Programs of Behavioural Science: Research in Human Survival', in J. Galtung (ed.) *Peace: Research, Education, Action. Essays in Peace Research Vol. 1*, Copenhagen: Ejlers, 167–87.

Galtung, J. (1985) 'Twenty-Five Years of Peace Research: Ten Challenges and Some Responses', *Journal of Peace Research*, 22.2, 141–58.

Galtung, J. (1990) 'Cultural Violence', *Journal of Peace Research*, 27.3, 291–305.

Gamba, A. (2003) 'Managing Violence: Disarmament and Demobilisation', in J. Darby and R. Mac Ginty (eds) *Contemporary Peacemaking: Conflict, Violence and Peace Processes*, Basingstoke: Palgrave.

Gambill, G. (2009) 'Islamist Groups in Lebanon', in B. Rubin (ed.) *Lebanon: Liberation, Conflict and Crisis*, Basingstoke: Palgrave Macmillan.

Geslin, L. (2006) 'Dix ans après Dayton: la Bosnie-Herzegovine a l'heure du bilan', *Confluences Mediterranee*, 1.56, 173–82.

Geyer, R. and Rihani, S. (2010) *Complexity and Public Policy*, London: Routledge.

Gibson, J. (2004) *Overcoming Apartheid: Can Truth Reconcile a Divided Nation?* New York: Russell Sage Foundation.

Gibson, J. (2006) 'The Contributions of Truth to Reconciliation: Lessons from South Africa', *Journal of Conflict Resolution*, 50.3, 409–32.

Gilbert, M. (2007) *The Routledge Atlas of the Arab–Israeli Conflict*, London: Routledge.

Gillespie, G. (1998) The Sunningdale Agreement: Lost Opportunity or an Agreement Too Far? *Irish Political Studies*, 13, 100–14.

Gillespie, R. (1999) 'Peace Moves in the Basque Country', *Journal of Southern Europe and the Balkans*, 1.2, 119–36.

Glenny, M. (1996) *The Fall of Yugoslavia*, London: Penguin.

Goodhand, J. and Korf, B. (2011) 'Caught in the Peace Trap? On the Illiberal Consequences of Liberal Peace in South Africa', in J. Goodhand, B. Korf and J. Spencer (eds) *Conflict and Peacebuilding in Sri Lanka*, London: Routledge, 1–15.

Gordon, D. (1980) *Lebanon: The Fragmented Nation*, London: Croom Helm.

Gordon, N. (2008) *Israel's Occupation*, Berkeley, CA: University of California Press.

Gormley-Heenan, C. and Byrne, J. (2012) 'The Problem with Northern Ireland's Peace Walls', *Political Insight*, December, 4–7.

Gow, J. (1997) *Triumph of the Lack of Will: International Diplomacy and the Yugoslav War*, New York: Columbia University Press.

Gowan, P. (1999) 'Placing Serbia in Context', *Journal of Southern Europe and the Balkans*, 1.2, 171–82.

Greenhill, K. and Major, S. (2006–7) 'The Perils of Profiling: Civil War Spoilers and the Collapse of Intrastate Peace Accords', *International Security*, 31.3, 7–40.

Guelke, A. (2001) 'Northern Ireland: International and Island Status', in J. McGarry (ed.) *Northern Ireland and the Divided World*, Oxford: Oxford University Press, 228–52.

Guelke, A. (2003) 'Negotiations and Peace Processes', in J. Darby and R. Mac Ginty (eds) *Contemporary Peace Making: Conflict, Violence and Peace Processes*, Basingstoke: Macmillan, 53–64.

Guelke, A. (ed.) (2010) *The Challenges of Ethno-Nationalism: Case Studies in Identity Politics*, Basingstoke: Palgrave Macmillan.

Gunasinghe, N. (1989) 'Ethnic Conflict in Sri Lanka: Perceptions and Solutions', in H. Alavi and J. Harriss (eds) *Sociology of Developing Societies: South Asia*, Basingstoke: Macmillan, 247–55.

Gurr, T. (1970) *Why Men Rebel*, Princeton, NJ: Princeton University Press.

Gurr, T. (1993) *Minorities at Risk: A Global View of Ethnopolitical Conflict*, Washington, DC: United States Institute for Peace.

Gurr, T. (1995) 'Transforming Ethnopolitical Conflicts: Exit, Autonomy or Access?' in K. Rupesinghe (ed.) *Conflict Transformation*, London: Macmillan.

Haass, R. (1988) 'Ripeness and the Settlement of International Disputes', *Survival*, 30.3, 232–51.

Hadden, T. (2005) 'Integration and Autonomy: Minority Rights and Political Accommodation', in I. O'Flynn and D. Horowitz (eds) *Power Sharing: New Challenges for Divided Societies*, London: Pluto.

Hain, P. (2012) *Outside In*, London: Biteback.

Ha'ivri, D. (2010) Interview, available at http://arielzellman.wordpress.com/2010/10/11/interview-with-david-haivri-shomron-spokesman/, accessed 21 October 2013.

Halilovic, S. (1998) *Lukavia Strategija*, Sarajevo: Matica.

Hamdan, O. (2011) 'The Palestinian Cause Has Been Betrayed. But No More', *The Guardian*, 26 January.

Harbom, L. and Wallensteen, P. (2010) 'Armed Conflicts, 1946–2009', *Journal of Peace Research*, 47.4, 501–9.

Harbom, L., Hogbladh, S. and Wallensteen, P. (2006) 'Armed Conflict and Peace Agreements', *Journal of Peace Research*, 43.5, 617–31.

Harik, J. (2005) *Hezbollah: The Changing Face of Terrorism*, London: I.B. Tauris.

Harik, J. (2010) 'Force of Arms and Hizbullah's Staying Power in Precarious Lebanon', in K. Mulaj (ed.) *Violent Non-State Actors in World Politics*, London: Hurst, 137–56.

Harris, W. (1997) *Faces of Lebanon: Sects, Wars and Global Extensions*, Princeton, NJ: Markus Wiener.

Harris, W. (2007) 'Lebanon's Roller Coaster Ride', in B. Rubin (ed.) *Lebanon: Liberation, Conflict and Crisis*, Basingstoke: Palgrave Macmillan, 63–82.

Hayes, B. and McAllister, I. (2001) 'Who Voted for Peace? Public Support for the 1998 Northern Ireland Agreement', *Irish Political Studies*, 16.1, 73–93.

Hayes, B. and McAllister, I. (2013) *Politics and Society in Northern Ireland over Half a Century*, Manchester: Manchester University Press.

Helmick, R. (1988) 'Internal Lebanese Politics: The Lebanese Front and Forces', in H. Barakat (ed.) *Toward a Viable Lebanon*, London: Croom Helm, 306–23.

Heraclides, A. (1998) 'The Ending of Unending Conflicts: Separatist Wars', *Millennium*, 26.3, 679–708.

Herman, E. and Peterson, D. (2010) *The Politics of Genocide*, New York: Monthly Review Press.

Hewstone, M., Cairns, E., Voci, A., Hamberger, J. and Niens, U. (2006) 'Intergroup Contact, Forgiveness and Experience of "The Troubles" in Northern Ireland', *Journal of Social Issues*, 62.1, 99–120.

Hiro, D. (1993) *Lebanon: Fire and Embers: A History of the Lebanese Civil War*, London: Weidenfeld and Nicolson.

Hoglund, K. and Orjuela, C. (2011) 'Winning the Peace: Conflict Prevention after a Victor's Peace in Sri Lanka', *Contemporary Social Science*, 6.1, 19–37.

Holmes, M., Gutierrez de Pineres, S. and Curtin, K. (2007) 'A Subnational Study of Insurgency: FARC Violence in the 1990s', *Studies in Conflict and Terrorism*, 30, 249–65.

Holt, S. (2011) *Aid, Peacebuilding and the Resurgence of War: Buying Time in Sri Lanka*, Basingstoke: Macmillan.

Horgan, J. (2013) *Divided We Stand: The Strategy and Psychology of Ireland's Dissident Terrorists*, Oxford: Oxford University Press.

Horgan, J. and Gill, P. (2011) 'Who Are the Dissidents? An Introduction to the ICST Violent Dissident Republican Project', in P. Currie and M. Taylor (eds) *Dissident Irish Republicanism*, London: Continuum, 43–64.

Horgan, J. and Morrison, J. (2011) 'Here to Stay? The Rising Threat of Dissident Republicanism in Northern Ireland', *Terrorism and Political Violence*, 23.4, 642–69.

Horowitz, D. (1985) *Ethnic Groups in Conflict*, Berkeley, CA: University of California Press.

Horowitz, D. (2001) 'The Northern Ireland Agreement: Clear, Consociational and Risky', in J. McGarry (ed.) *Northern Ireland and the Divided World: Post Agreement Northern Ireland in Comparative Perspective*, Oxford: Oxford University Press.

Horowitz, D. (2002) 'Constitutional Design: Proposals versus Processes', in

A. Reynolds (ed.) *The Architecture of Democracy: Constitutional Design, Conflict Management and Democracy*, Oxford: Oxford University Press, 89–108.

Hroub, K. (2006) *Hamas*, London: Pluto.

Hudson, M. (1988) 'The Problem of Authoritative Power in Lebanese Politics: Why Consociationalism Failed', in N. Shehadi and D. Mills (eds) *Lebanon: a History of Conflict and Consensus*, London: I.B. Tauris, 224–39.

Husseini, R. (2010) 'Hezbollah and the Axis of Refusal: Hamas, Iran and Syria', *Third World Quarterly*, 31.5, 803–15.

Independent Commission on Policing (1999) *A New Beginning: Policing in Northern Ireland*, Belfast: HMSO.

International Institute for Democracy and Electoral Assistance (2006) *Democracy, Conflict and Human Security: Pursuing Peace in the 21st Century*, Stockholm: IDEA.

Irish Times (1998) 'Basque leader sees peace process as the way forward', 31 October.

Irish Times (2012) 'Republic Takes More Relaxed Approach to Dual Identity across the Border', 27 November, http://www.irishtimes.com/newspaper/ireland/2012/1127/1224327144275.html, accessed 16 December 2012.

Irvin, C. (1999) *Militant Nationalism: Between Movement and Party in Ireland and the Basque Country*, Minneapolis, MN: University of Minnesota Press.

Irwin, C. (2012) *The People's Peace*, Charleston, SC: Createspace.

Ismail, Q. (2005) *Abiding by Sri Lanka: On Peace, Place and Postcoloniality*, Minneapolis, MN: University of Minnesota Press.

Jeong, H-W. (2010) *Conflict Management and Resolution*, London: Routledge.

Jeyaratnam Wilson, A. (1974) *Politics in Sri Lanka 1947–1973*, Basingstoke: Macmillan.

Johnson, G. (1976) *Conflicting Concepts of Peace in Contemporary Peace Studies*, Beverly Hills: Sage.

Jones, C. and Murphy, E. (2001) *Israel: Challenges to Identity, Democracy and the State*, London: Routledge.

Joshi, M. (1996) 'On the Razor's Edge: the Liberation Tigers of Tamil Elam', *Studies in Conflict and Terrorism*, 19.1, 19–42.

Judah, T. (2000) *The Serbs: History, Myth and the Destruction of Yugoslavia*, New Haven, CT: Yale University Press.

Justice, J. (2005) 'Of Guns and Ballots: Attitudes towards Unconventional and Destructive Political Participation among Sinn Féin and Herri Batasuna supporters', *Nationalism and Ethnic Politics*, 11.3, 295–320.

Kaplan, R. (2005) *Balkan Ghosts: A Journey through History*, London: Picador.

Kaufmann, C. (1996) 'Possible and Impossible Solutions to Ethnic Civil Wars', *International Security*, 20.4, 136–75.

Kaufmann, C. (1998) 'When All Else Fails: Ethnic Population Transfers and Partitions in the Twentieth Century', *International Security*, 23.2, 120–56.

Kemp, A. (1985) 'Image of the Peace Field: An International Survey', *Journal of Peace Research*, 22.2, 129–40.

Kent, G. (1971) 'The Application of Peace Studies', *Journal of Conflict Resolution*, 15.1, 47–53.

Kerr, M. (2005) *Imposing Power Sharing: Conflict and Coexistence in Northern Ireland and Lebanon*, Dublin: Irish Academic Press.

Kerr, M. (2009) 'A Culture of Power Sharing', in R. Taylor (ed.) *Consociational Theory: McGarry and O'Leary and the Northern Ireland Conflict*, London: Routledge: 206–20.

Khairallah, D. (1994) 'Secular Democracy: A Viable Alternative to the Confessional System', in D. Collings (ed.) *Peace for Lebanon: From War to Reconstruction*, London: Lynne Rienner, 259–72.

Khalaf, S. (2002) *Civil and Uncivil Violence in Lebanon*, New York: Columbia University Press.

Kimmerling, B. and Migdal, J. (1992) *Palestinians: The Making of a People*, New York: Free Press.

Kleiboer, M. (1994) 'Ripeness of Conflict: A Fruitful Notion?' *Journal of Peace Research*, 31.1, 109–16.

Klieman, A. (2005) 'Israeli Negotiating Culture', in T. Wittes (ed.) *How Israelis and Palestinians Negotiate: A Cross-Cultural Analysis of the Oslo Peace Process*, Washington, DC: United States Institute for Peace, 81–132.

Kliot, N. (1987) 'The Collapse of the Lebanese State', *Middle Eastern Studies*, 23.1, 54–74.

Knudsen, A. (2010) 'Acquiescence to Assassinations in Post-Civil War Lebanon?', *Journal of Mediterranean Politics*, 15.1, 1–23.

Kumar, R. (1997) 'The Troubled History of Partition', *Foreign Affairs*, 75, 22–34.

La Calle, L. and Miley, T. (2008) 'Is There More Assimilation in Catalonia Than in the Basque Country? Analysing Dynamics of Assimilation in Nationalist Contexts', *European Journal of Political Research*, 47, 710–36.

Lacina, B. (2006) 'Explaining the Severity of Civil Wars', *Journal of Conflict Resolution*, 50.2, 276–89.

Landau, D. (2007) 'Two-State Salvation', *Ha'aretz*, 27 December.

Lederach, J. (1997) *Building Peace: Sustainable Reconciliation in Divided Societies*, Washington, DC: United States Institute of Peace.

Lederach, J. (2003) 'Cultivating Peace: a Practitioner's View of Deadly Conflict and Negotiation', in J. Darby and R. Mac Ginty (eds) *Contemporary Peacemaking: Conflict, Violence and Peace Processes*, Basingtoke: Palgrave Macmillan, 30–7.

Lemarchand, R. (1993) 'Burundi in Comparative Perspective: Dimensions of Ethnic Strife', in J. McGarry and B. O'Leary (eds) *The Politics of Ethnic Conflict Regulation*, London: Routledge, 151–71.

Lesch, D. (2008) *The Arab–Israeli Conflict: A History*, Oxford: Oxford University Press.

Letamendia, F. and Loughlin, J. (2006) 'Learning from Other Places: Northern Ireland, the Basque Country and Corsica', in M. Cox, A. Guelke and F. Stephen (eds) (2006) *A Farewell to Arms? Beyond the Good Friday Agreement*, Manchester: Manchester University Press, 377–94.

Lieberman, R. (2009) 'The "Israel Lobby" and American Politics', *Perspectives on Politics*, 7.2, 235–57.

Lieven, A. (2011) *Pakistan: A Hard Country*, London: Allen Lane.

Lieven, A. (2012) 'An end to illusion', *Financial Times* (Life and Arts Section), 31 March, p. 12.

Lijphart, A. (1968) *The Politics of Accommodation*, Berkeley, CA: University of California Press.

Lijphart, A. (1969) 'Consociational Democracy', *World Politics*, 21.2, 207–25.

Lijphart, A. (1975) 'The Northern Ireland Problem: Cases, Theories and Solutions', *British Journal of Political Science*, 5.1, 83–106.

Lijphart, A. (1977) *Democracy in Plural Societies: A Comparative Exploration*, New Haven, CT: Yale University Press.

Lijphart, A. (1984) *Democracies: Patterns of Majoritarian and Consensus Government in Twenty-One Countries*, New Haven, CT: Yale University Press.

Lijphart, A. (2002) 'The Wave of Power Sharing Democracy', in A. Reynolds (ed.) *The Architecture of Democracy: Constitutional Design, Conflict Management and Democracy*, Oxford: Oxford University Press, 37–54.

Little, A. (2009) 'Sunningdale for Slow Learners? Towards a Complexity Paradigm?' in R. Taylor (ed.) *Consociational Theory: McGarry and O'Leary and the Northern Ireland Conflict*, London: Routledge, 252–63.

Livni, T. (2012) 'A Terrorist is a Terrorist. Europe Got it Wrong', *The Times*, 31 July.

Lundy, P. (2012) 'Research Brief: Assessment of the Historical Enquiries Team (HET) Review Processes and Procedures in Royal Military Police (RMP) Investigation Cases', available at http://eprints.ulster.ac.uk/21809/, accessed 26 November 2012.

Lustick, I. (1979) 'Stability in Deeply Divided Societies: Consociationalism versus Control', *World Politics*, 31, 325–44.

McAuley, J., Tonge, J. and Mycock, A. (2011) *Loyal to the Core? Orangeism and Britishness in Northern Ireland*, Dublin: Irish Academic Press.

McEvoy, K. (1998) 'Prisoner Release and Conflict Resolution: International Lessons for Northern Ireland', *International Criminal Justice Review*, 8, 33–61.

McGarry, J. (2004) 'The Politics of Policing Reform in Northern Ireland', in J. McGarry and B. O'Leary (eds) *The Northern Ireland Conflict: Consociational Engagements*, Oxford: Oxford University Press, 371–403.

McGarry, J. and O'Leary, B. (1993) 'Introduction: the Macro-Political Regulation of Ethnic Conflict', in J. McGarry and B. O'Leary (eds) *The Politics of Ethnic Conflict Regulation*, London: Routledge, 1–40.

McGarry, J. and O'Leary, B. (1995) *Explaining Northern Ireland*, Oxford: Blackwell.

McGarry, J. and O'Leary, B. (2009) 'Response: Under Friendly and Less-Friendly Fire', in R. Taylor (ed.) *Consociational Theory: McGarry and O'Leary and the Northern Ireland Conflict*, London: Routledge, 333–88.

Mac Ginty, R. (1999) 'Biting the Bullet: Decommissioning in the Transition from War to Peace in Northern Ireland', *Irish Studies in International Affairs*, 10, 237–47.

Mac Ginty, R. (2006) *No War, No Peace: The Rejuvenation of Stalled Peace Processes and Peace Accords*, Basingstoke: Palgrave Macmillan.

McGovern, M. (2008) 'Liberia: The Risks of Rebuilding a Shadow State', in C. Call and V. Wyeth (eds) *Building States to Build Peace*, Boulder, CO: Lynne Rienner, 335–64.

McGrattan, C. (2010) *Northern Ireland 1968–2008: The Politics of Entrenchment*, Basingstoke: Palgrave Macmillan.

McIntyre, A. (1995) 'Modern Irish Republicanism: The Product of British State Strategies', *Irish Political Studies*, 10, 97–122.

McIntyre, A. (2001) 'Modern Irish Republicanism and the Belfast Agreement: Chickens Coming Home to Roost or Turkeys Celebrating Christmas?', in R. Wilford (ed.) *Aspects of the Belfast Agreement*, Oxford: Oxford University Press, 202–22.

McIntyre, A. (2008) *Good Friday: The Death of Irish Republicanism*, New York: Ausubo.

MacQueen, N. (2006) *Peacekeeping and the International System*, Abingdon: Routledge.

Mack, A. (2005) *War and Peace in the 21st Century: Human Security Report 2005*, Oxford: Oxford University Press.

Mack, A. and Nielsen, Z. (eds) (2008) *Human Security Brief 2007* (Burnbaby, BC, Human Security Project), available online at http://www.humansecuritybrief. info/HRSP_Brief_2007.pdf/.

Makdisi, U. (2007) 'Understanding Sectarianism', in N. Hovsepian (ed.) *The War on Lebanon: A Reader*, Moreton-in-Marsh: Arris, 20–7.

Makdisi, S. (2008) *Palestine Inside Out: An Everyday Occupation*, New York: W.W. Norton.

Malcolm, N. (1994) *The Serbs*, London: Pan.

Malcolm, N. (2002) *Bosnia: A Short History*, London: Pan.

Malhotra, D. and Liyanage, S. (2005) 'Long-Term Effects of Peace Workshops in Protracted Conflicts', *Journal of Conflict Resolution*, 49.6, 908–24.

Malia, J. (1994) 'The Ta'if Accord: An Evaluation', in D. Collings (ed.) *Peace for Lebanon: From War to Reconstruction*, London: Lynne Rienner, 31–44.

Manor, J. (ed.) (1984) 'Introduction', in J. Manor (ed.) *Sri Lanka in Change and Crisis*, London: Croom Helm, 1–32.

Mansvelt Beck, J. (1999) 'The Continuity of Basque Political Violence: A Geographical Perspective on the Legitimation of Violence', *Geojournal*, 48.2, 109–21.

Martinez-Herrera, E. and Miley, T. (2010) 'The Constitution and the Politics of National Identity in Spain', *Nations and Nationalism*, 16.1, 6–30.

Mattes, M. and Savun, B. (2009) 'Fostering Peace after Civil War: Commitment Problems and Agreement Design', *International Studies Quarterly*, 53.3, 737–59.

Mearsheimer, J. and Walt, S. (2008) *The Israel Lobby and US Foreign Policy*, London: Penguin.

Mees, L. (2001) 'Between Votes and Bullets: Conflicting Ethnic Identities in the Basque Country', *Ethnic and Racial Studies*, 24.5, 798–827.

Mees, L. (2003) *Nationalism, Violence and Democracy: The Basque Clash of Identities*, Basingstoke: Palgrave Macmillan.

Menkhaus, K. (2008) 'Somalia: Governance versus Statebuilding', in C. Call and V. Wyeth (eds) *Building States to Build Peace*, Boulder, CO: Lynne Rienner, 187–215.

Meyer, E. (1984) 'Seeking the Roots of the Tragedy', in J. Manor (ed.) *Sri Lanka in Change and Crisis*, London: Croom Helm, 137–52.

Milosevic, G. (2008) 'It is wrong to sound alarms about a "Bosnian powder keg"', *The Guardian*, 31 October, available at http://www.guardian.co.uk/commentis-free/2008/oct/31/balkans, accessed 31 March 2013.

Milton Edwards, B. (2006) *Contemporary Politics in the Middle East*, Cambridge: Polity.

Mitchell, C. (2003) 'Mediation and the Ending of Conflicts', in J. Darby and R. Mac Ginty (eds) *Contemporary Peacemaking: Conflict, Violence and Peace Processes*, Basingstoke: Palgrave Macmillan, 77–86.

Mitchell, G. (2000) *Making Peace*, Berkeley, CA: University of California Press.

Mitchell, G. (2009) Secretary's Remarks: Special Envoy for the Middle East, *The Guardian*, 23 January, available at http://www.scoop.co.nz/stories/WO0901/S00489.htm, accessed 3 January 2013.

Mitchell, P., Evans, G. and O'Leary, B. (2009) 'Extremist Outbidding in Ethnic Party Systems is Not Inevitable: Tribune Parties in Northern Ireland', *Political Studies*, 57.2, 397–421.

Mooradian, M. and Druckman, D. (1999) 'Hurting Stalemate or Mediation? The Conflict over Nagorno-Karabakh, 1990–95', *Journal of Peace Research*, 36.6, 709–27.

Moreno, L., Arriba, A. and Serrano, A. (1997) *Multiple Identities in Decentralised Spain; the Case of Catalonia*, Instituto de Estudios Sociales Avanzados Working Paper 97-06, Madrid: CSIC.

Morris, B. (1988) *The Birth of the Palestinian Refugee Problem*, Cambridge: Cambridge University Press.

Morris, B. (2010) *One State Two State: Resolving the Israel/Palestine Conflict*, Boston, MA: Yale University Press.

Morrison, J. (2011) 'Why Do People become Dissident Irish Republicans?', in P. Currie and M. Taylor (eds) *Dissident Irish Republicanism*, London: Continuum, 17–42.

Morrow, D. (2005) 'Breaking Antagonism? Political Leadership in Divided Societies', in I. O'Flynn and D. Russell (eds) *Power Sharing: New Challenges for Divided Societies*, London: Pluto, 45–58.

Mowles, C. (1986) 'The Israeli Invasion of South Lebanon', *Third World Quarterly*, 8.4, 1350–60.

Mueller, J. (2005) 'Six Rather Unusual Propositions about Terrorism', *Terrorism and Political Violence*, 17.4, 487–505.

Murden, S. (2009) *The Problem of Force: Grappling with the Global Battlefield*, Boulder, CO: Lynne Rienner.

Muro, D. (2008) *Ethnicity and Violence: The Case of Radical Basque Nationalism*, London: Routledge.

Murray, G. and Tonge, J. (2005) *Sinn Féin and the SDLP: From Alienation to Participation*, London: Hurst.

Najem, T. (2012) *Lebanon: The Politics of a Penetrated Society*, London: Routledge.

Neumayer, E. (2009) 'A New Moral Hazard? Military Intervention, Peacekeeping and Ratification of the International Criminal Court', *Journal of Peace Research*, 46.5, 659–70.

Newman, E. and Richmond, O. (2006) 'Peace Building and Spoilers', *Conflict, Security and Development*, 6.1, 101–10.

Nir, O. (2009) 'The Lebanese Shi'a as a Political Community', in B. Rubin (ed.) *Lebanon: Liberation: Conflict and Crisis*, Basingstoke: Palgrave Macmillan, 177–93.

Nissan, E. (1996) *Sri Lanka: A Bitter Harvest*, London: Minority Rights Group.

Nolan, P. (2012) *Northern Ireland Peace Monitoring Report, Number One*, Belfast: Community Relations Council.

Nordquist, K. (1985) 'Contradicting Peace Proposals in the Palestine Conflict', *Journal of Peace Research*, 22.2, 159–73.

Norris, P. (2008) *Driving Democracy: Do Power-Sharing Institutions Work?* Cambridge: Cambridge University Press.

Northern Ireland Life and Times Survey (1998) Community Relations, available at http://www.ark.ac.uk/nilt/1998/Community_Relations/NINATID.html, accessed 16 March 2013.

Northern Ireland Life and Times Survey (2010a) Political Attitudes, available at http://www.ark.ac.uk/nilt/2010/Political_Attitudes/NIRELND2.html, accessed 16 March 2013.

Northern Ireland Life and Times Survey (2010b) Community Relations, available at http://www.ark.ac.uk/nilt/2010/Community_Relations/NINATID.html, accessed 16 March 2013.

O'Donnell, C. (2007) *Fianna Fail, Irish Republicanism and the Northern Ireland Troubles 1968–2005*, Dublin: Irish Academic Press.

O'Dowd, L. (2009) 'Debating the Agreement: Beyond a Communalist Dynamic?', in R. Taylor (ed.) *Consociational Theory: McGarry and O'Leary and the Northern Ireland Conflict*, London: Routledge, 295–308.

O'Flynn, I. (2009) 'Progressive Integration (and Accommodation too)', in R. Taylor (ed.) *Consociational Theory: McGarry and O'Leary and the Northern Ireland Conflict*, London: Routledge, 264–78.

O'Kane, E. (2007) *Britain, Ireland and Northern Ireland since 1980*, London: Routledge.

O'Leary, B. (2013) 'Power Sharing in Deeply Divided Places: An Advocate's Introduction', in J. McEvoy and B. O'Leary (eds) *Power Sharing in Deeply Divided Places*, Philadelphia, PA: University of Pennyslvania Press, 1–66.

Ollapally, D. (2008) *The Politics of Extremism in South Asia*, Cambridge: Cambridge University Press.

Oren, M. (1992) 'The State, Ethnic Relations and Democratic Stability: Lebanon: Cyprus and Israel', *Geo-Journal*, 28.3, 319–32.

Orjuela, C. (2008) *The Identity Politics of Peacebuilding: Civil Society in War-Torn Sri Lanka*, London: Sage.

Owen, D. (1995) *Balkan Odyssey*, London: Weidenfeld and Nicolson.

Ozerdem, A. (2002) 'Disarmament, Demobilization and Reintegration of Former Combatants in Afghanistan: Lessons Learned from a Cross-Cultural Perspective', *Third World Quarterly*, 23.5, 961–75.

Paolini, S., Hewstone, M., Cairns, E. and Voci, A. (2002) 'Effects of Direct and Indirect Cross-Group Friendships on Judgements of Catholics and Protestants in Northern Ireland: The Mediating Role of an Anxiety-Reduction Mechanism', *Personality and Social Psychology Bulletin*, 30, 770–86.

Pape, R. (2003) 'The Strategic Logic of Suicide Terrorism', *American Political Science Review*, 97.3, 341–63.

Pappalardo, A. (1981) 'The Conditions for Consociational Democracy: A Logical and Empirical Critique', *European Journal of Political Research*, 9.4, 365–90.

Pappe, I. (2006) *The Ethnic Cleansing of Palestine*, Oxford: Oneworld.

Parades Commission for Northern Ireland (2011) *Annual Report and Financial Statements for 2011*, Belfast: Parades Commission, available at http://www.parades commission.org/fs/doc/publications/2011-ar-final.pdf, accessed 17 December 2012.

Parker, R. (1978) *Peace Research: A Questionnaire-Based Assessment*, St Louis, MI: Peace Research Lab.

Patomaki, H. (2001) 'The Challenge of Critical Theories: Peace Research at the Start of the New Century', *Journal of Peace Research*, 38.6, 723–37.

Patterson, H. (1997) *The Politics of Illusion: A Political History of the IRA*, London: Serif.

Patterson, H. (2011) 'Beyond the "Micro Group": The Dissident Republican Challenge', in P. Currie and M. Taylor (eds) *Dissident Irish Republicanism*, London: Continuum, 65–96.

Pavlowitch, S. (1999) 'Yugoslavia: the Failure of a Success', *Journal of Southern Europe and the Balkans*, 1.2, 163–70.

Perez-Agote, A. (2006) *The Social Roots of Basque Nationalism*, Reno, NV: University of Nevada Press.

Petritsch, W. (2001) 'Islam is Part of the West Too: The EU Should Reach Out to Muslims in Europe', *New York Times*, 20 November, available at http://www.ohr.int/ohr-dept/presso/pressa/default.asp?content_id=6385, accessed 31 March 2013.

Phares, W. (1995) *Lebanese Christian Nationalism: The Rise and Fall of an Ethnic Resistance*, London: Lynne Rienner.

Picard, E. (1996) *Lebanon: A Shattered Country*, New York: Holmes and Meier.

Police Service of Northern Ireland (2012a) 'Workforce Composition Figures', available at http://www.psni.police.uk/index/updates/updates_statistics/updates_workforce_composition_figures.htm, accessed 18 December 2012.

Police Service of Northern Ireland (2012b) Security Situation Statistics, available at http://www.psni.police.uk/security_related_incidents_cy.pdf, accessed 18 December 2012.

Quandt, W. (2005) 'Israeli–Palestinian Peace Talks: From Oslo to Camp David II', in T. Wittes (ed.) *How Israelis and Palestinians Negotiate: A Cross-Cultural Analysis of the Oslo Peace Process*, Washington, DC: United States Institute for Peace, 13–38.

Rabin, Y. (1996) *The Rabin Memoirs*, Berkeley, CA: University of California Press.

Rabinovich, I. (1985) *The War for Lebanon*, Ithaca, NY: Cornell University Press.

Ramet, S. (2005) *Thinking about Yugoslavia*, Cambridge: Cambridge University Press.

Ramsbotham, O., Woodhouse, T. and Miall, H. (2005) *Contemporary Conflict Resolution*, Cambridge: Polity.

Rapoport, A. (1970) 'Can Peace Research Be Applied?' *Journal of Conflict Resolution*, 14.2, 277–86.

Rapoport, A. and Chammah, A. (1965) *Prisoner's Dilemma*, Ann Arbor, MI: University of Michigan Press.

Rapoport, D. (2012) 'The Four Waves of Modern Terrorism', in J. Horgan and K. Braddock (eds) *Terrorism Studies: A Reader*, London: Routledge.

Rifaat Hussain, S. (2010) 'Liberation Tigers of Tamil Eelam (LTTE): Failed Quest for a "Homeland"', in K. Mulaj (ed.) *Violent Non-State Actors in World Politics*, London: Hurst, 381–412.

Rinehart, M. (1995) 'Understanding the Concept "Peace": A Search for Common Ground', *Peace and Change*, 20.3, 379–96.

Robinson, P. (2012) Leader's Speech to Democratic Unionist Party annual conference, La Mon hotel, 24 November 2012.

Rolston, B. (2007) 'Demobilisation and Reintegration of Ex-Combatants: the Irish Case in International Perspective', *Social and Legal Studies*, 16.2, 259–80.

Ross, C. (1996) 'Nationalism and Party Competition in the Basque Country and Catalonia', *West European Politics*, 19.3, 488–506.

Rummel, R. (1995) 'Democracy, Power, Genocide and Mass Murder', *Journal of Conflict Resolution*, 39.1, 3–26.

Saad-Ghorayeb, A. (2002) *Hizbu'llah: Politics, Religion*, London: Pluto.

Salam, N. (2004) 'Reforming the Electoral System: A Comparative Perspective', in N. Salam (ed.) *Options for Lebanon*, London: I.B. Tauris, 1–22.

Saliba, N. (1988) 'Syrian–Lebanese Relations', in H. Barakat (ed.) *Toward a Viable Lebanon*, London: Croom Helm, 145–59.

Salla, M. (1997) 'Constructing the "Ripe Moment" in the East Timor Conflict', *Journal of Peace Research*, 34.4, 449–66.

Sanchez-Cuenca, I. (2007) 'The Dynamics of Nationalist Terrorism: ETA and the IRA', *Terrorism and Political Violence*, 19.3, 289–306.

Sanchez-Cuenca, I. (2010) 'The Persistence of Nationalist Terrorism: The Case of ETA', in K. Mulaj (ed.) *Violent Non-State Actors in World Politics*, London: Hurst, 69–92.

Sand, S. (2010) *The Invention of the Jewish People*, London: Verso.

Sayed, H. and Tzannatos, Z. (2007) 'The Economic and Human Costs of the War', in N. Hovsepian (ed.) *The War on Lebanon: A Reader*, Moreton-in-Marsh: Arris, 316–42.

Schenker, D. (2009) 'America and the Lebanon Issue', in B. Rubin (ed.) *Lebanon: Liberation: Conflict and Crisis*, Basingstoke: Palgrave Macmillan, 213–37.

Schmid, A. (1993) 'The Response Problem as a Definition Problem', in A. Schmid and R. Crelinsten (eds) *Western Responses to Terrorism*, London: Frank Cass, 7–13.

Schwarzer, G. (1998) 'The Peaceful Settlement of Interstate Conflict: Saar, Austria, and Berlin', *Journal of Peace Research*, 35.6, 743–57.

Sebag Montefiore, S. (2011) *Jerusalem: the Biography*, London: Phoenix.

Shafer, J. (1998) '"A baby who does not cry will not be suckled": AMODEG and the Reintegration of Demobilised Soldiers', *Journal of South African Studies*, 4.1, 207–22.

Shaw, J. (2009) 'Irish Republicans and Basque Abertzales: To What Extent is the Irish Peace Process an Effective Model for a Basque Peace Process?'. Unpublished MA thesis, University of Central Lancashire.

Shaw, M. (2011) 'Review of *The Politics of Genocide* (Herman and Peterson)', *Journal of Genocide Research*, 13.3, 353–8.

Shearer, D. (1997) 'Exploring the Limits of Consent: Conflict Resolution in Sierra Leone', *Millennium Journal of International Studies*, 26.3, 845–60.

Sherman, M. (2008) 'Nationally-Led Statebuilding', in C. Call and V. Wyeth (eds) *Building States to Build Peace*, Boulder, CO: Lynne Rienner, 303–34.

Shields, V. (2008) 'Political Reform in Lebanon: Has the Cedar Revolution Failed?', *Journal of Legislative Studies*, 14.4, 474–87.

Shirlow, P. and McEvoy, K. (2008) *Beyond the Wire: Former Prisoners and Conflict Transformation in Northern Ireland*, London: Pluto, 2008.

Shirlow, P., Tonge, J., McAuley, J. and McGlynn, C. (2010) *Abandoning Historical Conflict? Former Political Prisoners and Reconciliation in Northern Ireland*, Manchester: Manchester University Press.

Shlaim, A. (2010) 'This Time in Washington, Honest Brokerage is Not Going To Be Enough', *The Guardian*, 27 September.

Silber, L. and Little, A. (1995) *The Death of Yugoslavia*, London: Penguin/BBC.

Silva, N. (ed.) (2002) *The Hybrid Island: Culture Crossings and the Invention of Identity in Sri Lanka*, London: Zed.

Simms, B. (2002) *Unfinest Hour: Britain and the Destruction of Bosnia*, London: Penguin.

Singer, J. (1971) 'Modern International War: From Conjecture to Explanation', in A. Lepawsky, E. Buehrig and H. Lasswell (eds) *The Search for World Order*, New York: Appleton-Century-Crofts, 47–71.

Singer, J. (1972) 'The Correlates of War Project: Interim Report and Rationale', *World Politics*, 24.2, 243–70.

Sisk, T. (2003) 'Power Sharing after Civil Wars: Matching Problems to Solutions', in J. Darby and R. Mac Ginty (eds) *Contemporary Peacemaking: Conflict, Violence and Peace Processes*, Basingstoke: Palgrave Macmillan, 139–50.

Smith, C. (2011) 'The Military Dynamics of the Peace Process and its Aftermath', in J. Goodhand, B. Korf and J. Spencer (eds) *Conflict and Peacebuilding in Sri Lanka*, London: Routledge, 74–91.

Smith, D. (2007) *Palestine and the Arab–Israeli Conflict*, Basingstoke: Palgrave Macmillan.

Snyder, J. (2000) *From Voting to Violence: Democratization and Nationalist Conflict*, New York: W.W. Norton.

Snyder, J. and Vinjamuri, L. (2003) 'Trials and Errors: Principle and Pragmatism in Strategies of International Justice', *International Security*, 28.3, 5–44.

Spyer, N. (2009) 'Israel and Lebanon: Problematic Proximity', in B. Rubin (ed.) *Lebanon: Liberation: Conflict and Crisis*, Basingstoke: Palgrave Macmillan, 194–212.

Stedman, S. (1991) *Peacemaking in Civil War: International Mediation in Zimbabwe 1974–1980*, Boulder, CO: Lynne Rienner.

Stedman, S. (1997) 'Spoiler Groups in Peace Processes', *International Security*, 22.2, 5–53.

Stedman, S. (2003) 'Peace Processes and the Challenges of Violence', in J. Darby and R. Mac Ginty (eds) *Contemporary Peacemaking: Conflict, Violence and Peace Processes*, Basingstoke: Palgrave.

Steiner, J. (2009) 'In Search of the Consociational "Spirit of Accommodation"', in R. Taylor (ed.) *Consociational Theory: McGarry and O'Leary and the Northern Ireland Conflict*, London: Routledge, 196–205.

Stevens Report (1990) *The Report of the Deputy Chief Constable of Cambridgeshire into Allegations of Collusion between the Security Forces and Loyalist Paramilitaries*, London: HMSO.

Stevens Report (1994) *Second Report of Inquiry into Allegations of Collusion between the Security Forces and Loyalist Paramilitaries*, London: HMSO.

Stevens Report (2003) *Third Report of Inquiry into Allegations of Collusion between the Security Forces and Loyalist Paramilitaries*, London: HMSO.

Sullivan, J. (1988) *ETA and Basque Nationalism: The Fight for Euskadi 1890–1986*, London: Routledge.

Svensson, I. (2007) 'Bargaining, Bias and Peace Brokers: How Rebels Commit to Peace', *Journal of Peace Research*, 44.2, 177–94.

Svensson, I. (2009) 'Who Brings Which Peace?' Neutral versus Biased Mediation and Institutional Peace Arrangements in Civil Wars', *Journal of Conflict Resolution*, 53.3, 446–69.

Taheri, A. (2007) 'Hamas-land and Fatah-land at War', *Times*, 16 June.

Taheri, A. (2010) *Persian Night: Iran under the Khomeinist Revolution*, London: Encounter.

Ta'if Accord (1989) available at http://www.al-bab.com/arab/docs/lebanon/taif.htm, accessed 1 August 2012.

Tamimi, A. (2006) *Hamas: Unwritten Chapters*, London: Hurst.

Taylor, M. and Horgan, J. (2006) 'A Conceptual Framework for Addressing Psychological Process in the Development of the Terrorist', *Terrorism and Political Violence*, 18.4, 585–601.

Taylor, R. (2009a) 'Introduction: the Promise of Consociational Theory', in R. Taylor (ed.) *Consociational Theory: McGarry and O'Leary and the Northern Ireland Conflict*, London: Routledge, 1–12.

Taylor, R. (2009b) 'The Injustice of a Consociational Solution to the Northern Ireland Problem', in R. Taylor (ed.) *Consociational Theory: McGarry and O'Leary and the Northern Ireland Conflict*, London: Routledge, 309–29.

The Guardian (2011), 'The Palestine Papers', 24–28 January, available at http://www.guardian.co.uk/world/palestine-papers, accessed 23 February 2012.

Thomas, R. (1998) *Serbia under Milosevic*, London: Hurst.

Tilley, V. (2005) *The One-State Solution: A Breakthrough for Peace in the Israeli–Palestinian Deadlock*, Manchester: Manchester University Press.

Tilley, V. (2007) 'Israel in Lebanon: The Foreign Policy Logic of Jewish Statehood', in N. Hovsepian (ed.) *The War on Lebanon: A Reader*, Moreton-in-Marsh: Arris, 287–301.

Tir, J. (2005) 'Dividing Countries to Promote Peace: Prospects for Long-Term Success of Partitions', *Journal of Peace Research*, 42.5, 545–62.

Tonge, J. (2000) 'From Sunningdale to the Good Friday Agreement: Creating Devolved Government in Northern Ireland', *Contemporary British History*, 14.3, 39–60.

Tonge, J. (2004) '"They haven't gone away y'know": Irish Republican "Dissidents," and "Armed Struggle"', *Terrorism and Political Violence*, 16.3, 671–93.

Tonge, J. (2005) *The New Northern Irish Politics?* Basingstoke: Palgrave.

Tonge, J. (2006) *Northern Ireland*, Cambridge: Polity.

Tonge, J. (2011) 'An Enduring Tradition or the Last Gasp of Physical Force Republicanism? "Dissident" Republican Violence in Northern Ireland', in P. Currie and M. Taylor (eds) *Dissident Irish Republicanism*, London: Continuum, 97–118.

Tonge, J. (2012) '"No-one likes us: we don't care": Dissident Irish Republicans and Mandates', *Political Quarterly*, 83.2, 219–26.

Tonge, J. and Evans, J. (2010) 'Northern Ireland: Unionism Loses More Leaders', in A. Geddes and J. Tonge (eds) *Britain Votes 2010*, Oxford: Oxford University Press, 158–75.

Tonge, J., Shirlow, P. and McAuley, J. (2011) 'So Why Did the Guns Fall Silent? How Interplay, not Stalemate, Explains the Northern Ireland Peace Process', *Irish Political Studies*, 26.1, 1–18.

United Nations (2005) *Report of the International Independent Commission Established Persuant to Security Council Resolution 1595 (Mehlis Report)*, New York: United Nations.

United Nations (2011) *Report of the Secretary General's Panel of Experts on Accountability in Sri Lanka*, New York: United Nations.

Uyangoda, J. (2011) 'Government-LTTE Peace Negotiations in 2002–2005 and the Clash of State Formation Projects', in J. Goodhand, B. Korf and J. Spencer (eds) *Conflict and Peacebuilding in Sri Lanka*, London: Routledge, 16–38.

Van den Dungen, P. and Wittner, L. (2003) 'Peace History: An Introduction', *Journal of Peace Research*, 40.4, 363–75.

Vocke, H. (1978) *The Lebanese War: Its Origins and Dimensions*, London: Hurst.

Wall, J. and Druckman, D. (2003) 'Mediation in Peacekeeping Missions', *Journal of Conflict Resolution*, 47.5, 693–705.

Wallensteen, P. (2011) *Understanding Conflict Resolution: War, Peace and the Global System*, London: Sage.

Wallensteen, P. and Sollenberg, M. (2001) 'Armed Conflict 1989–2000', *Journal of Peace Research*, 38.5, 629–44.

Walter, B. (2002) *Committing to Peace: The Successful Settlement of Civil Wars*, Princeton, NJ: Princeton University Press.

Weinberg, L. (1991) 'Turning to Terror: The Conditions under which Political Parties Turn to Terrorist Activities', *Comparative Politics*, 23, 423–88.

Whiting, S. (2012) '"The Discourse of Defence": "Dissident" Irish Republican Newspapers and the "Propaganda War"', *Terrorism and Political Violence*, 24.3, 483–503.

Whittaker, D. (ed.) (2003) *The Terrorism Reader*, London: Routledge.

Whittaker, D. (ed.) (2007) *The Terrorism Reader*, 2nd edn, London: Routledge.

Wiggins, H. (1995) 'Sri Lanka: Negotiations in a Secessionist Conflict', in W. Zartman (ed.) *Elusive Peace: Negotiating an End to Civil Wars*, Washington, DC: Brookings Institution, 35–58.

Wilson, R. (2009) 'From Consociationalism to Interculturalism', in R. Taylor (ed.) *Consociational Theory: McGarry and O'Leary and the Northern Ireland Conflict*, London: Routledge, 221–36.

Winslow, C. (1996) *Lebanon: War and Politics in a Fragmented Society*, London: Routledge.

Winslow, D. and Woost, M. (2004) 'Articulations of Economy and Ethnic Conflict in Sri Lanka', in D. Winslow and M. Woost (eds) *Economy, Culture and Civil War in Sri Lanka*, Bloomington, IN: Indiana University Press, 1–30.

Wittes, T. (2005) 'Conclusion: Culture as an Intervening Variable', in T. Wittes (ed.) *How Israelis and Palestinians Negotiate: A Cross-Cultural Analysis of the Oslo Peace Process*, Washington, DC: United States Institute for Peace, 133–48.

Wolff, S. (2005) 'Electoral-Systems Design and Power-Sharing Regimes', in I. O'Flynn and D. Russell (eds) *Power Sharing: New Challenges for Divided Societies*, London: Pluto, 59–74.

Wolff, S. (2006) *Ethnic Conflict: A Global Perspective*, Oxford: Oxford University Press.

Wolff, S. (2009) 'Peace by Design: Towards "Complex Power Sharing"', in R. Taylor (ed.) *Consociational Theory: McGarry and O'Leary and the Northern Ireland Conflict*, London: Routledge, 110–21.

Woodward, S. (1994) *Balkan Tragedy: Chaos and Dissolution after the Cold War*, Washington, DC: Brookings Institution.

Woodworth, P. (2001) *Dirty War, Clean Hands: ETA, the GAL and Spanish Democracy*, Cork: Cork University Press.

Young, C. (2003) 'Explaining the Conflict Potential of Ethnicity', in J. Darby and R. Mac Ginty (eds) *Contemporary Peacemaking: Conflict, Violence and Peace Processes*, Basingstoke: Palgrave Macmillan, 9–18.

Zartman, W. (1986) 'Ripening Conflict, Ripe Moment, Formula and Mediation', in D. Bendahmane and J. McDonald (eds) *Perspectives on Negotiation*, Washington, DC: Center for the Study of Foreign Affairs, 205–27.

Zartman, W. (1989) *Ripe for Resolution: Conflict and Intervention in Africa*, Oxford: Oxford University Press.

Zartman, W. (ed.) (1995) *Elusive Peace: Negotiating an End to Civil Wars*, Washington, DC: Brookings Institution.

Zartman, W. (2003) 'The Timing of Peace Initiatives: Hurting Stalemates and Ripe Moments', in J. Darby and R. Mac Ginty (eds) *Contemporary Peacemaking: Conflict, Violence and Peace Processes*, Basingstoke: Palgrave Macmillan, 19–29.

Zimmerman, W. (1999) *Origins of a Catastrophe: Yugoslavia and its Destroyers*, New York: Times Books.

Zisser, E. (2000) *Lebanon: The Challenge of Independence*, London: I.B. Tauris.

Zisser, E. (2009) 'Hizballah in Lebanon', in B. Rubin (ed.) *Lebanon: Liberation: Conflict and Crisis*, Basingstoke: Palgrave Macmillan, 155–76.

Žižek, S. (2009) 'Quiet Slicing of the West Bank Makes Abstract Prayers for Peace Obscene', *The Guardian*, 18 August.

Zunes, S. (2007) 'Washington's Proxy War', in N. Hovsepian (ed.) *The War on Lebanon: A Reader*, Moreton-in-Marsh: Arris, 93–118.

Index